SPIRIT STONES

Spirit Stones

BY Dianne Ebertt Beeaff

Five Star Publications Inc.
A Resource for Every Author & Publisher Since 1985

Chandler, Arizona

Linda F. Radke, President
Five Star Publications, Inc.
P.O. Box 6698
Chandler, AZ 85246-6698

www.SpiritStonesBook.com

Library of Congress Cataloging-in-Publication Data

Beeaff, Dianne Ebertt.
Spirit stones : unraveling the mysteries of Western Europe's prehistoric monuments / by Dianne Ebertt Beeaff.
p. cm.
ISBN 978-1-58985-198-6
eISBN 978-1-58985-049-1
1. Megalithic monuments–Europe, Western. 2. Europe, Western–Antiquities. 3. Sacred space–Europe, Western. 4. Mystery. 5. Spiritual life. 6. Europe, Western–History, Local. I. Title.
GN790.B43 2011
936–dc22
2011011233

Printed in the United States of America

Electronic edition provided by
www.eStarPublish.com

the eDivision of Five Star Publications, Inc.

Editor: Jennifer Christensen
Cover Design: Kris Taft Miller
Interior Design: Linda Longmire
Project Manager: Sue DeFabis
Photos Courtesy of the Author

For Dan, Danielle and Dustin,
who have lived with it all
for so long.

V

TABLE OF CONTENTS

THE STONES REMAIN;
their stillness can outlast
the skies of history
hurrying overhead."

– Siegfried Sassoon (*The Heart's Journey*)

Introduction

REACHING FOR A SHADOW

I'm standing in the wind, rain and cold of an early June morning on the west coast of the heath-covered Isle of Lewis in the Outer Hebrides. The thin slabs of rock that make up Callanish Stone Circle rise up around me from a wild, yet peaceful moorland landscape of low rocky hills and shimmering lochs (PLATE 1).

Callanish (Tursachan Calanais) is the most exceptional and impressive prehistoric monument in the west of Scotland. Aloof and silent, it dominates the southern end of a low, uneven ridge on the edge of the scattered crofts of Callanish Village. Together, the stones and I look out northwest to the inky, olive-green seawater of East Loch Roag.

My first impression of Callanish is one of awe. The haunting, twisted stones exude a powerful presence. Thirteen graceful stones of whitish Lewisian gneiss, marked with lumps of greenish/black hornblende and patches of red-orange feldspar, form a small circle with a central cairn. An avenue of parallel stones stretches to the north. Three short arms, aligned approximately to the remaining points of the compass, fan out from the tallest stone, a lofty eight-foot monolith inside the circle (PLATE 2). The entire design resembles a Celtic cross, as I can clearly see when I climb a nearby rocky outcrop and am nearly swept into the sea by a gale-force Lewisian wind.

Like so many other stone monuments that are steeped in the atmosphere of distant memory, Callanish has a matchless appeal. I can so easily feel the dark shadow of its past as its monoliths rise up below me, human forms in a brooding and lonely landscape. They call up the wonder of life even if they can never be adequately explained.

The prehistoric stone monuments of the world form a huge jigsaw puzzle from which we will always be missing most of the pieces. In the end, we can only fully understand and admire them as living monuments to the spirit and aspirations of the people who built them. Kevin Crossley-Holland writes in his book, *The Stones Remain*, "To come as close as possible to understanding stones, we must gather the facts and then we must dream."

There is much we can learn about living in the present from the standing stones of our ancient past; ways to apply the powerful concentration of life they embody, connect with and be enriched by the elements and ideas they suggest. This is what I've aimed for in this book – to fully appreciate an ancestral heritage in a contemporary human context; to bring the stones to life again.

If we want to appreciate the world's megalithic monuments, we have to start with an attempt to understand and connect with the prehistoric mentality that created them. Though specific shapes may differ, stone building was prominent for thousands of years in Malta, Sicily, Germany, Scandinavia, France, Spain, Portugal, Great Britain, Ireland, the Baltic, Turkey and Mesoamerica.

The megalithic builders of our ancestry were a sturdy and unsentimental lot, intelligent and inquisitive, deserving of our respect. Their lives were short, insecure and filled with suffering. But they laughed and cried just as we do, and they must have found their world as full of wonder, cruelty, beauty and violence as we do ours. They were interested in the fertility of the Earth and her creatures, in ensuring favorable weather, in appeasing the elements, forces or gods that controlled their lives. Even after their gradual shift from hunting to raising crops and domesticating animals, they still needed to store food, note boundaries and honor ancestors. We often think of them as superstitious people. And yet we know from our own experience that any belief in the supernatural, in coincidence or chance, accepts that there are modes of life our human minds have not yet fully grasped. In a very real sense, they are us and we are them.

What the people of our past left behind suggests to us what they thought was especially important. That these ancient lives from our ancient past appear strange is really just a matter of perspective. We're looking at them from our own point of view in an isolated present. Societies arise from both environment and inheritance. We impinge on each other and intermingle, retaining things carried from our distant past. One culture subverts or adapts the magic and ritual of the one it follows. We are left with a continuity of tradition from which the fears, beliefs and sentiments of past generations are carried forward to our present. The past, the present and the future are all woven as one fabric.

Like some of you, I have walked the Ridgeway Path to Wayland's Smithy's Chambered Tomb in Oxfordshire, England, tracing in that muddy but still viable track-way the course of 300 generations right down to my own. In the nineteenth century, an entire family was living in Ireland's Haroldstown Dolmen. A Viking named Bjorn etched his name in runes on a monolith in the Orkney Islands' Ring of Brodgar (PLATE 3) in the twelfth century — 5000 years after that stone circle had been raised. The burial chamber of Maes Howe, also on the Orkney Islands, was sacked by Vikings in the twelfth century. One of the raiders scrawled on the wall in Runes, "Ingeborg is the most beautiful of women." About 800 years later, I saw "Miree Lydon is a babe" spray-painted on a shop wall in Kirkwall, the Orkneys' capital. Similar tagging on subway corridors, city walls and idled boxcars appears to us every day.

Megalithic monuments have been given any number of meanings through the ages. Extra-terrestrials built them; Atlanteans or Egyptians. We've been told they were racecourses, processional pathways, guideposts, astronomical markers, ancestral shrines, cenotaphs, calendars, Druid temples, assembly points. Pious Medieval peasants buried some of them. Others were blown up by landlords, dragged off in land clearances, incorporated into field walls or used as shooting hides. We have no shortage of information regarding stone monuments. What we're missing is any certainty of interpretation. Nothing is written in stone, so to speak. We just don't know. And we never will.

The world of megaliths is vast. There are more than 900 known stone circles in the British Isles alone, more than in any other country in Europe. More than eighty chambered tombs have been discovered on the small archipelago of Scotland's Orkney Islands. Single stones stand in the thousands. Consequently, I've had to apply some arbitrary limitations to this book. Geographically, I've restricted it to England, Wales, Scotland, Northern Ireland, the Republic of Ireland and Brittany; architecturally to standing stones, stone circles and burial chambers; and functionally by limited theory and use.

In Part I: Fact, we're going to talk about our Neolithic and Bronze Age past, the worlds to which prehistoric stone monuments belong. While there, we'll look at *culture, architectural design, medium and motif,* and *sacred space.* In Part II: Fancy, we'll focus on four major areas of human interpretation: *Life and Death, Heaven and Earth, Secular and Sacred,* and *Body and Soul.* I've closed most chapters with a special section I call *Spiritual Fitness,* in which I've suggested applications to our present day living. This is, after all, the foundation for any continuous connection to our megalithic ancestors.

We are each the product of a boundless past. Stone monuments, as part of that past, can renew our sense of the mystery and wonder of life, of the great gift of being and the continuity of the human spirit. There's no shortage of books on either megalithic prehistory or spiritual growth. What we celebrate in this book is their connection.

SPIRIT STONES

Unraveling the Mysteries of Western Europe's Prehistoric Monuments

by Dianne Ebertt Beeaff

PART I:

FACT

CHAPTER I

ROCK OF AGES
MEGALITHS IN TIME

> "ASK NOT THE REASON
> FROM WHERE IT DID SPRING.
> FOR YOU KNOW VERY WELL,
> IT'S AN OLD ANCIENT THING."
>
> – CORNISH CHRISTMAS WASSAILING SONG

I F YOU AND I WERE TO WANDER THROUGH
London's Highgate Cemetery — and I think you should
if you ever get the chance — we'd find a stunning
collection of moss-draped stone angels, carved burial urns
and faceless sculpted mourners. To more fully appreciate
this imagery, we should ideally know something about the
upper class of the Victorian Era that created it. The same
holds true for earlier stone monuments. Cultural change
moves slowly, rarely with any clear demarcation. Some
elements can overlap for hundreds, even thousands of
years. Before we look at the attributes, interpretation and
inspiration of ancient stone monuments, we ought to have
a little bit more material information to help us along. How
did they come to be? What were the times like in which they
were built?

For nearly 7000 years, megalithic monuments raised
by our European ancestors have dotted the western edge
of Europe from Portugal to Scandinavia and deep into
Southern France. The periods in which these monuments
were built are called the Neolithic Era, or New Stone Age,
and the Bronze Age, after the nature of the weapons and
tools used at the time.

Scientists use pollen analysis, thermo-luminescence in
fired pottery and Carbon-14 to date archeological remains.
All of these methods are already imprecise, and none of
them can be applied to stone. We can only guess, therefore,
at the age of any rock monument from something datable,
such as charred wood or burned seeds, that we might find
on or near it or buried beneath it. Only after about 5000
BCE (Before the Common Era) did humans leave any
lasting markers on the Western European landscape. What
prehistoric communities did leave behind depends on the

materials they used. Stone and metal outlast wood and fabric, so that their presence at archeological sites might leave us with a false impression about the dominance of technology. Still, experts have been able to make some assumptions about food production, burial customs and seasonal farming rituals that can shed light on these areas of our prehistory. Further examination of our ancient ancestors' culture can help us more deeply appreciate the heritage they left behind.

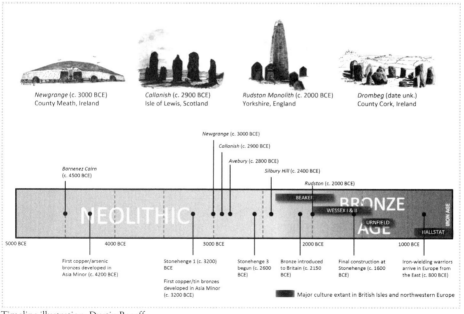

Newgrange (c. 3000 BCE)
County Meath, Ireland

Callanish (c. 2900 BCE)
Isle of Lewis, Scotland

Rudston Monolith (c. 2000 BCE)
Yorkshire, England

Drombeg (date unk.)
County Cork, Ireland

Newgrange (c. 3000 BCE)

Callanish (c. 2900 BCE)

Avebury (c. 2800 BCE)

Silbury Hill (c. 2400 BCE)

Barnenez Cairn
(c. 4500 BCE)

Rudston (c. 2000 BCE)

BEAKER

WESSEX I & II

URNFIELD

HALLSTAT

NEOLITHIC

BRONZE AGE

IRON AGE

5000 BCE   4000 BCE   3000 BCE   2000 BCE   1000 BCE

First copper/arsenic bronzes developed in Asia Minor (c. 4200 BCE)

Stonehenge 1 (c. 3200) BCE

First copper/tin bronzes developed in Asia Minor (c. 3200 BCE)

Stonehenge 3 begun (c. 2600 BCE)

Bronze introduced to Britain (c. 2150 BCE)

Final construction at Stonehenge (c. 1600 BCE)

Iron-wielding warriors arrive in Europe from the East (c. 800 BCE)

Major culture extant in British Isles and northwestern Europe

Timeline illustration: Dustin Beeaff

11

THE NEOLITHIC ERA OR NEW STONE AGE

The Neolithic or New Stone Age was a lengthy prehistoric period in which agriculture dominated the economy and stone was used for warfare, industry and survival. The use of metal that identifies the Bronze Age came into some areas well before 2000 BCE. But in other areas, stone-age technology lingered on far longer. For convenience sake, we're going to place the Neolithic Era at 5000 to 2000 BCE.

The Neolithic Age grew out of a Mesolithic or Middle Stone Age culture of semi-nomadic hunter/gatherers that blossomed at the end of the last ice age, about 10,000 years ago. Sea levels rose, and people living in Ireland and Great Britain became isolated from the rest of Europe. Forests expanded, and the herding animals our European ancestors had stalked for millennia began to disappear. Still hunting wild fowl and remaining woodland animals such as red deer and wild boar, Mesolithic people boosted their food supply with plants, nuts and berries and began to increasingly rely on fish and shellfish, which they gathered at seasonal seaside or lakeside camps. This subtle change in lifestyle is currently the best marker we have of late Mesolithic culture. Tools remained of flint, stone, bone and antler.

Unlike their Neolithic descendants, Mesolithic populations put great emphasis on the skill and experience of individuals. Great Britain probably supported about 30,000 people living in small family groups of two to eight. Some Southern gatherings could have had as many as twenty-five members, while, by contrast, there may only have been 150 to 200 people in all of Scotland.

By the time our predecessors entered the Atlantic Period – a post-glacial warming that took place from about 6500

BCE into the early centuries of the Neolithic Era – higher temperatures brought more rainfall. Thick deciduous forests spread across the British landscape. Elms and alders prospered where we now have moorland, with birch, pine and hazel in the North. Travelers moved about in dugout canoes similar to those used in the Scottish Highlands well into the eighteenth century. Dangerous waters, such as Scotland's Mull of Kintyre or the Gulf of Corryvrechan, with its infamous whirlpool, were probably avoided by portages. The beginnings of animal husbandry and a heavier use of stone axes to clear land mark the close of this Mesolithic Period.

A sedentary, agricultural economy of mixed farming, crop production and the further domestication of animals signals the period we call the Neolithic Era or New Stone Age. This transformation to a settled agricultural existence from a nomadic or semi-nomadic lifestyle, where small groups of people survived at the mercy of the environment, may be the single most significant feat we humans have ever accomplished.

One wild July day in the late afternoon, I wandered along the muddy hillside track that connects the Neolithic's Wideford Hill Chambered Cairn on the heathery Orkney Mainland to its companion mound, Cuween Chambered Cairn. I watched a tawny, short-eared owl hunting over the marshy bottomland. Below me, a landscape continuously farmed for more than 5000 years stretched westward toward the choppy Bay of Firth. The fields were no doubt smaller in those ancient times, mere ragged pockets in a thick forest. But the enduring extent of this unparalleled transformation was palpable to me.

Our ancestors in the Eastern Mediterranean became agriculturalists around 6500 BCE. Scattered groups of immigrants from Western Europe came to Southern England in skin boats around 5000 to 4300 BCE, either as traders or as farming colonists. Agriculture then spread north and west in the British Isles and was prevalent in all areas by about 3800 BCE. Under the clearer skies of a warm and somewhat drier Sub-Boreal climate, these early farmers grew rye and barley, together with their principal crop, a strain of wheat we now know as emmer. They cleared away forest and scrub using fire and wooden or stone tools, cultivating the high, well-drained land first and building dry-stone walls to separate their fields.

On the Hebridean Islands of Scotland, in the west of Ireland, in Cornwall and in the Scottish Highlands, you can still see dry-stone field walls climbing up mist-shrouded hillsides, disappearing in heathery peat bogs or literally dropping over cliffs. My husband Dan and I once made the incomparably scenic climb up to the saddle that divides Brandon Head in the west of Ireland from 3000-foot Mount Brandon next door. The remnant wall there skirts the edge of a drop-off that plunges hundreds of feet directly into the Atlantic. Portions had long since crumbled into the abyss and I couldn't help but wonder if some sheep hadn't followed. When the mist comes up on the mountain, a local farmer we met on the way down told us — and Irish mist is almost as omnipresent as L.A. smog — farmers must herd their sheep back from the cliff's edge or they'd all be lost.

The ash that resulted from the Neolithic burning of vegetation enriched the land. In fragile spots, we can see that this farming technique fused with climate change and in time produced Britain's ever-present heaths and bogs. By about 3000 BCE, much of the north country of the British Isles was as treeless as it is in great part today. In other places, great forests in varied mixtures of pine, oak, willow, birch, alder, ash, elm, hazel and lime were reduced. In some cases, they vanished altogether.

In addition to raising cereal crops, our Neolithic farming ancestors had domesticated dogs. They raised sheep and goats in communal pastures and penned cattle, deer and oxen. Pigs, being able to break up bracken infestations, grew in importance as climate and over-cultivation changed the face of the land. Pigs also had large, fast-growing litters that made for a rather reliable food source. But over time, the sheep and the goats won out over the cattle and the pigs. Today, it's hard for us to imagine any significant stretch of the present British countryside without its scattering of sheep.

Neolithic settlers built mostly near water. Occasionally gathered into small villages, most families lived in rectangular stone or timber huts, on self-sufficient farmsteads. Many of us may have read about one Neolithic settlement in particular, the largest found thus far in the British Isles. Unearthed near Durrington Wells on the Salisbury Plain, this hamlet is thought by some to be the village in which the first builders of Stonehenge lived. Amid the ruins, outlines of wooden box beds and cupboards were excavated in houses laid out exactly like the Neolithic houses we find at Skara Brae, far to the north in Scotland's Orkney Islands.

Skara Brae itself is an astonishing place to visit. One night in 1850, a monster storm dislodged the sandy dunes on the Bay of Skaill on the Orkney Mainland, revealing fragments of tools, weapons, richly decorated pottery and a collection of huts linked by interconnecting underground passageways. The six rectangular homes and one workshop here were occupied for over 500 years, from about 3100 to 2600 BCE. The blackhouse, a traditional home used in the Highlands and Hebrides well into the 1970s, is much the same in style, though further elongated in the manner of a Viking longhouse. The central hearths and the stone beds and cupboards of both the blackhouse and the longhouse, are direct descendants of those uncovered at Neolithic Skara Brae. The entire complex was buried in a midden of ashes, shells, bones and sand. Pasturage and meadowlands, dotted in summer with low-lying wildflowers, still surround the village, just as they did in its heyday, though the sea is much closer now.

If you go to Skara Brae, only occasionally are you allowed to walk down off the walls. In one small nook stands a rune stone. When I was last there in the late 1990s, a blackbird had built a nest in the wall nearby and was busy feeding her young. Strolling afterwards on the wide sandy beach, my husband picked up an identical miniature version of the flat sandstone monoliths that make up the nearby Neolithic Ring of Brodgar, a monument probably built by the inhabitants of Skara Brae.

In some cases, we find Neolithic houses built directly on Mesolithic sites, suggesting immigration or a transformation in the existing population. Between 4000 and 2000 BCE, these ancient people began making pottery. By about 3000 BCE, they had created a useful, ornamented style we call Grooved Ware. They made all their own utensils, tools and clothing and strung beads of bone, shell and stone into necklaces. Both men and women averaged about five and a half feet tall, and, with a possible life span of just twenty-five to thirty years, their lives were ones of general physical misery; full of the fractures, abscesses and osteoarthritis we find later in the peasantry of the Dark Ages.

Neolithic trade networks moved pottery, knives from Welsh flint mines and polished stone axes from factories in Cornwall and the Lake District, deep into Europe. This required extensive track-ways like the Ridgeway Path we touched on earlier.

The Ridgeway is Britain's — and possibly Western Europe's — oldest established roadway. In continuous use for at least 5000 years, it wends its way on chalk ridges from very near the Neolithic stone circle of Avebury, near Marlborough Downs at the edge of the Salisbury Plain, crosses the Thames and then heads into the woodland groves of the Chiltern Hills. When we walk the Ridgeway Path — and we can do so today for some eighty miles — we have history and prehistory literally underfoot. We move in the very footsteps of our ancient ancestors.

New Stone Age populations were organized, communal, tribal societies. Small, scattered family groups formed the basis of a social structure that emphasized centralization, unlike the individualists of their Mesolithic past. We can envision esteemed elders consolidating control over ritual, knowledge and ideology, a process that probably gave rise to ancestor cults and a general reverence for the past.

But sedentary populations will just naturally accumulate more and more, a process that increases the likelihood of confrontation. The Neolithic Era was never as peaceful as we once thought, and feuding eventually resulted in fortified settlements like Britain's Hambledon Hill and Crickley Hill (3200 BCE), some of which show evidence of having been attacked by archers and even burned.

By about 3000 BCE, late Neolithic society began to form elite chiefdoms such as the ones we later find ruling the Dark Ages. Wealth, based on new and competitive trade networks, accumulated in dominant lineages. Through patronage and indebtedness, powerful individuals became ever more prominent. Trade focused more and more on personal adornment, ornamental or symbolic, a reflection of the prestige and power of such personages. Where our early Neolithic ancestors appear to have stressed communal, intergenerational and tribal connections and obligations, the economic and social changes of the Late Neolithic ushered in the embryonic forms of the powerful chiefdoms we now recognize as a defining feature of the more populous warrior societies of the Bronze Age.

THE BRONZE AGE

The Bronze Age began when our ancient ancestors started using metal for their implements of warfare, industry and general living. Once again, for convenience sake, we're going to place the Early Bronze Age at 2200-1500 BCE, the Late Bronze Age at 1500-600 BCE. These dates are, of course, very fluid. In parts of Scotland, for example, the Bronze Age lingered on well into the second century BCE.

A single definitive time in which societies used one metal exclusively over another does not exist. Our ancestors produced and used copper, bronze and iron — sometimes at the same time — in different places, and in different quantities, from either accident or experimentation. The earliest metallurgists were the scientists and researchers of their day. Beyond that, they could liquefy stone and then turn it into something even stronger and harder. This is the stuff of magic. Those age-old myths many of us read in high school, of otherworldly metal smiths with magical golden chalices, probably date back to this period. Certainly many Celtic legends about enchanted cauldrons had their origin in the Bronze Age. Food from the Cauldron of Dagda, for example, one of the treasures of the mythological Celtic people known as the Tuatha Dé Danann, was said to never run out. Whoever ate of it would be restored their strength and energy.

We sometimes call the early centuries of the Bronze Age the Chalcolithic or Copper-Stone Period because of the emphasis on pure copper. Well before 4000 BCE, we were using meteoric iron with small nuggets of natural or "pure" soft metals like gold, silver and copper to make beads or amulets. We shaped them into ornaments and trinkets by cutting, grinding or hammering. Gold was preferred for jewelry.

By about 3000 BCE, all the techniques familiar to jewelers today had been perfected – inlay, stamping, repoussé, raising, soldering, riveting, granulation and surface coloring, as well as the lost wax method for complicated castings. Though too soft for most weapons, copper hardened when hammered, allowing our predecessors to shape it into sickles and daggers. Every ancient metal culture we know of today began with the use of native gold and/or copper.

The art of smelting pure copper is thought to have originated independently in Turkey and the Balkans about 5000 BCE, and in Mesopotamia – roughly present day Iraq – about 4000 BCE. Copper objects were traded into Northern Europe much earlier, but by 3000 BCE, we find the art widely spread in the Near East and moving westward into the Neolithic cultures of Europe. By 2000 BCE, Cyprus produced copper so extensively and deposits were so highly valued that the struggle for control of the island brought constant warfare, and Cyprus fell in turn to Egypt, Assyria, Phoenicia, Greece, Persia and Rome. Copper and, later, tin producers were the equivalent of the oil barons of our day. Controllers of a finite and coveted natural resource, they became extremely wealthy.

The oldest piece of bronze we know of is a rod found in the collapsed pyramid of Medum, south of Giza, which dates to 2700 BCE. Bronze is harder and more workable than copper, and with a much lower melting point, it is far superior to pure copper for casting. By smelting mixtures of copper and arsenic bearing ores, the ancients began producing very early bronzes between 4000 and 3000 BCE. Tin bronzes, the mixture of copper and tin which is the true marker of the Late Bronze Age, were in use by about 1500 BCE.

From Mesopotamia and Egypt, the use of bronze spread throughout the Mediterranean, just as the use of copper had. With the discovery of more tin deposits in the late third millennium BCE, communities could produce even more bronze.

Much of the knowledge of metalworking was spread by sea-faring Phoenicians, who brought their tin from India and Spain and moved on to exploit rich Cornish deposits in southwest England. British tin was used throughout the second millennium BCE and is responsible for the huge number of bronze objects we've since discovered all over Europe.

Tin and copper often had to be carried over long distances and thus became valuable trade items. Bronze products were so expensive that at the end of the second millennium BCE, cheaper iron goods began to take their place, replacing them entirely in most of Europe by the seventh century BCE. The early Celtic Iron Age Austrian culture we now know as Hallstatt, took fully 500 years to reach England, a distance of just 500 miles. Once again, we see that prehistoric change moves at a snail's pace, but is significant nonetheless.

With these economic developments, power began to accumulate over time with wealthy copper and tin merchants, or with chieftains who otherwise controlled metal technology. The trend toward chiefdoms that we saw in the late Neolithic continued into the Bronze Age. With the elite in control of supplies and transport, we find the late Bronze Age increasingly hierarchical and militaristic.

For a long time, scholars thought copper-working technology came to Britain between 2500 and 2000 BCE, with members of a group of obscure cultures we collectively call Beaker Culture. The name is taken from a unique style of ceramic cup associated with beer. One branch of Beaker Culture fused a Late Neolithic native culture in Northern Europe with that of newcomers from the Asian Steppe Lands. A second branch, with bell-shaped drinking cups, probably came from the Iberian Peninsula and spread along the west coast of Spain and France to mix with North European Beakers of the Rhineland and Holland. Members of Beaker Culture seem to have been of different physical stature than native Neolithic people. Neolithic skulls are generally elongated, while those associated with Beaker Culture are more rounded. Neolithic burial chambers are similarly elongated, while those associated with Beaker Culture are more circular.

It's equally possible, of course, that we're reading all of this wrong and that the Beakers were not a distinct cultural subtype at all. Their unique ceramic cups and burial customs may simply have been a regional way of expressing individual prestige. The shape of a skull may reflect this same impulse. Head binding, as found in ancient Nubia and Egypt, results in elongated skulls.

Wherever they originated, Beaker cultural elements blended in the south of England to become what we now call the Wessex Culture, an advanced society represented by a series of rich graves, the earliest dating to about 1800 BCE. The people buried here were probably the Rockefellers and Carnegies of their day, Bronze Age tin traders or wealthy middlemen in an ever-broadening Bronze Age trade network that reached into Ireland, Scottish Argyll, Brittany, Egypt, Crete, Central Europe and Mycenaean Greece.

A "heroic" and adventurous society in its upper-most ranks, Bronze Age warrior cultures displayed their dominance with personal adornment and specialized weaponry. By the late Bronze Age, trade and industry were booming. Demand for metal and metal goods like knives, awls, pins, daggers, earrings, button caps, cauldrons, buckets, jewelry and ritual shields (combat shields were made of leather or wood), advanced trade markets well beyond earlier Neolithic networks. We can find evidence of amber traded from Jutland and the Baltic, shale from Dorset, jade axe-heads from the German Alps, copper and porcelainite axes from Ireland and jet necklaces from England's Yorkshire coast.

Much as it does today, increased trade created a specialized workforce. In the case of our Bronze Age ancestors, this included miners, metalworkers, carpenters and potters. As we see in our own time, the more we become dependent on others for our food, our clothing, our worldly goods and even for our housing, the more our self-sufficiency as a society declines. In the Bronze Age, this spurred on territorial divisions and economically motivated peace treaties.

Besides the increase in metal tools, weapons and ornaments, we don't know much more about everyday life in the Bronze Age. Individuals and families probably lived much as they had before, only now they did so under powerful overlords. Animals were raised as they had been in the Neolithic period, and farmers show a preference first for barley and then for wheat. Scattered populations lived predominantly in circular houses rather than the rectangular homes of their Neolithic predecessors.

We've had a good many excavations of Bronze Age circular hut complexes and hill forts over the years, among them Paxton Pits in the Ouse Valley of Sussex, England; Curraghatoor in Ireland's County Tipperary; Merrivale on Dartmoor, England; Landau-Southeast in Southern Germany; the River Canche estuary settlements near Pas-de-Calais, France; Friago in the Eastern Austrian Alps; Ganglegg in the South Tyrol of Italy; and Ty Mawr at the foot of Holyhead Mountain in North Wales.

Merrivale, off the road to Tavistock, is one of the most extensive of these, a sprawling complex scattered about in short-grass common lands grazed by sheep and goats. These eyed me suspiciously from behind boulders the early September morning I visited. A jumble of squared stones and fallen walls, it was at first difficult to distinguish Merrivale's burial cists from stone cairns or hut circles. Limestone was propped up and strewn about everywhere. But the huts soon became recognizable from their entranceways, and several cairns had monoliths at their cores. Two splendid double rows of standing stones climbed up the slope of a nearby hill, and a clear, cold creek from a spring near Rundlestone flowed down through the choppy grasses to the River Walkham far below. I felt transported in time, as if at any moment a handful of Merrivale's ancient villagers might top the ridge above me.

The Ty Mawr Hut Circles at the base of Holyhead Mountain in North Wales are another fine example of Bronze Age domestic architecture. Ty Mawr, which was used from the late Neolithic period through to the Iron Age Romans, is comprised of a small settlement stretched over fifteen to twenty acres along a gorse and bracken-covered hillside. There are about eight homesteads, just two or three of which were ever occupied at the same time. The settlement sits well back from the vertical cliffs of the South Stack, which were thick with sea pinks the summer I walked them. High, gnarly thickets of butter yellow gorse surrounded each hut's foundation. Ty Mawr, too, left me feeling very close to a distant past.

The cultural and economic trends of the Bronze Age were aided and abetted by another formidable player — the weather. The Sub-Boreal Period, which began about 4100 BCE, continued through much of the Early Bronze Age. By 2000 BCE, we know that temperatures had begun to drop slightly, and from about 1500 BCE on, weather conditions deteriorated. There was less sun and more rain, a pattern that continued until the climate changes of our present day, largely brought on by global warming.

Recorded in ice sheets, massive volcanic eruptions in Iceland in the late twelfth century BCE raised clouds of ash and dust that darkened the sun, dropped atmospheric pressure and brought even heavier rains that boosted growing blankets of peat bog. Eventually, we find that high-ground settlements had to be abandoned.

One of the most impressive of these is Grimspound, which I had the opportunity to view on a drive through England with my mother in the fall of 1991. A four-acre, late Bronze Age settlement situated on Dartmoor in Devon, England, in the high valley between Hameldown (Hamel Down) Tor and Hookney Tor, Grimspound has at least twenty-four hut circles with L-shaped porches, all surrounded by a low granite wall. In its time, this wall must have been massive. I could see that, in places, its ruins were more than fifteen feet wide. Each hut had been built with a double ring of granite slabs infilled with rubble and possibly peat, a technique still used in dry-stone walling today. Some of these huts were probably used for storage or for penning livestock.

The village's entranceway faccs south, uphill toward Hameldown, on the slopes of which the inhabitants had their pasturage. On the northern edge of the site rises the West Webburn, the main water source for the settlement. When I was there, this seep was a mere trickle through tangled gorse and heather. The acidic soils of Dartmoor have destroyed any organic material that might have been left at Grimspound, but it is still a striking site.

In some cases — especially in the north of Scotland — acid rain probably sterilized the fields, sending tribes southward in search of more productive farmland. Literally thousands of years of long summers, mild winters and generally calm seas, during which our farming forbearers felled vast tracts of forest, came to an end. Earthquakes, tidal waves and volcanic activity throughout the Mediterranean also mark this period. Santorini, north of Crete, erupted in 1626 BCE. The violent changes as people fled this devastation could easily have fueled the collapse of such rich areas as Wessex in southern England, Schleswig-Holstein on the continent and Nordic Jutland.

In the Early Bronze Age, the sowing of winter barley had provided a year-round food supply for these ancient cultivators, and populations had swelled. By the Late Bronze Age, however, climate change had reduced the growing season by as much as five weeks in many areas. Agriculture was plagued by bad farming practices, soil depletion, a shortened growing season, flooding and blanket bog. Settlements no longer accumulated surpluses. Food shortages, starvation and disease followed.

In bared and exhausted farmland, wind erosion became a serious problem, and farmers could only watch helplessly as scrub, bracken and weeds crept across their derelict fields. By about 1400 BCE, the Yorkshire Moors had been stripped of productive soils; by 1200 BCE, Cotswold valleys had filled with alluvial leeched from the fields above; by 900 BCE, southwest Ireland saw a marked decline in human activity, and much of northern Scotland was abandoned.

By the Middle Bronze Age, the availability of productive land had shrunk. Our ancestors thus began a shift toward stock rearing. Cattle complexes grew, eventually leading to a new commercial money-maker; the rock salt deposits that would dominate Iron Age society by the eighth to sixth centuries BCE. Celtic legends such as The Cattle Raid of Cooley, which involved the theft of prize bulls, probably date from this period.

Between 1200 and 1000 BCE, most of the prosperous and powerful civilizations of southeast Europe and the Near East collapsed violently. Cities like Troy, Miletus, Tarsus, Thebes, Pylos and Mycenae were burned. Trade was stifled, and large groups of people were uprooted. The highly centralized Mycenaean and Cretan kingdoms disappeared, and the population of Greece declined by about seventy-five percent. The Hittite Empire in Anatolia and northern Syria likewise collapsed, likely in large part due to food shortages. Egypt's New Kingdom was severely diminished.

By the eighth century BCE, mounted warriors armed with the spears and long swords that would become a staple of the age of iron, surged into Europe from the east, pushing native tribes westward. Warfare, famine, plague and pestilence took their toll, leaving behind ever more aggressive and insecure survivors, who were already under pressure from over-population, under-production of food, dwindling farmland and failed harvests.

We know that hill forts, defended farmsteads and hamlets with fortified gateways and walls grew in number from the middle Bronze Age. Eventually, they merged with those built in the Iron Age, when an aggressive and warlike population – hidden away when threatened in defensive fortresses such as Castell Henllys in Wales, Chysauster and Chun Castle in Cornwall, Maiden Castle in Dorset, Crickley Hill in Gloucestershire and dozens of others – became more or less the norm.

The Iron Age was dominated by Celtic-speaking people who appear to have evolved from European tribes of the thirteenth and twelfth centuries BCE and were therefore neither a separate culture nor race. In upcoming pages, we're going to talk about the well-known Celtic veneration of water, because it's likely that votive offerings to water were brought from the Bronze Age as a way of controlling rising floodwaters and growing peat bogs. Water is also a common feature in megalithic architecture. However, because there's no evidence that megalithic ceremonial centers of any kind were built in the British Isles after about 1500 BCE, the Iron Age, and thus true Celtic society, remain outside the scope of this book.

Iron technology spread from the Asian Steppe Lands and reached Great Britain in the late eighth century BCE. But it's safe to say that the seeds of the Iron Age – the settlement patterns, the economy, religion and tribal organization — were planted in the Bronze Age. Before we speculate on what stone building may have meant to our Neolithic and Bronze Age ancestors, it's important to examine the legacy of dazzling megalithic architecture they left behind.

CHAPTER 2

FORM AND FUNCTION
MEGALITH
ARCHITECTURE

"THE SUREST TEST OF THE
CIVILIZATION OF A PEOPLE . . .
IS TO BE FOUND IN
THEIR ARCHITECTURE."

– WILLIAM HICKLING PRESCOTT

Now that we know something about the background against which our ancient ancestors raised the great stone monuments of Western Europe, it's insightful to take a quick look at what exactly they built. As with any other prehistoric timescale, we don't have any definitive datelines between megalithic architectural styles. One flows easily into the next as elements are adjusted and ideas overlap. If we were to visit Cairnpapple Hill in the Lowlands of Scotland, for example, we'd see changes in human burial customs that span 4000 years, from 3500 BCE to CE (Common Era) 500. Near a Neolithic henge and circle, we'd also find Bronze Age cist burial cairns and a Late Iron Age Cemetery.

THE NEOLITHIC OR NEW STONE AGE

In the earliest centuries of the Neolithic Age, there's not much evidence of any stone tradition at all, though the Late Mesolithic/Early Neolithic people of Brittany apparently interred their dead together, males and females of all ages, in stone-lined pits. The building of stone monuments began soon after European tribes took up farming, probably while they were still partly nomadic.

We have no way of knowing if monumental stone architecture traveled as part of Europe's farming culture, or if it developed straight out of the Mesolithic Age through architectural migration. Most Western European stone tombs are older than the Eastern civilizations we once thought inspired them. The Neolithic period of great communal tomb building ranges from about 5000 to 3200 BCE. Egypt's pyramids date only to about 2500 BCE.

Therefore, the tribes of Western Europe may well have been the first people to build monumentally in stone, though this theory has been challenged in recent years by the discovery of a megalithic complex near Urfa in southeastern Turkey. Here, massive, elaborately carved limestone standing stones believed by many scholars to date to 9000 BCE were found arranged in circles on the hilltop of Gobekli Tepe.

In general, stone architecture in the Neolithic Age includes monumental, inhumation, earthen long-barrow tombs, and impressive stone-built chambered tombs like Ireland's Newgrange and Brittany's La Table de Merchand Chambered Tomb (PLATE 4) and Gavrinis (PLATE 5). In later years, giant stone circles such as Avebury and the Stones of Stenness in the Orkney Islands of Scotland were prominent.

Our Bronze Age ancestors raised most single standing stones (menhirs) and stone alignments, a great crop of small stone circles, and most round cist cairns such as the 300-plus around Stonehenge, which date to between 1700 and 1400 BCE, although we can also find all of these elements in the Late Neolithic.

As we've already seen, the Neolithic Age was a fragmented society probably based on extended families. The great tomb was the focus of a community, a religious/cult monument that marked a local group's territory. It was also a burial place and sanctuary that likely honored certain family or tribal members who were elevated in time to the status of revered ancestors. We have only to catch a glimpse of one of these magnificent tombs to know that they were meant to be seen from a great distance.

East of Slane Hill, in the Irish Republic, the River Boyne makes a loop to the south. There, in the semi-circle it forms, are three great glacial mounds that support the massive Neolithic chambered tombs of Dowth, Knowth and Newgrange. The most famous of these, Newgrange

(PLATE 6), dates to about 3200 BCE and has a corbelled roof that has been watertight for more than 5000 years. Newgrange had a massive, white-stone façade — now reconstructed — that glistened under both the sun and the moon and could easily be seen from many miles away. When I was there in 2007, the wet weather suddenly cleared to a deep blue sky filled with sunshine and high, wind-rushed clouds. The mound, once covered with stones, is now green and grassy, but its brilliant white-quartz frontage gleamed as ever in the sunlight. Even in a bank of Irish mist, it could never have been very well hidden.

In some cases, these great mounds, which vary from eighty to more than 200 feet in length, were used for more than a thousand years. They were the cathedrals or parish churches of their day and are common predominantly along the Atlantic seaboard. The earliest are found in Malta, Brittany, Southern France, Scandinavia and the Iberian Peninsula, with Holland, Germany and the British Isles closely following.

The dead might have been laid out in a separate timber-built mortuary house or in an enclosure at the front of the barrow. Alternatively, they may have been placed atop portal stones — massive entrance slabs supported by two or three uprights — where they would be protected from most wild animals. These portal stones may have been incorporated into larger burial mounds, from which gallery and passage graves eventually developed. If left open to the elements until the flesh was gone, selected bones were probably removed for burial on a particularly auspicious occasion, such as the Summer Solstice, or a full moon.

Beyond the odd stone axe, scraper or fragment of burnt or broken pottery, we've found very few grave goods in most early stone chambers. As cremation gradually replaced inhumation, bone and shell necklaces subsequently cracked from funeral pyres were buried with the dead, along with pottery fragments, animal bones, shells and the remains of what may have been ritual meals.

Now and again, old bones may have been cleared from a tomb to make room for new ones. Hundreds of people for thousands of years must have been buried like this. Once sealed, these tombs — some being first cleared of remains, some with from a handful to more than fifty bodies still inside — remained unopened until they were vandalized centuries later or discovered by archeologists. This unearthing, in some cases, was unfortunately the same thing.

Our Neolithic ancestors showed great diversity in the material and construction of their graves. On the rich alluvial soils of Brittany's coastal plain, they erected passage graves (Gavrinis) and long mounds with decorated menhirs (Locmariaquier). In Ireland, in addition to the massive passage graves of the Boyne Valley, we find court cairns with long-mounds and forecourts (Creevykeel); open portal dolmens with stone chambers and slanted capstones (Poulnabrone); and wedge tombs with rectangular chambers concealed inside a wedge-shaped mound (Gleninsheen, PLATE 7). The earliest wedge tombs date to around 3000 BCE. They were still being raised in the Irish counties of Cork and Kerry thirteen centuries later and were possibly still in use as late as 900 BCE, when the use of monumental tombs had long been phased out in the rest of Western Europe.

In the Cotswolds and the lower Severn Valley in England, our Neolithic ancestors fancied stone rotunda tombs with a central cist. Uncovered portal dolmens surrounded by a low platform were popular in Cornwall and the west of Wales. Passage graves, a means of interment possibly introduced from continental Europe around 3500 BCE, were also favorites in the north and west of both Wales and Scotland. Along with rebuilding and conversions of pre-existing burial chambers, we find regional variations everywhere.

At Wayland's Smithy's Chambered Tomb, for example, a long barrow was added on to a small earlier structure, possibly a simple cist cairn, perhaps in response to a growing population.

In general, the barrows of southern and eastern Britain were built of earth and rubble, while the chambered tombs of the north and west were made of stone. Those classic Mid-Neolithic tombs of the Brú Na Bòinne — Newgrange, Knowth and Dowth —date to 3200 or 3300 BCE and may have influenced the later massive chambered tombs of the northern Scottish Isles, such as Maes Howe in the Orkneys. There, a squared burial chamber with side cells echoes the houses at Skara Brae, the contemporary settlement nearby where the houses had similarly shaped rooms and side cells.

Such enclosed ritual sites, where access to the sacred is restricted, may reflect a growing control of spiritual matters, by, in this case, an elite group of tribal elders. Despite their awesome exteriors, the monumental tombs of the Neolithic Age all have small, dark central chambers where there is room for a mere handful of people. Just as the choir screens of our medieval cathedrals later shielded a privileged few from the common masses, so did the forecourts, anti-chambers and passageways of Neolithic burial chambers.

Arthur Norway, writing in the late nineteenth century, describes the Yorkshire Wolds as "a strange, lonely district, abounding in traces of some long-vanished people who, in days before the dawn of history, scattered their camps and funeral mounds over every slope and valley of the hills." In the Wolds, those ancient remnants have long since vanished under farmland and settlements. In other areas, they eroded into rising seas.

But even accounting for this — and the periodic cleaning out of old bones — it seems only a small percentage of people were actually buried in these communal graves. About twenty were found at Knowth. The Carrowkeel chambers in Ireland held about thirty bodies each. What was required of our ancestors for burial here? Did they have to be members of a chiefly or sacred clan? Did they draw lots? Were they chosen by talent or appearance? Or, was it just that whatever spiritual power lay in human remains, fewer and fewer were needed to gain that power until eventually, the monument alone was enough?

Whatever the reasoning, the construction of these great megalithic tombs and earthen long barrows reached its height in Ireland, in Scotland (north and west of the Highlands) and in the far west of Cornwall and Wales just as it was coming to an end elsewhere. With few exceptions and across several centuries, the tradition ceased altogether around 3000 BCE. Some tombs were permanently sealed. Others were used a short time longer; but by about 2250, BCE people were not even making offerings at them anymore. Abandonment seems to have come with a general spirit of reverence, final human remains being protected with layers of rubble, earth or shells.

At Cairn Holy II, out of Gatehouse of Fleet in Scotland, (PLATE 8), the last ceremony held there apparently involved the breaking of Beaker pottery. A huge mound with several exposed standing stones, Cairn Holy II is similar to a group of burial chambers on either side of the Irish Sea and along the Clyde estuary. Used from 3000 to 1800 BCE by both our Neolithic and Bronze Age ancestors, Cairn Holy II was excavated along with its companion, Cairn Holy I, in 1949. Because of the acidic soils, few relics beyond the broken pottery were found – though a jadeite axe of a blue-green stone from the Alps was uncovered at Cairn Holy I. As I sat there alone above Kirkdale Glen on a darkly clouded afternoon, it was easy to envision a torch lit funeral procession – the dancing, the chanting, the ritual release of the spirit of some sacred vessel that may have accompanied the spiriting away of the dead.

In the end, though, we really have no clear idea why the massive stone tombs of our Neolithic ancestors were abandoned. Local clan cults may have been combined under a more centralized authority. Given the apparent failing of their ancestral spirits to protect them from rising water and creeping bog, our ancestors may have turned away from a reverence for the dead in favor of some other expression of holiness. In any case, local power centers were eliminated altogether or were grafted onto new traditions, just as Christianity would later bring something of the past into the present, enclosing pagan burial chambers in the chapels of parish churches, adding crosses to solitary "pagan" standing stones and raising up churches and cathedrals on prehistoric holy ground, sometimes inside the remains of a stone circle.

Other monuments of the Neolithic period — earthen henges and causewayed camps — seem to have been sites periodically or seasonally occupied for markets, meetings or festivals of great communal feasting. As their populations grew, our Neolithic ancestors had a greater need for suitable spots — like causewayed camps — to exchange goods, information and even marriage partners. Fashioned in circular areas with encompassing ditches and entrance causeways, these ancient sites are often associated with axes. This suggests that they could have been marketplaces for the axe trade. Because the axe was a prominent Neolithic artistic motif, it may have been a symbol of the link between tribal members and their distant ancestors, those who had cleared the land long ago.

We've found more than 300 henge monuments in the British Isles. Circular or oval enclosures, each with a ditch and a bank, henges were constructed between about 3250 and 2200 BCE. Most have two entranceways and show a greater uniformity of design than do tombs. Henges appear to have been the precursors of the great Late Neolithic stone circles like Long Meg and Her Daughters and the Stones of Stenness, though in some cases, such circles seem to have been raised independently of other ritual monuments. One of the earliest rings, dating to about 3300 BCE, once surrounded the megalithic passage grave of Newgrange in Ireland. Today, we have only the occasional standing stone to serve as a reminder.

Early British circles such as Castlerigg and Swinside, both in Cumbria, date to about 3200 BCE, and a more beautiful setting than Castelrigg's would be hard to imagine. Some thirty-eight stones, not all upright, stand in a pear-shaped circle on the open fells east of Keswick, surrounded by the grassy highlands of the Lake District. The first time I saw Castlerigg, in the late 1980s, I'd narrowly missed a loaded tour bus. The sun lit up successive rusted-bracken hillsides like a giant spotlight, and ragged clouds shredded themselves overhead.

When I saw the stones next, more than ten years later, my husband and I had just come from a late supper at the Skiddaw Hotel in Keswick, and we reached Castlerigg well after dark on a clear moonless night. In the near distance, urban lights painted the mist over the town a pale pink. We sat for some time on the stones, some of which were reflected in pools of black rainwater, while a million stars glittered overhead. It was a truly magical experience.

Above Morecambe Bay, Swinside Stone Circle (also in the Lake District's Cumbrian Fells) stands a mile or so down a muddy track by Swinside Farm and across several fields. When Dan and I walked the path that same year, "Beware of Bull" signs had been posted all along the way. Two or three male calves were grazing in one field, and a large, docile black bull rested in a gathering of cows in the next.

Swinside, also known as Sunken Kirk, is one of the best-preserved circles in Western Europe. The stones are porphyritic slate quarried from the nearby fells, a rock known locally as "grey cobbles." Fifty-five of a possible sixty stones remain, thirty-two of them still standing. The tallest, directly to the north, tapers off at seven feet, six inches high. The stones were raised in an almost perfect circle, ninety feet in diameter, on a leveled earthen platform cut into the hillside. The name Sunken Kirk (Sunken Church) has been applied to a number of stone circles. At night, it's said, the devil pulls down the stones of a church being built during the day. Under overcast skies, I found Swinside — stately, powerful and isolated in its broad, walled field — yet another enchanting experience.

All of such circular monuments have more or less distinct entrances, cover a great deal of ground, and are made up of a large number of fair-sized stones spaced relatively closely together. In Ireland and Scotland, stone circles are often recumbent. Stone pillars are arranged in ascending height toward a large stone — the recumbent — which is placed horizontally between two flanking stones, Loanhead of Daviot is an example (PLATE 9). Some circles, such as those at Carrowmore Cemetery in Ireland, are really just the remains of despoiled cairns, or even the kerbstones that once surrounded them.

THE BRONZE AGE

The majority of stone circles must be placed in the early Bronze Age. Here we find two main types — circles that are open, with no pits or other ritual features, and circles associated with burial. All of them probably served the same function as henges. Many more were likely made of wood and have not survived, though in 1998, a Bronze Age circle of oak stumps, unearthed by the North Sea from a layer of peat moss, was discovered in East Anglia and named Seahenge or Holme-next-the-Sea.

During a 2000-year period, from about 3200 BCE to

about 1200 BCE, these circular monuments spread out over more than 300,000 square miles of the British Isles, from the Shetlands to Cornwall and from Aberdeenshire to the west of Ireland. They all have a general uniformity of pattern, yet also show remarkable diversity. We have small stones, large stones, evenly spaced stones and stones standing shoulder-to-shoulder. We can also see egg-shaped monuments and ellipses, center stones, outliers, concentric circles, flattened rings and "four-posters" made up of just four stones. Some circles were built inside henges. Some were erected next to long mounds and chambered tombs. Some have associated alignments, and some were built using rubbish banks.

Though likely part of the same series of formations that began with causewayed camps and henges, Bronze Age circles are generally smaller than their Neolithic counterparts, and their stones are more evenly spaced. The Merry Maids, also known as Dans Maen or Stone Dance, outside of Mousehole on the road to Land's End, is a good example.

The Merry Maids, the best known, best preserved and most accessible of the many stone circles at the western end of Cornwall, is an exact circle, with each of its nineteen well-weathered granite stones standing about four feet high. Today, the Merry Maids has a steady stream of summer visitors. A woman from Germany I met there, an artist and healer, had found the stones and their center in the pitch black of the previous night. Using a guidebook, my own approach was far more mundane.

As weather conditions deteriorated and traditional rituals failed, chambered tombs were sealed and ritual activity shifted to these open-air spaces. The rising tribal leaders of the Bronze Age may have raised stone circles as enhancements to henges, to siphon off some of the power of the local ancestor cults. While there's no obvious connection to death and burial among most circles and henges built between 2500-1100 BCE, there were quite likely other significant purposes for these circles. As rainfall increased and fields became waterlogged, the veneration of ancestors may have been abandoned in favor of a strong *living* individual who could mediate for humanity directly between the mortal and the Divine. The celestial aspects of stone circles may have then developed as a way of eclipsing or replacing ancestral power. In our Neolithic past, many of the departed could have become honored ancestors. By contrast, in the aggressive warrior societies of the Late Bronze Age, just a select few could become a chieftain or a priest.

As we see in Callanish, Carnac and Cork, the entire standing stone tradition appears to have moved from the stately circles of Cumbria and the Orkneys to increasingly complicated structures involving avenues, multiple, single or shortened stone rows, and simple paired stones.

An exception might be the single standing stone, or menhir. We know of at least 1200 of these still standing in northwest France alone. We can assume that single monoliths were used from the earliest of times to mark graves, springs, landfalls, meeting points, market places or boundaries. Some, such as the gnarly monument at St. Peter's, Peterchurch, Herefordshire, or the impressive monolith of Rudston out of Bridlington in Yorkshire — which, at twenty-six feet is the tallest standing stone in Britain — still stand in churchyards, a measure of the reverence they inspire. Countless others throughout Western Europe, denounced by the church, were blown up, buried, desecrated or otherwise eliminated.

Extensions to the single standing stone design began in Britain and northwest France about 3200 BCE. Stone rows reached their apex from about 2100-1600 BCE, and there are still more than a hundred remaining in Brittany alone. Stones stand as simple pairs, in short rows, long rows, double rows and multiple rows. The massive complex at Carnac has over 3000 grey-stone granite boulders arranged in four groupings, now walled in for their protection. The stones of some alignments rise in height as they approach a cairn, and there are stone rows that may have been extended entrances leading to circles or other ritual enclosures. Despite the circus atmosphere of their surroundings – the mini-rail tourist trams, the endless souvenir stalls and carnival barkers – the stones of Carnac are still an awesome sight.

A central feature of Bronze Age Europe is the small circular burial mound or cairn. These come in many shapes and sizes, and they formed the cemeteries of their day. In the Kilmartin Valley of Scotland, a round cairn cemetery dating to about 2000 BCE lies to either side of the great passage tomb of Nether Largie. Similarly, more than 300 round cairns were raised between 1700 and 1400 BCE for the cemetery around Stonehenge. Round barrows in the south of England were built mostly on grass surfaces or on field boundaries. Their cores are often turf heaps infused with the remains of snail shells. Snails are usually found in an open landscape, and their fossilized presence suggests that these barrow soils may once have been farmed.

In the Late Neolithic, a single adult male might have been buried with a flint club, a heavy, antlered mace-head or some other prestigious weapon. In the Early Bronze Age, as evidenced in the rich graves of England's Wessex Culture (about 1800 BCE) and those of Brittany, powerful, aristocratic chieftains, priests or metal workers apparently dominated the tribes, and we've found personal goods like bronze daggers or copper axes buried with the dead under small, individual tumuli. Clearly, these single burial mounds had taken the place of the large family tomb. By 1200 BCE, even the construction of round barrows had ceased.

From the Middle Bronze Age, cremation became more popular. We find cinerary urns buried in the sides of barrows or in urn cemeteries that often grew up around a single monolith. This Urnfield Culture was prominent in the flat lands of southern and central England and dates to between about 1500 and 1200 BCE.

By the Late Bronze Age (1100-600 BCE), 3000 years of a continuously developing stone-building tradition among our European ancestors came to an end. Circles, burial mounds and henges all went out of use. More than that, from the Middle Bronze Age onward, they were often treated with little respect. Stones were leveled for agriculture. Field walls were built across stone avenues. The Neolithic henge monument at Moncrieff in Perthshire, which had been turned into a ring cairn in the Bronze Age, became a forge in the Iron Age. It might seem fitting that metalworking should take place inside a mystical stone ring, but the cremation urns unearthed at the time appear to have been purposefully smashed.

Even so, the fact that myths and legends of heroes and gods living in the ancient tombs of the Neolithic and Bronze Age lingered on among the Iron Age Celts who were their likely descendants, suggests some continuity in beliefs about death and fertility. Yet the same destructive pattern that came out of the Middle Bronze Age continued through the Roman period and beyond. Agriculture impinged on and destroyed many of the stone monuments of our prehistoric past. In Celtic mythology, the stones were sometimes regarded as the work of an alien race. Humans were warned to stay clear of them for fear of transformation or even death. We sense this same detachment from human prehistory in the work of the Roman writer Pliny the Elder, who died in the eruption of Mt. Vesuvius in CE 79. Pliny claimed that stone axes placed in Romano/British temples, were thunderbolts from the god, Jupiter. In the Middle Ages, these same axes became fairy missiles.

Beginning about 1200 BCE, probably in response to the

dire effects of heavy rainfall, water spirits came into vogue and rose in popularity into the Iron Age. Fine weapons and other metal goods were offered to lakes, rivers, meres and bogs to appease the vengeful water gods, and wet places became the focus of an emerging water cult. By then, of course, those far off, forgotten days when our prehistoric ancestors had raised up great stone monuments had long passed into the mists of time.

CHAPTER 3

FRAGMENTS OF INFINITY
MEGALITHIC ART

"A WORK OF ART ONCE COMPLETED
STANDS AS A
FINAL STATEMENT FOR ALL TIME."

– ENCYCLOPEDIA BRITANNICA

WHEN I FIRST SAW WESTERN IRELAND'S massive portal dolmen of Poulnabrone (PLATE 10) in the heart of the Burren, I was deeply impressed. Its dramatic capstone of slender limestone extends high over the entrance and gives it the sculptural quality of a work of art. All around lay the pale gray to grayish-blue limestone of the 340-million-year-old seabed that makes up the Burren, crisscrossed by joints that were in many places deep, dark and empty that summer day, and in others brimming with grasses, mosses and wildflowers – daisies, bloody-cranesbill and bluebells.

The vertical stones of Poulnabrone, held in place like a house of cards by the weight of a capstone, were erected directly on the bedrock. Popular with tourists, who've set up miniature replica dolmens in all directions, Poulnabrone was excavated in 1986. The remains of about twenty-eight people were found buried there sometime between 3800 and 3200 BCE, one of them a newborn baby. All but one of the adults had died before the age of thirty.

Most megalithic monuments are similarly visual. Faulty restoration, the shifting of surrounding soils or the incursion of vegetation may have altered their shapes, yet most still have an aesthetic quality we can all appreciate.

While our literate societies emphasize the written word, people with no written language use music or art as their primary form of expression. A language of images and symbols, art makes the present permanent to some degree. The mind and the imagination of the artist recreate an experience in visual, verbal or auditory form. The mind and the imagination of the observer respond with a set of personal images and impressions.

Throughout the ages, we can best see the fusion of artistic

form and function in architecture. Our buildings today must be practical for their purpose, while still dealing with mass and space, color, the flow of light and the quality and texture of our materials. The stone buildings of our Neolithic and Bronze Age past are no exception. Their builders paired stones of different shapes, lengths and colors. They placed a squat gray granite boulder beside a lofty red sandstone monolith. They used the square and the circle to define sacred space, and they directed the light of the sun or the moon.

As we move on with our discussion, we're going to look not only at stone, the most obvious and enduring building material of our prehistoric past, but also at wood, which may have been just as popular with our ancestors. We'll examine color and design through artistic motif and shape, with emphasis on the circle, our most evident unit of sacred space, and the purist, simplest and most all-encompassing artistic form. After each section, under the heading of *Spiritual Fitness*, we'll then talk a little bit about applications to contemporary spiritual growth inspired by these ancient expressions in stone. They have a fascinating relevance to our everyday living.

STONE

"I sometimes choose to think
that man is a dream,
thought an illusion and
only rock is real."

— Edward Abbey

Rock is the basic building material – the skeleton – of the Earth's crust. Some experts think that a shell of granite lies under the Earth's lithosphere. Igneous rocks such as granite, gabbro and basalt are crystallized from magma. Sedimentary rocks such as conglomerates, sandstones, shale, limestone, marble, dolomite and travertine are formed from the deposits of both organic and inorganic debris. Metamorphic rocks, including slate, quartzite, gneiss, schist and serpentine, are produced when sedimentary or igneous rock is re-crystallized under extreme temperature and/or pressure.

It's a stone's business to be durable. The bones of Mother Earth appear to us as tough, stable, solid and long lasting. An emblem of suffering and survival, rock deals stoically with the elements – weathered by stream, lake and seawater; assailed by wind, rain, dissolved salts and ground moisture; eaten away slowly by the carbonic, nitric and sulfuric acids produced by fungi, lichens and mosses.

Some stones give us a hint of special power. When wet, for example, crystalline rock quartz glitters and gleams in the sunlight. Aboriginal shamans thought of quartz crystals as power-bearers or a form of "solidified light." We know of monoliths that retain the warmth of the sun long after dark and of others that leave a tingling or prickling sensation in the hand when touched. Rock can be rough or smooth or luminous, soft or hard, light or heavy. In contrast to our own uncertain and fragile lives, rock is stalwart and everlasting. To touch a stone of noted power is to touch the eternal and perhaps –just maybe – acquire a measure of divine virtue.

From the very earliest of times, humans have linked stone with the sacred. Gods like the Roman Mithras were born from stone. The Chaldean god Anu was represented by a single upright standing stone, a symbol also used by early Semitic people to mark a spot where a deity had manifested. The cosmic center of the Islamic world is the black meteorite in Mecca known as the Kaaba Stone.

The stone builders of our prehistoric past rarely quarried or dressed their stones. They chose the boulders, slabs and glacial erratics that were close at hand and set them up in their natural state. In an animistic world, all things have life, and to alter a stone physically diminishes its spiritual power and reduces its potency. Stone alone must have been inherently attractive to our ancestors, as a good number of megalithic monuments were raised in places that were then rich in timber.

Just as we do today, the builders of prehistory chose stone for its mineral composition, color and texture. A porous, uniform grain size produces a finer product than one without, and rock has an unlimited variety of color, the shade determined by the dominant mineral, the grain size and adhesive and the adjacent minerals. Colors can range from the pinks of potassium and feldspar to the reds, browns and yellows of iron minerals such as hematite and limonite; greens from magnesium and iron silicates; blue from titanium; and white and gray from carbon, quartz, calcite and clay minerals.

IGNEOUS ROCK

Some igneous rocks, including granite, gabbro and diorite, are cooled slowly beneath the earth or intruded from its surface. Their crystals are coarse-grained and textured. Rocks cooled rapidly at or near the surface, like basalt and porphyry, are finer-grained, harder and stronger. The color of igneous rock is stable and depends largely on feldspars that usually make up from fifty to seventy-five percent of the total rock. Dark-colored igneous rock, like diorite and basalt, can be medium gray to black, depending on its iron content. Hornblendes of the iron-magnesium-

47

silicate group produce colors from green to black, while traces of titanium give us igneous rocks with a bluish tint. The dark feldspars that dominate gabbro have made this rock one of a number we commonly call "black granite."

Our prehistoric ancestors most often used granite in its natural shape and size. For example, in the Cumbrian countryside, the magnificent Late Neolithic stone circle of Long Meg and her Daughters (PLATE 11) — located east of the Eden Valley on a gentle slope near Little Salkeld — is made up of sixty-nine granite glacial erratics arranged in an expansive oval, with twenty-seven of them still standing. In the light of a falling English sky, they are usually a dark grey. Long Meg, the tallest stone at twelve feet, is an outlier of red sandstone.

Feldspars, and sometimes hornblendes, determine the color of most granite, which varies from flesh-colored or pink and white, to beige, light tan, deep red and even grays and greens. Crystallized silica — quartz — makes up from ten- to thirty-five- percent of granite, depending on the amount of silica that was in the magma when it crystallized. Imperfections, such as air bubbles trapped in cooling crystals, produce a glassy gray or white sheen. We also see opalescent blue, pearl or rose-colored quartz. With its abundance and great variety of color and texture, granite has traditionally been, and still is, our most common building stone.

SEDIMENTARY ROCK

Sedimentary rock forms when organic or inorganic debris accumulates from chemical precipitation or from the action of wind, waves, rain or flowing streams. We most often see these rocks deposited in flat layers called bedding. Beaches and sand dunes form fine-grained sandstone;

stream action builds coarse sandstone and conglomerates; and dissipated calcium from shelled sea creatures becomes limestone. The minerals in sedimentary rock come, of course, from the sediment's source.

Except where the original rock source contained some igneous component such as feldspar or quartz, the generally warm colors of sedimentary rock are often unstable. Ferric, or iron oxide, is the most common and most powerful pigment in sedimentary rock. Soft, warm colors from deep red to orange, yellow, brown, tan and bluish green result from the concentration and degree of oxidation of the iron in the rock. A mere fraction of one percent can add a warm touch to a sedimentary rock's hue. Ferrous carbonate produces shades of white or light cream that oxidize to yellow. Grays and blacks come from organic substances like carbon, and clay minerals produce a dull white to medium gray.

The megalithic builders of our ancient past favored sedimentary rocks, including sandstone and limestone. Sand-sized grains of quartz or feldspar, cemented with silica, calcium carbonate or clay, dominate most sandstone, which is colored white to buff-red and dark brown. We also find calcite, mica and hornblende. A porous rock, sandstone is easily eroded by water and wind. The trilithons of Stonehenge are made of sarsen, a sandstone brought from the Marlborough Downs.

Bluestone is a hard, gray sandstone made mostly of dark feldspar. Just two of the so-called "bluestones" of Stonehenge are actually sandstone. One of the misnamed stones is limestone, and the others are dolerite, a fine to medium-grained dark gray/blue igneous rock of basaltic composition. Dolerite is another of the dark-colored rocks we call "black granite." Brownstone, a brownish or reddish-brown sandstone, is produced in harsh, hot desert environments, and it weathers to clay very rapidly. The fiery red sandstones of the American Southwest are the work of iron hydroxide absorbed as a thin coating on the quartz crystals of sandstone. Other red sandstones take on the color of their inter-grain cement.

The Ring of Brodgar in the Orkney Islands of Scotland (PLATE 12) is a prime example of a Neolithic sandstone ring. Brodgar is the third largest stone circle in the British Isles, next to Avebury and Stanton Drew, and it was probably one of the last to be built. Twenty-seven of a possible sixty stones still stand in a perfect circle on the Ness of Brodgar, the low-lying strip of land between the lochs of Harray and Stenness. We can easily see that Brodgar's tan-colored monoliths, once called the Temple of the Sun, were taken from layered bedding. Rising up from the heather, many of them have deep fractured fissures running the length of the stones. In England, the three impressive stone circles of Stanton Drew, near Bath, are also large, undressed sandstone.

Limestone and dolomite, the most versatile of all sedimentary rocks, are often found in horizontal beds, which are easily quarried. Limestone — calcium carbonate with less than five-percent impurities — is a soft, fine-textured rock colored white to cream and gray. It's often stained yellow or brown by iron oxides or can be colored bluish to black by organic matter or iron disulfide.

METAMORPHIC ROCK

Metamorphic rock results from heat and/or pressure being applied to a sedimentary, igneous or other metamorphic rock. If metamorphic processes are low, clay or shale becomes slate, limestone turns into strong, fine-grained marble, and granite becomes gneiss, a rock similar to granite but with banded mineral grains. Higher processes produce stones such as coarse-grained marble and schist, a rock that resembles gneiss but has thinner bands.

Strong foliation – the quality of being easily split – makes most metamorphic rock, with the exception of slate, unsuitable for building. Slate is produced from fine, clayey sedimentary rock containing a high volume of sand or volcanic dust, and so it splits easily into strong, thin slabs. The durability of slate has made it perfect for roofing tiles, and we have quarries all over the world producing a great variety.

Most metamorphic rock has a naturally cold color. Slates can be gray, red, green, black, blue, purple or mottled. Dark slates contain carbonaceous material or iron. Chlorite produces green slate; hematite, red and purple. Greenstone, a metamorphic igneous rock primarily made of basalt, takes its color from hornblende and chlorite. Gneisses and schists inherit stable minerals from their igneous rock sources and thus have stable colors. But for the most part, sedimentary limestones, sandstones and conglomerates undergo color changes during metamorphic processes, and warm tones such as tan, buff, cream and ochre become colder.

The magnificent Callanish complex is constructed of indigenous metamorphic Lewisian gneiss (PLATE 13). The name derives from the Isle of Lewis, the outer Hebridian island on which Callanish stands. Lewisian gneiss is among our most ancient rocks, dating back around 300 million years. If we could look in on the Earth's lower continental crust, we'd quite likely find similar gneisses.

When I visited Callanish last, in the wildest Scottish weather – sheep were very nearly being blown into the sea by gale winds – all that slashing wind and rain came nowhere near to diminishing the sentient beauty of this rock. The overall color of these tall thin stones is a dovish gray highlighted with striking specks of color: chunks of black/green hornblende, chips of terra-cotta feldspar and glassy

white quartz. The rocky undulating landscapes of much
of the Outer Hebrides, their black tarns and low heathery
crags, their skerries and reefs, are all typical of the dramatic
form and sharp texture of the Lewisian gneiss of which they
are formed.

PUTTInG ROCK TO WORK

The hammer as a tool and a weapon was civilization's
most common use of stone in the prehistoric period,
beginning with the hammers of our Paleolithic ancestors.
We've since used stone to hold down thatched roofs or
cover chimneys; as anchors or sinkers, wayside markers,
memorials, milestones or boundaries; as a scratching post
for field animals; and, of course, for building. Shamans use
hollow concretions filled with loose pebbles as rattles, and
hot rocks added to water in stone-lined pits have been used
for cooking.

Very early in our history, humans recognized the
outstanding properties of certain rocks for axes and jewelry;
Bronze Age jet and amber necklaces, for example. Black
stones like coal or jet and wet slabs of dark slate are still
used to induce the psychic visions of the altered state of
consciousness called scrying.

Because stone is mysterious and everlasting, its use has
long been prominent in defining sacred spaces, designating
meeting places and housing the dead. It has also been widely
used in healing, health and fertility rituals. Where frost is
deep, stones multiply in cultivated fields as new stones are
heaved up from lower levels by successive freezing and
thawing, a process that suggested fertility to our ancestors.
Aetites or "eagle stones" — claystone cores surrounded by
clay/ironstone concretions of shell that are often found
in eagles' nests — are still emblems of fertility, believed to

ensure breeding success.

Stones have a variety of healing functions that will be more fully addressed in upcoming pages. Briefly, pumice removes bunions and calluses; smooth or water-born "worry stones" have a tranquilizing effect; a small stone under the tongue offsets thirst. For health and protection or to ward off disease or malevolence, many of us might wear or carry a stone of specific shape, color or composition as a talisman.

The most credible example of a healing stone we have is probably the quartz crystal. Quartz produces an electric current when under pressure or tension and vibrates when influenced by an electrical field. These qualities make it invaluable for resonators and oscillators, and we may eventually find that it influences the human body in ways we've not yet uncovered. Quartz has long been considered a powerful tool in aboriginal medicine, and clear or white quartz stones are often offered at holy wells to increase their potency. In the north of Ireland, gold or yellow crystalline quartz, which appears to house its own light, is valued as a symbol of the essence of spirituality.

Many of our rituals, both past and present, have involved stone. Bullauns —hemispherical depressions cut in rock — have been used in Ireland for generations, extending into modern times. A coconut-sized "turning" or "cursing" stone placed in the bullaun is rotated in a manner specific to local tradition, for prayer, healing or cursing. Public cursings used to be known as "Turning the Stones." In the nineteenth century, with the approach of a British gunboat sent to evict the tenants of Tory Island off the coast of County Donegal, the local cursing stone was activated. Consequently — or so the story goes — the gunboat sank, and its entire crew drowned.

Dry-stone altars known as "leachta" were often part of old Celtic monasteries. Wishes were made by rotating a collection of stones on the altars, eleven of which still stand on the Irish island of Inishmurray. Each of these leachtas bears its own name. The one for curses is called Clochabreacha.

Celtic labyrinths carved on small portable slate slabs called Troy Stones were once used by visionary women to communicate with other worlds. By continually tracing a finger over the lines of the labyrinth — a symbol of the path from the outer to the inner world — these women reached an altered state of consciousness.

Well into the nineteenth century, the eternal quality of stones made them popular for sealing oaths. One of these, the Odin Stone — a holed stone at Croft Odin in the Orkney Islands — was, unfortunately, purposely destroyed in 1814. Another, the Blessed Stone of St. Columba on Scotland's Holy Island of Iona, granted any supplicant a single wish. Oath-binding stones also appear in Christian scripture. "And Joshua . . . took a great stone and set it up there under an oak that was by the sanctuary of the Lord," the Bible says. "And Joshua said unto all the people 'Behold this stone shall be a witness unto us; for it hath heard all the words of the Lord which he spake unto us.'"

In our mythology and legends, stones walk, dance, drink, wash and even eat. Such powerful entities appealed to us in defining sacred spaces. For the Old Norse, a vébond — a sacred enclosure surrounded by standing stones — had a great many uses, among them oath-taking and ritual combat.

Stones from holy ground are energized by their place of origin. The green stones found on the Holy Island of Iona, for example, are believed to promote healing and blessing. The bluestones of Stonehenge that came from the Prescelly Hills in Wales may have been revered for the magical and protective properties they brought with them from their mountain home. Some of us may have seen libations, shells and wildflowers offered at stone circles. I was once at Long Meg and Her Daughters just after the Summer Solstice and found a fresh bouquet of purple saxifrage lying at the base of Long Meg. Handfuls of snail shells had been placed reverentially on several of her Daughters.

In many cultures, stone is an emblem of the sacred mountain, which itself symbolizes the axis of the universe. Travelers in Tibet add stones to holy cairns in mountain passes, and certain shrines of the Hottentots in Africa are made up of heaps of stones dedicated to the god Heitsi-Eibib, who battles darkness. In the United States, a few well-placed stones outline the sacred area of a shrine on one of the holy mountains of Santa Clara Pueblo in New Mexico.

For Neolithic cultures, the great chambered tomb may have been the holiest place of all. Sixteenth and seventeenth century manuscripts tell us of dolmens in the Channel Islands called "altars of the gods of the sea." Hallowed by their nearness to ancestral spirits, the stones of these dolmens may have become guardians and protectors of the tombs themselves. As time passed and our ancestors abandoned the tombs, the people of the cultures that followed them were prohibited by their religious leaders from approaching them at night, when they were believed to have been occupied by gods and spirits or, in the case of the Irish, the "Little People." Today we would say they were haunted. Despite such superstition, the long and rich tradition of megalithic sites being used for worship and spiritual guidance continued well into historical times.

We've also seen that stones had a place in the actual burial practices of our forbearers. Among the grave goods found in Poulnabrone — a stone axe, disc beads and flint scrapers — were two large quartz crystals. In Ulster and the Western Isles, a handful of quartz pebbles called "godstones" were often left on graves or in tombs as an offering that would carry off the prayers of those who had placed them there. Well into the 1950s, the Irish buried unbaptized infants in "killeens"—"little churches or churchyards." These unconsecrated, but nonetheless sacred grounds could be identified by the pieces of white quartz that surrounded them, similar to the white pebbled façade of Newgrange.

Such scatterings of white quartz were possibly associated with the moon and may well represent our attempt to reflect the moon's mystic light onto the dead. This practice was known among the ancient Greeks as "drawing down the moon." For ancient Semites, certain gods could be called upon by erecting a feldspar monolith known as a moonstone. In Hinduism, these feldspars are believed to be made of condensed moonbeams. We'll be looking more closely at the complex and intriguing connections between the moon and prehistoric stone monuments in a later chapter.

SPIRITUAL FITNESS

"One who values stones
is surrounded by treasures wherever
he goes."
– Pär Lagerkvist, Dvärgen

"This hand size rock inhabits the outline
of itself on the sand . . .
Honor it, touch it with awe."
– Virginia Hamilton Adair "Godstone"

Around CE 600, Japan imported a discipline called Suiseki – the Art of Stone Appreciation – from China, where it had originated several centuries earlier. Small, especially beautiful stones were set on stands to represent the legendary islands and mountains associated with the Buddha or the Tao.

Suiseki is a Japanese word meaning "water stone," derived from the early custom of displaying the stones in trays of water. First collected from ancient rivers, Suiseki stones may be from just a few inches to more than a foot and a half in length. Most are small and have the distinctive shapes of mountains, waterfalls or islands. They may also have similar images or scenes patterned on their surfaces. Suiseki are traditionally set on carved wooden stands called "daizas" or in shallow trays called "dobans," where they can be admired as true works of art; perhaps imparting a sense of spiritual inspiration to the viewer. When combined with bonsai, they become the vision of a far-off mountain.

In Suiseki tradition, we, too, can collect our own stones, chosen by color, texture, shape or place of origin, and place them by a hearth, in a display case or on a small personal altar. Our collections can be used for meditation on particularly hard issues in our lives. We might want to contemplate suffering and survival, strength, spiritual potency, longevity, endurance, the beauty of nature or the miracle of life, all attributes of stone. What in our lives feels secure and well grounded? What feels heavy and immovable? We might also focus on the moments and experiences when we've felt as eternal and unalterable as stone. A solitary crystal might simply invoke clarity. A special smooth or water-borne stone may serve as a "worry stone."

The use of a talisman is another way we can honor stone. We might carry a specific stone — found or purchased for the attribute with which it is associated — as an item of jewelry or in a leather pouch. Amethyst, for example, is the stone of spiritual power. The biblical priest Aaron, by divine command, put an amethyst in the center of his breastplate. *The Book of Stones: Who They Are and What They Teach* by Robert Simmond and Naisha Ahsian, and *Stone*, by Andy Goldsworthy, are just two of a number of books that can help you find the amulet you're looking for.

WOOD

"I HAVE HAD NO OTHER MASTERS
BUT THE BEECHES AND THE OAKS."
— St. Bernard of Clairvaux

From archeological evidence, we've discovered that the pattern of our ancestors' stone circles and burial chambers may have come from structures they originally built of wood, which may have been their material of first choice. But because wood rarely survives the passage of time, few timber relics remain.

Two miles northeast of Stonehenge, however, we've found a Neolithic ring of timber called Woodhenge. Oval in shape, its long axis is aligned with the Midsummer sunrise. The holes of its posts, in six concentric circles of about 168 posts, are now marked with cement pillars. In just the past few years, other wooden henges have been uncovered, one at Durrington Wells near Stonehenge and another at Stanton Drew near Bristol. The last of these is comprised of between 400 and 500 posts set in nine concentric rings more than 300 feet in diameter.

Today, wood is, of course, one of our primary building materials. But we also have many other uses for trees. Their foliage gives us shade and protection. Trunks and branches provide us with fuel. We can eat and drink their fruits, nuts and juices, and their leaves and flowers bring added beauty into our lives. From the near white of holly to the jet-black of ebony, the colors of wood appeal to us. Dark woods pale when lit and light woods darken.

Trees are a marvel, but they must have been utterly bewildering in our earliest days. Bare, wasted and seemingly lifeless in winter, they transformed themselves in spring to become vast ripe summer canopies of deep shade and shelter. In fall they dropped their leaves, dead again to winter, to be renewed in springtime. The tree, changing with the seasons, is the very mirror of our human lives. A tree's roots dig deep into the earth. Its branches reach upward into other worlds. Trees are natural mediators between Heaven and Earth. With reflected root and branch systems, they are the physical representation of the ancient mystic adage, "As above, so below."

To many cultures, the natural flow of tree sap demonstrates that sacred or cosmic forces are at work. The tree is one of our archetypes, an "elementary idea," the scholar and storyteller Joseph Campbell has written in his Harvard University book, *The Hero with a Thousand Faces*. The stylized Tree of Life of the Jewish Kabbalah is a virtual map of creation.

When our human ideal has been the tree, it's easy to understand why we've honored it. As natural holy centers, trees were perhaps our earliest temples. In many mythologies, trees are not only sacred but are directly connected to the birth of humankind. Ancient Romans, for instance, believed that oaks produced the first people. Some early cultures deposited their dead in trees or used trees in human sacrifice. The Norse god Odin was hung on a tree and stabbed with a spear, as was Christianity's Jesus of Nazareth.

Tree worship was common to our ancient ancestors. In the city of Dedu, in Egypt, the god Osiris manifested in a wooden pillar (originally the trunk of a cedar tree) which came to be identified with him. Dionysus appears in Greek iconography as a tree and was often called Dendrites, "He of the Tree." The Omaha, a Native American tribe, erected a sacred pole known as the "Mystery Tree," which was the center of the four winds and the home of the legendary Thunderbird. Into the early nineteenth century, Arabs worshipped sacred trees called Manahil, which were believed to grow in places where angels – jinn – had descended to Earth.

Specific tree species gave their name to a number of Celtic tribes: the Eburovices (People of the Yew), the Arverni (People from the Land of the Alder) and the Lemovices (People of the Elm). The Celtic Tree Calendar consisted of twelve sacred trees, along with ivy. Each was revered for its unique attributes, with one plant representing each month of the Celtic year as reckoned by the moon. In one form of contemporary Celtic divination, a twig from each of these sacred plants is tossed into a small circle. In response to a posed question, the diviner then interprets the scatter pattern as the twigs relate to each other. Christianity often blessed ancient trees and built altars and churches near them.

People have valued and used many species of trees over the years. From the Bronze Age forward, early Britons made voyages in boats made of willow, a tough, light, workable, elastic wood. With animal skins stretched over a framework of willow withies, these coracles, with weighted nets hung between them, were used for salmon fishing. A wood that could bend without breaking, willow also made an excellent shield. Our ancestors looked on spiky holly and white thorn as natural guardians, and hawthorn made a fine scepter for early Celtic kings. Forked twigs are still used for water divination and dowsing. In the mid-1950s, my father found the well for our summer cottage in Southern Ontario by dowsing with a forked willow branch.

Among the most powerful of all trees are the *ash*, the *oak* and the *yew*. Each with its own symbolic significance, they are known throughout Celtic and Greek history for properties of healing, blessing and strength.

ASH

One of the most exquisite ash trees I've had the good fortune to see was in the Cheviot Hills of southern Scotland. The hilltops were wild with rusty bracken the blustery fall day I traveled the long, thin black road to Hermitage Castle. Aberdeen Angus cattle dotted small green fields in bottomlands that glowed with the occasional shaft of sunlight.

Hermitage Castle is a Medieval Douglas ruin built on earlier foundations. The emptiness surrounding it was palpable, all lonely hill and fell with fall-tinged grasses whipping about in the wind and a tea-colored burn trickling by just below the castle walls. The building was empty except for a couple of workmen. At the gateway, under a falling sky in a swirl of red-brown grass, a single noble mountain ash bright with red berries leaned majestically against a grizzled stone wall.

Most ash trees belong to the olive family and have deciduous leaves generally pinnately compound, which means their leaves range up and down a long stem opposite each other. The European Ash grows throughout Europe and Asia Minor. The Flowering Ash, also indigenous to Europe and Asia, can grow up to fifty feet tall. Its bark exudes a sweet resin called manna. The manna or "bread of heaven" found in the Bible's Book of Exodus, was likely a wind-borne lichen, though elsewhere in the Bible, manna refers to resins from desert trees and shrubs similar to the

Flowering Ash. In the past, these resinous ash mannas were used both as a mild laxative and as an expectorant.

In Finnish mythology, the arcane Mountain Ash or Rowan – an ash of the rose family – symbolized the wife of Ukko, the god of Thunder, who was himself represented by an oak tree. The Teutonic Tree of Life, Yggdrasil – "The Horse of Yggr, the Terrible One" – was a giant ash that grew by the Well of Mimir. Yggdrasil supported the entire universe and typified existence for the Old Norse. Sometimes called Irminsul or "the Mighty Pillar," its roots were said to grow through all the many worlds of both the living and the dead. A "life-giving mead-like dew" – manna – fell on the earth from Yggdrasil's branches, an eagle sat in its boughs, a winged dragon gnawed at its roots and a squirrel roamed up and down the trunk stirring up trouble between the two.

⊙AK

One of the hardest, heaviest, toughest and most durable of our construction woods, oak is the common name for more than 600 trees and shrubs around the world, more than 300 of which belong to the beech family. Oaks have simple leaves – deciduous in some species, evergreen in others – with lobed or toothed margins. These trees have a distinctive fruit, the acorn, which is a common food for small game animals. Acorns were once used as a primary feed for domesticated pigs.

During the French Revolution, the Tree of Liberty was often depicted as an oak. In Britain, the oak has been a symbol of the monarchy since the seventeenth century, when the Boscobel Oak in Worcestershire hid Charles II from capture by Cromwell's troops.

Vast tracts of dense oak forest, now largely lost to agriculture and settlement, once covered much of Northern and Central Europe, including the British Isles. Some of the finest forests are in England's Lake District. One of my favorite walking paths there meanders from Crummock Water to the tiny village of Buttermere. Mill Beck, lined with maple trees, rushes to Crummock Water below Nether How Wood, which is thick with gnarly old oaks scattered on soft green hillocks. Across sheep-filled Buttermere Meadow, a styled bridge over Mill Beck brings hill walkers into oak-filled Long How Wood, where worn stone steps climb up to the parking lot at Craig Farm in Buttermere. In early September, the oaks of both these woods, some of which have three or four mossy trunks apiece, were already changing their color for fall and masses of chestnut brown leaves rustled on their angular limbs or crunched underfoot.

Through the ages, we've valued oak for its fine timber and have used the bark of all species, which contains tannic acid, to tan leather. Brown or English Oak, the only species indigenous to Great Britain, has a rich, fine-grained, brown heartwood once used to build the English navy. The shrine of Edward the Confessor in Westminster Abbey is likewise made of English Oak.

Our Greek, Roman, Near Eastern and European ancestors all worshipped the oak. In fact, the Celts and the Greeks identified their chief deity — a god connected to thunder — with an oak tree. The original site of the ancient Greek Oracle of Dodona was on nearby Mount Tomaros, where priests interpreted the rustling of leaves in a grove of oaks considered sacred to Zeus. In ancient Prussia, oaks were oracles inhabited by gods who would answer questions put to them. Even the Old Testament records a sacred oak or terebinth growing at Shachem, and near Fritzlar, in northern Hesse, Germany, St. Boniface, in CE 722, chopped down an oak tree sacred to Thor, the Anglo-Saxon god of thunder, and built a chapel to St. Peter with the wood. The Druids — the priesthood of the Celts — probably took their name from the sacred oak. Their Celtic name "Duirwydd" means "oak-seer."

Strong and long lasting, an oak can reach an immense age and size. The Conqueror's Oak at Windsor Castle has been dying for more than 300 years. Most of the old giants still alive in Great Britain today date to the Late Middle Ages. The Little Porter Oak at Welbeck Abbey in Nottinghamshire, for example, is known to be nearly 500 years old. A large oak can weigh thirty tons, cover 2000 square yards with ten miles of twigs and branches and grow to upwards of one hundred feet. The trunk of one Sessile Oak at Croft Castle in Herefordshire has a girth of thirty-seven feet above its lowest branch.

In the days when our ancestors connected objects with divinity more often than we do now, the mighty oak, prone to lightning strikes, seemed to have been chosen by God – sacred, and sometimes even equal, to the Divine. Lightning spirals downward through oak, a powerful pattern in many cultures both ancient and modern. Mistletoe and ivy, both parasites of oak, appear to partake of this divinity and were gathered for sacred service by the Druids.

The ancient Anglo-Saxon ritual of "Bringing Home the May," involved a night out in the woods and a morning gathering flowers for garlands and Maypoles. Young girls would wash their faces in May Day dew, a cure for a variety of ailments and a potent charm for successful husband hunting. This May Day dew was thought particularly effective if collected from under the limbs of an ancient oak tree.

YEW

We apply the name yew to a small group of evergreen shrubs and trees of a family called Taxaceae, which has about nineteen different species. All of these have flattened needlelike leaves that resemble conifers, except that their seeds are protected in fleshy coverings called arils instead of in cones. Yews are also dioecious, individual plants being either male or female.

Our most widely distributed yew is the Common, European or English Yew, which still grows wild in Great Britain. Fossil evidence tells us that the Common Yew is scarcer now than it was in the past, though its range still extends from the British Isles across Europe and Asia as far as the Himalayas and southward into Africa.

For the past 10,000 years, Common Yew has been a dominant species in European forests. From place names such as Eboracum ("Yewtown") — the Roman name for York, in the north of England — we know that it once grew more widely. Ireland has had a long-standing fondness for yew, too. The Irish town of Newry ("Yewtree") was probably named for a columnar form of the European species called Irish Yew. The largest wild wood of yews in Ireland is a forest near Killarney that was once described as "black as a monk's cowl."

Yew is slow growing, slow burning and long lived. Its sapwood — white, cream or pinkish-colored — is tough, fine-grained and heavy. Its heartwood is amber to brown. In the eighteenth century, the Rev. Gilbert White, who studied an ancient yew in his churchyard at Selbourne, Hampshire, estimated the tree's growth rate at three feet in 200 years. Pliable yew wood is easily carved and polished, and through the years we've found it an excellent material for making tool handles, furniture and other implements that call for strength and durability. The Romans logged yew for chariot axlcs, spears, lances, bows and arrows.

The oldest wooden implement we know of — a spear of yew found in Clacton-on-Sea, Essex, England — is believed to be at least 50,000 years old. Another spear of yew was discovered embedded between the ribs of a straight-tusked elephant in Lower Saxony, Germany. A sturdy, rot-resistant wood, only moderately susceptible to insect infestation and heavy enough to sink, yew was also popular for votive offerings at springs, lakes and holy wells.

The Greeks, Romans and Druids, along with the indigenous people of Japan, Russia, China, Southeast Asia, North America and India, used yew as an abortifacient and as a treatment for bronchitis and scurvy. Since the 1960s, Taxol, one of about forty taxane compounds found in yew, has shown great promise in cancer treatment. The only Taxol source we've developed to any extent is the bark of the Pacific Yew found on the West Coast of the United States.

Yew trees regenerate themselves. Their branches root in the earth to produce an ever-widening circle of new trees. These vast natural groves, which remain green all year, were probably holy places that may have inspired the megalithic builders of our Neolithic and Bronze Age past to re-create their circles with wooden posts or raised stones.

The average yew tree grows up to thirty feet — though a good-sized tree can be fifty to seventy-five, or even ninety feet tall — and two to three feet in diameter. Under the best of conditions, its girth may exceed twenty feet. A yew tree three feet in diameter is probably around 600 years old.

More than 250 yew trees in England and Wales are as old, or older, than the churchyards in which most of them are found. A few are 1500 to 3000 years old. The yew tree in the churchyard at Crowhurst in Surrey, for example, has a girth of nearly thirty-one feet and was certified in 1990 to be at least 4000 years old. The church itself dates only to the twelfth century. With a hollow interior space about six feet in diameter, the Crowhurst Yew was fitted in the nineteenth century with a door, a table and a bench that sat twelve people. Another yew tree in Shropshire held twenty-one men standing upright. Unfortunately, many of the ancient trees of the British Isles, venerable yews among them, were lost in the violent gales of the 1990s.

Despite its widespread acclaim, the yew tree has another, more sinister, side as well. A poisonous alkaloid in its foliage and seeds, mentioned by both Caesar and Virgil, can kill horses and cattle. Only the red berry surrounding the seed is harmless. Juice or oil from crushed leaves, bark or seeds was used to tip arrows for poisoning fish or small animals. It's also quite likely that yew figured in the occasional murder or suicide. This weighty attribute, along with the yew's evergreen nature, longevity and imposing presence, made it a holy tree to many cultures, among them the Greeks, Romans, Danes, Saxons and Celts. The yew was also understandably useful in occult practices. Because religious rites firmly linked it with cemeteries, ghosts, life and death, eternity and the afterlife, the yew tree is still a potent emblem of immortality. In the classical world, sprigs of yew were used in funeral rites and as a sign of mourning. Celtic and pre-Celtic societies associated the yew tree with the Triple Goddess — maiden, matron and crone — just as they did the waxing, full and waning moon.

Yews were particularly honored on the Iberian Peninsula, where they were more numerous than oak trees. If the stone building of our European ancestors moved northward from Iberia, which is not unlikely, Iberian immigrants may have brought the veneration of the yew tree with them. The Celts especially revered yew trees that grew near burial mounds or megalithic monuments, believing that they held the spirit of the person buried there. They hung offerings, including human sacrifices and the severed heads of their enemies, on these trees. Celtic priests and shamans probably used yew branches as rune rods or magic wands. The Druids called the

Winter Solstice —representing the divine cycle of death and rebirth — "the Day of the Yew."

Many yew trees that we see in the British Isles today grow in Christian churchyards. In the 1990s, I was privileged to see one of the most famous of these, the Fortingall Yew, which grows in the churchyard of the peaceful village of Fortingall at the mouth of Scotland's lonely Glen Lyon.

The Parish Church of Fortingall dates only to the 1900s, when Sir Donald Curie of Garth had it built in a place that has been holy since at least the seventh century, and doubtlessly far longer. A remnant of the primeval forest that once stood there, the Fortingall Yew, at about 5000 years of age, is believed to be the world's oldest living thing. Tradition has it that Pontius Pilate was born in Fortingall and slept under this mighty tree. More than 200 years ago, it had a circumference of fifty-six-and-a-half feet. Since then, the trunk has fragmented into three parts. Two stand in a walled area and shield the graves of the Stewarts of Garth. Sir Donald himself is buried under the third section. The church was not open when I was there, but I was not disheartened. I'd come primarily to see that massively majestic yew, and it was all that I thought it would be — the thick impenetrable darkness, the stalwart nobility, the heft, the timelessness and so much more.

As the Fortingall Yew demonstrates, yew trees, already gracing sacred places and associated with the Divine, were readily adapted by Christianity. Churches were built in or near yew groves, which were seen as fitting guardians for both the living and the dead. A ruined church in Knowlton, Dorset, was built inside a circular bank covered almost entirely by yews. Two yews in the churchyard at Mells in Somerset grow on mounds that may well be prehistoric barrows.

We can easily find reasons yew trees and churchyards might have fit so well together. A fourth century Welsh poem recorded in the thirteenth century, the *Cad Goddeau* or "*Battle of the Trees*," describes solar deities wresting power from Earth goddesses. Could this have been some poetic expression for the Christian faith's battle against the "heathen?" Did the yew tree in a churchyard serve as a symbol for this struggle? Were yew trees associated with protection from evil or black witchcraft? Did their long-lived and hardy presence prevent free-ranging cattle from grazing on church grounds? And, at a time when the nobility and the clergy claimed most of the countryside, could prime yew wood for commoners' bows and arrows be taken from communal church property?

Many of our folk tales revolve around the power of the yew tree. In one of these, the yew sends its roots into the throats of the buried dead, pulling up untold secrets, which are turned into whispers blown loose from foliage by the wind. In the Irish Celtic legend of Deirdre of the Sorrows, we have one of the most touching and forceful examples of the weighty influence of the yew tree. Against the wishes of King Conor of Navan, Deirdre, the daughter of Conor's storyteller, ran off to Scotland with a young fellow with whom she'd fallen in love. The pair took with them her lover's two brothers. The King pleaded for their return, yet when they came back, he promptly had all three young men put to death.

Deirdre, overcome with grief, spent an entire year without a single smile lighting her face. Never once did she even look up from the ground. Finally, King Conor gave her away in marriage. But as she was leaving Navan, she let out a heartbreakingly mournful cry and threw herself from her chariot, hitting her head against a stone. The earth swallowed up her lifeless body, and out of her grave grew a yew tree. The branches spread across the land, stopping only when they met those of a second yew tree, the one that had grown up from her lover's grave.

SPIRITUAL FITNESS

"TODAY I HAVE GROWN TALLER FROM
WALKING WITH THE TREES."

— KARLE WILSON

"EACH TREE GROWS IN TWO
DIRECTIONS AT ONCE,
INTO THE DARKNESS AND OUT TO THE LIGHT."

— JOHN O'DONOHUE

We can easily appreciate the power and beauty of wood by simply becoming more aware of the trees around us, particularly those that are deciduous. We can celebrate both their continuity and their seasonal changes. Spring buds inspire personal renewal after winter's hibernation — lessons to be learned and new beginnings. We can honor this rebirth by starting a new project or bringing wreaths or flowering boughs into our homes, in imitation of the May Day traditions of our ancestors.

With summer's abundance and high energy, we celebrate the great gift of life. Where are we in our lives? Where do we want to go? What's the best way to get there? Where does the true wealth in our life lie?

Autumn's quiet maturity reminds us of the importance of harvesting our insights and sharing the accumulated abundance of summer. We might choose to volunteer with a charitable organization. We can simplify our lives. We can give away what we no longer need.

Winter sees the death of the old in preparation for the birth of the new. Is there something in our lives or living that needs to be ended or let go of?

Tenm Laida is a method of Celtic divination that involves the spiritual understanding that comes from creating poems. In many ways Tenm Laida is similar to the "power song" of Native Americans or to a Buddhist mantra — a short repeated chant that's easy to remember. We can each create a personal poem that encapsulates the eternal yew and the fleeting rose, the balanced representation of all life. "The moment of the rose and the moment of the yew tree are of equal duration" (T.S. Eliot).

We might also like to decorate an outdoor tree for Christmas. The evergreens of Christmas are probably remnants of our tree-worshiping past. In our ancestral past, oaks associated with "pagan" thunder gods like Thor and Jupiter were often worshiped themselves, and gifts were sometimes left at their bases for their guardians. Such trees are even mentioned in the Hebrew Scriptures. "For one cutteth a tree out of the forest, the work of the hands of the workman, with the ax. They deck it with silver and with gold; they fasten it with nails with hammers, that it move not" (Jeremiah 10:3-4). We might cover our tree with images of the things we wish for in the coming year.

The greenery of the yew symbolizes hope for the sun's return. We can think of Yule logs as sympathetic magic to lure the sun back. Is there something in our lives that needs to change in the New Year, as the sun returns? Write it down on a slip of paper and burn it in a Yuletide fire.

The Bonsai tree is an art form that teaches us patience and promotes a centered, more contemplative life. As part of Taoism's search for growth, fulfillment and harmony between man and nature, the Bonsai tradition began as "Penjing" in China, nearly 2000 years ago. We cultivate self-discipline, a peaceful state of mind and happiness in spite of limitations when we plant and tend a bonsai. According to Penjing Master Wu Yee-Sun, each tree in its landscape is like a painting, an expression as uniquely powerful and creative as a poem.

Another very simple way to honor the trees in our midst is to use a collection of driftwood or other gracefully-shaped natural wood for meditation, with emphasis on the magical tenet, "As above, so below." We can use larger pieces as walking sticks.

A tree is a tree is a tree, whether it grows in Brooklyn or Belize. We must learn to pay careful attention to the "urban forests" in our neighborhoods. The Western World uses an average of four to six trees per person per year. By planting a tree, we can begin to replace some of the many we've lost.

COLOR

"COLORS ARE THE DEEDS AND SUFFERINGS OF LIGHT."– GOETHE

People have used color for decorative purposes from the earliest of times. Color as a thing of beauty itself probably dates only to the Renaissance; though ancient Celtic texts filled with adjectives like "rusty-red," "blood-red," "blue-gray," "grayish-brown," "auburn" and so on do show a clear appreciation.

Beauty undoubtedly existed for our ancestors, but when artwork is focused on the symbolic, artists are first and foremost *mystics*. Moved by magic and mystery, their creations are symbols of the universe rather than freestanding aesthetic expressions. In our prehistoric past, people of all cultures probably wore amulets and jewelry to benefit their dead, to help them lead charmed lives or to worship their gods.

This same spiritual impulse likely led us to build great megalithic monuments of varied texture and color. If we were to visit the five stone circles on Machrie Moor on the Isle of Arran in Scotland, for example, we'd find squat gray granite boulders raised dramatically beside lofty red sandstones. At Auchagallon, also in Scotland, the kerbstones of a barrow are all comprised of red sandstone, while the recumbent and its opposite are both of pale gray granite. The stone circle at East Aquhorthies is made of pink porphyry and red jasper, with two gray granite pillars flanking a recumbent slab of red granite. Megalithic builders clearly considered color a part of their overall design.

The human color palette has grown over time. As we can see from their extraordinary, naturalistic work in caverns like Lascaux Cave in France and in the Cave of Altamira in Spain, individual Paleolithic artists used a palette that was simple, direct, richly hued and magical. They produced their pigments from chalk, clay and minerals, including black from soot; red, black and dark brown from oxides of iron or manganese; and a dull yellow or brown from iron carbonate.

Our Neolithic and Bronze Age ancestors had only slightly more knowledge of how to make color. Their simple palette of yellow/gold, red, green, blue, black and white is common in Africa, Asia Minor, Asia, Europe and Mesoamerica. As pigments, these colors are vigorous and vivid.

In spite of this, and despite the fact that humanity has witnessed the spectrum of a rainbow and the other endless and varied colors of nature for millennia, color has always been somehow less marked among "primitive" people. Our ancestors were instead preoccupied with practical matters, dealing with the forces that allowed for their very existence, achieving harmony with the gods and spirits of the natural world, looking for rain or a healthy harvest, pleading for relief from disease or preparing for the afterlife.

In the Egyptian papyrus of Eber, which dates to about 1500 BCE, we find a reference to red and yellow clays and minerals like malachite that were highly prized for healing purposes. Navajo sand-painters still use white, red, yellow, blue and black for shamanistic cures.

As late as the recording of Old English poetry or Early German and Old French texts, rarely do we find any mention of hues created from mixing pigments with white or black. Society's perception of color instead looked at other factors, including a shade's degree and brightness of light. Old English, for example, has few words for specific colors. But there's a rich vocabulary to describe the effects of light on objects — "shining," "gleaming," "glittering," "glowing," "shimmering" and so on.

In every culture, many factors determine the meaning ascribed to a particular color. But there are a few instances where one interpretation appears dominant. For the megalithic builders of the Neolithic and Bronze Age, the same symbolism we now give most often to red and white may have carried the most weight.

RED

The most important coloring agents we have in all rock types are the reddish ferric forms of iron. For most of us, red is the color of passion, high energy and tension. Red raises our blood pressure, quickens our pulse and excites our brain. It's the first color we notice as children. Red is life itself, symbolizing blood and fertility.

In keeping with the duality of much of traditional thought, red can also represent death, destruction and humankind's struggles against nature. For the ancient Chinese and the early Hebrews, red was the color of fire. In the fifth century BCE, it was the hue of Greek heroes. Red and yellow were once marriage colors in both Egypt and the Orient, as they still are in parts of Russia and the Balkans.

Our Neolithic and Bronze Age ancestors made their red pigments from crushed hematite, an oxide of iron, or from the ground iron ore called ochre. Disarticulated bones, appropriately stained with red ochre, have been found in many megalithic burial chambers.

WHITE OR GRAY

White is most often the color of truth, purity and divine protection. In prehistoric times, white probably also represented the moon, whose actual color can range from white to gray, a yellowish beige and even a pale blue. In our Neolithic and Bronze Age past, mourners may have placed the white quartz pebbles sometimes found in tombs as a reflection of the power and light of the moon on the deceased. Blue, silver and black have also been associated with the moon.

For the ancient Celts, white or colorless stones were supernatural, and fairy animals such as snow-white hares or milky mares lured the overly curious into the spirit world.

The white pigments of our ancestors were made from carbonate of lime.

YELLOW

Yellow/gold, the most eye-catching color after red, often represents the sun. In Northern Ireland, yellow crystals, which seem to contain their own internal light, were valued as the ultimate spiritual essence. The Egyptian sun god Ra was depicted in gold, yellow and red. In palmistry, the ring finger is associated with the Greek sun god Apollo. Our wedding rings — usually made of gold — were placed on ring fingers because of the ancient belief that an energy line ran directly to the heart from that finger.

Reseda Luteola, a weedy plant of the Mignonette Family, with tall, slender spikes of greenish-yellow flowers, provided a bright yellow dye for our ancestors. Yellow paint was mixed from crushed ochre, a blend still used along with red ochre for contemporary pigments.

GREEN

Green is still our color of choice for growth, healing, nurturing and enchantment. Physiologically, green has a neutral effect on blood pressure and pulse. The floors of Egyptian temples were "as green as the meadows of the Nile," while their ceilings were deep blue.

Prehistoric green pigment was made from an oxide of copper.

BLUE

Blue, the cool color of sky and sea, now represents the Virgin Mary in Christianity. The color of spirituality and relaxation, blue lowers both blood pressure and heart rate.

Neolithic artists produced blue dye from the Danewort plant and made a blue paint pigment from copper oxide.

BLACK

In most cultures, black has most often been associated with the earth, though it represents water to the Chinese. Fifth century BCE Greeks used black to signify poverty, death and grief, as many Western cultures do today. Death is still very often viewed as a journey into darkness.

Soot and charcoal made up the black pigments of prehistory.

SPIRITUAL FITNESS
"EVERY COLOR IS A BIT OF TRUTH."
– Natalia Crane

Colors each have their own distinct vibration and properties and have a deep influence on our physical, mental, emotional and spiritual wellbeing. Once we've learned to appreciate how different colors affect us, we can make a conscious effort to incorporate them into our daily living – in the details of our homes, in the clothes we wear or in focused meditation.

If you want to know which colors work best for you, you can meditate on specific colors either in your mind's eye or by using small colored squares of paper or fabric. Note how each color makes you feel; reflect on what it does to or for you. And then apply that knowledge in your life.

MEGALITHIC DESIGN

"Civilization is . . . an artifact, made and
maintained by art."
— John F. Michell

Our impulse for artistic ornamentation springs from a
variety of collective objectives and personal needs. In
expressing the joys and fears of life, the art of our prehistoric
past, though often artistically attractive, probably had an
equally large number of aims. Historical accounts describe
the art of indigenous people like Australia's Aborigines
as representing elaborate maps, shamanistic dreams or
journeys into spirit worlds, ancestral tales, the trials and
tribulations of travelers, naturalistic observations, spiritual
propitiation, aspirations and worship and even the doodling
of infrequent leisure time. Some scientists theorize that the
abstract art of prehistory found in caves, rock shelters and
burial sites, is a reflection of visions induced by some altered
state of consciousness, a trance or hallucination brought on
by drugs or sensory deprivation.

The earliest paintings and carvings we know of date to
about 30,000 BCE. In Paleolithic Europe, humans created
figurines and wall paintings as far back as 25,000 BCE.
As climates improved, the quantity of that art increased,
declining about 11,000 BCE, perhaps due to the varied
effects of our last ice age. Another 3000 years and this
artwork would disappear altogether. Paleolithic and
Mesolithic art seem to harness hunting and fertility magic,
using anthropoid figures, animals and handprints. Probably
in large part because of extensive glaciation, we've found
little of this art remaining in Great Britain.

As we've already seen, Neolithic societies replaced a

Mesolithic emphasis on the individual with something more communal. As Mesolithic hunting and foraging cultures gave way to agriculture in the Neolithic and Bronze Ages, society's art forms, too, lost their individualistic realism, becoming stylized and geometric. Agricultural societies through time have been and continue to be dependent on invisible forces that bring us sunshine or rain, drought or flood, that control our own fertility, the fertility of our fields and of our domesticated animals. We largely represent these unseen powers with stylized ceremonial art, with masks and totem poles. Symbols "fix" the invisible. They give form to the intangible and transient. They may even be the means by which we inject a more human, *humane* element into a malevolent or indifferent world.

The agriculturalists of the Neolithic and Bronze Ages were no exception. They probably decorated many of their stone monuments with paintings or relief and engravings that have long since eroded. They may have embellished other constructs with tree branches, garlands or other vegetable fibers that have obviously not survived.

In general, Late Megalithic art peaked about 3000 BCE. We see this great work most clearly in the monumental tombs of the Boyne Valley in Ireland or in the alignments, solitary menhirs and burial chambers of the Golfe du Morbihan near Carnac in Brittany.

ARTISTIC MOTIF

"THE SOUL NEVER THINKS WITHOUT AN IMAGE."
– ARISTOTLE

Ireland has at least 576 decorated stones at fifty-one sites; England at least twenty-one such stones at seven sites.

These decorated menhirs are probably, for the most part, local statements. They may delineate some prominent burial, water source or festival site, for example. Yet some symbols appear to be more or less universal to megalithic architecture.

One of the most frequently found and earliest of these is the axe or axe-plough. Stone axes are associated with henges, causewayed camps and great Neolithic stone circles such as Stonehenge, the Ring of Brodgar and Avebury. Axes also decorate the oldest megalithic monuments of Brittany, which date from the fourth millennium BCE. Five polished axes were found there near the burial mound of Kermario. The ceiling slab of the Carnac area dolmen known as Le Table des Marchands (The Merchants Table), in Locmariaquer, is decorated with an axe-plough.

Over the years, our interpretation of the meaning and use of megalithic designs has been legion. Symbols are themselves empty. How we depict something might be seen as an expression of how much we value it. But those who observe the symbol are usually the ones to invest it with its greater meaning.

Of course, we have no way of knowing for certain what our prehistoric ancestors intended by their designs. Axes, for example, could symbolize a number of very different ideas. Along with the bow, the crook, the hammer and the plough — all of which are also elements in megalithic design — the axe may have symbolized male power. For example, if you visit Ri Cruin Cairn in the Kilmartin Valley of Scotland, you'll find an axe head design on one of its interior cist slabs. Similar to the stone swords added to effigies in medieval churches, the axe may have been the symbol of a great ancient warrior.

Or, since we sometimes find axes associated with female images in gallery graves, axes and hammers may have been part of the armor of some female goddess-guardian of the dead.

As the primary tool of early field clearance and cultivation, the axe may have also represented an important trade item or a symbol of human authority, as maces do today. In our past, we might have associated them with regeneration, blood sacrifice and replenishing the earth. Bronze Age axe depictions are often double or butterfly forms, and Late Bronze Age axes were often decorated with swastikas, wheels or other sun symbols.

In the art of our prehistoric ancestors, the hammer is quite often indistinguishable from the axe. In its capacity to destroy trees, animals and humans, the hammer may have been another symbol of power. The Norse god Thor carried a hammer to denote lightning. The hammer may have also been an emblem of safekeeping. As today's Christians wear a crucifix, Germanic tribesmen hung small hammers around their necks for protection. During the Roman occupation, Gaulish tombs were consecrated to guardian spirits with an axe symbol, along with the inscription "sub ascia" – "under the axe." In Medieval England, we considered Neolithic axe/hammers the thunderbolts of Thor. Bretons on occasion still use these "men-gurun" or "thunderstones" as talismans against lightning strikes.

We also find flowers, hands, feet and eyes in megalithic art. I visited Dark Age Dunadd Fort in the Kilmartin Valley of Scotland in the early 1990s and found there, at the top of the craggy knoll on which the sparse ruins lay, a single footprint carved deep into the bedrock (PLATE 14). I placed my foot in the carved depression – it was a perfect fit, by the way – and gazed out on the stunning grassy-green expanse of Crinan Moss below.

Dunadd was the traditional capital of the Scots, invaders from Ireland who established the Kingdom of Dalriada in Scotland under Fergus Mor about CE 500. The Dalriadic kings united Scotland by dominating the indigenous Picts, and their kings were inaugurated at Dunadd, which had been occupied for hundreds of years. On the steep Dunadd hillsides, remnants of the three main walled terraces were covered in bracken and rosy spikes of foxglove. In all likelihood, Dalriadic kings stood in this same spot, an ancient and enduring symbol of royal status, to be crowned and anointed with water from an adjacent rock basin.

By contrast, what we see in late Megalithic art even more often than these familiar objects, are fully abstract motifs. With variations, there are about eight basic forms – the *line*, *dot*, *grid*, *circle*, *spiral*, *lozenge*, *crescen*t and *U-shape*.

According to the altered-state theory, we commonly see five of these in the first phase of a trance – grids or lattices, dots, concentric circles, U-shaped lines and parallel, zigzag or meandering lines. We perceive all of these differently during altered states. A single dot, for example, becomes a cluster of dots; concentric circles warp into a tunnel or passageway. In Irish megalithic tombs, dots and arcs – generally engraved on stones outside the chamber – have been associated with altered states of consciousness in which a shaman contacted ancestors or other spirit beings through group rituals.

Circular motifs or spirals, lozenges or zigzags characterize Newgrange. Neighboring Knowth has about 250 similarly carved stones. Besides bows, axes and crooks, the chamber and passageway at Gavrinis in Brittany are covered with interlacing arcs and zigzag patterns.

Some researchers think that a single lozenge, chevron or diamond represented one whole entity – one whole day and night, one whole week, one month, one quarter year and so on. A string of three lozenges connected or cradled, therefore, meant three units. Other experts see lozenges as an image of the open birth position or as access to the spirit world. Lozenges with a single dot or many dots inside may have symbolized planted or seeded fields.

Lines or dots were probably used for the reckoning of time, each stroke or component of a zigzag or group of parallel lines being one unit. Alternatively, in ancient Chinese and Egyptian writing, a six-stroke zigzag line was the symbol for water, lightning often preceding rain. We might also see wavy lines as water, counted phases of the moon, light energy or snakes.

The grid or lattice shapes we find on the inner walls of Irish passage graves may have had a shamanic purpose as symbolic entrances into other worlds where the shaman might contact powerful entities on behalf of the deceased.

U-shaped lines cover entire wall surfaces in the superb passage tomb of Gavrinis (PLATE 15), on the southerly tip of Brittany's Ile de Gavrinis in the Golfe du Morbihan. Gavrinis is a dry-stone cairn 160 feet in diameter and almost twenty feet high. At the time Gavrinis was built, the Golfe did not exist. Three rivers converged there instead. The tomb was suddenly abandoned and purposefully hidden about 3000 BCE. A small wooden anti-chamber in front was burned down, and stones were piled up to block the entrance. The ceiling slab of Gavrinis is decorated with an ox and the partial depiction of another unidentified animal, the balance of which appears on the ceiling stone of the nearby Merchants Table, which also includes an axe-plough. The entrance corridor of Gavrinis is nearly forty-six feet long and leads to a single, almost square inner chamber.

By any account, Gavrinis is a magical and very powerful place. But it was the twenty-three passageway pillars decorated with gorgeous spirals and arched concentric U-shaped etchings that really dazzled me on a recent visit. Were these a counting mechanism? Symbols of the vault of heaven? The horns of sacred cattle?

Many engravings in the dark chambers of megalithic passage tombs seem to be an integral part of the interplay of light, stone and shadow. These decorated slabs were clearly meant to be seen by the illumination of the sun or the moon. If we were to enter Loughcrew in Ireland on the Spring Equinox, for example, we'd see a fragile beam of sunlight crawl in to frame a radial disc carved on a massive interior stone. Evidently contrived by the builders themselves, this unique design physically linked light with the radial image, magically bringing the reviving power of the sun into the dark resting place of the dead.

The crescent or arc, also in Loughcrew's burial chambers, appears to represent the phases of the moon. The largest body in the sky next to the sun, the moon — impressive and dramatic — attracts our attention by its constant change in shape, size and brightness. The moon affects our tides and our seasons and correlates with the human cycle of birth, growth, death and rebirth.

The circle and spiral dominate what are probably celestial themes in megalithic art, though circles and spirals have had other interpretations such as the magical eyes of an Earth Goddess. Our eyes resemble the sun, both in their form and in their connection to light. When we close our eyes in sleep, they mirror death. Some monoliths in Ireland's Loughcrew tombs have a design that looks very much like a body with two eyes. This has sometimes been interpreted as a guardian spirit.

There is also a slab in Newgrange on which a single large triple-spiral or triskele may have been designed to harmonize the sun, the moon and the stars. Spirals are found in caves and burial chambers in many parts of the world and have been interpreted as abstract maps of spiritual progress, the journey from death to rebirth or, in the case of the ancient Egyptians, the path of cosmic energy.

Beyond a natural fascination with the sun, the moon and the stars, our Neolithic and Bronze Age ancestors were farmers and probably used these orbs to keep track of time for agricultural activities and sacred rites. The unreachable, eye-dazzling sun is and has always been our dominant source of life. A phenomenon bright with divinity, we see the sun rise at dawn after the death of night. The sun is celebrated in summer and lured back in winter with the sympathetic magic of bonfires. I've witnessed these in many places, among them the hilltop of Menez Bré in Brittany, outside of Portree on the Isle of Skye and in the center of Pobull Fhinn stone circle in the Outer Hebrides.

We see the circle in its many manifestations as the simplest image depicting the life force of the sun. Radial, sundial, wheel or pie shapes may also have been used to describe the motion of the sun or to define both time and space. The sundial we see in the Irish chambered tomb of Knowth is divided into eight equal parts. A Neolithic passage tomb on the Iberian Peninsula features a stag's head formed by a rayed sun.

When asked to depict the sun, as children, we invariably draw a circle with the spokes of a wheel. Neolithic passage graves with spoked-wheel decorations were raised at least 2000 years before the wheel arrived in Western Europe. Such a symbol most probably represented the motion of the sun across the sky. We can also see the rayed circle as a star or as the drawing down of solar energy, a male principle in many cultures. In the Iron Age, we know that water birds, especially those with wide wingspans; horses and antlered stags, both swift and noble animals; and wheels that rolled across the sky all stood for the sun. The Celts represented renewal and rebirth with a rayed circle in the form of a sunflower or daisy. In all likelihood, these depictions were carried down from our Neolithic and Bronze Age ancestors.

Clusters of concentric circles, such as those we find in the great passage tombs of Ireland, have been interpreted as access points to otherworldly realms. The Celtic cross, which was first depicted, as far as we know, as a cross in a circle on Carpathian pottery about 3000 BCE, spread across

Europe over the next thousand years. It may have had a similar function to concentric circles, or it may simply have represented sunlight and shadow.

A final artistic component linked to megalithic architecture is important to examine before we move on, and that's the "*cup-and-ring*" formation — a circular indentation surrounded by one or more concentric circles. Cup-and-ring marks probably originated with our late Neolithic ancestors, but most are associated with Bronze Age sites of the second millennium BCE. We find most of them on horizontal or nearly horizontal rock outcroppings, on monoliths or on the stones of cist burials, especially those in Scotland and the north of England.

In the summer of 2009, I saw the supposed cup markings on several of the monoliths of the Scottish stone circle near Holywood on Ilkley Moor. At nearly thirty feet at its maximum diameter, The Twelve Apostles is the largest stone circle in mainland Scotland. In a broad green cow-filled field, eleven of the original twelve millstone grit stones have survived, and many of those were recumbent to begin with or have fallen. I was a bit skeptical about the authenticity of the cup and ring markings. They seemed entirely random to me, as though they were more a consequence of natural erosion by wind or water than by any conscious human activity.

Libations were poured into cup marks in Scotland in the early nineteenth century. At midnight, under a full moon, the cup-and-ring markings on Arthur's Stone — a passage tomb in Wales — received offerings of mead, honey and milk. For centuries, the wives of fishermen in the village of Roh-en-aod in Brittany would take hammers to a nearby dolmen and tap the stone's five cup-and-ring depressions in an effort to call up favorable winds for their husbands. Cup-and-ring marks have also been used in rainmaking, the grooves being filled with water to induce rain.

There's been no end of speculation as to what our prehistoric ancestors intended by these cup-and-ring designs. To various researchers, they represent spiritual doorways for communicating between the living and the dead, for consulting an oracle, for allowing the passage of spirits in and out of sacred stones as, for example, in aligning a woman's body to receive a spirit into her womb, with rings being added to ensure further children. We've interpreted them as solar symbols, cursing stones, gaming tables, depictions of the sun, moon and stars, molds for making metal rings, maps of religious sites, alignment markers, prospectors' imprints, mixing vessels, measuring gauges, clocks, route markers, memorials, oath-taking devices and knife-sharpening objects. They might have been any one of these, all of them or none.

SHAPE

"So full of shapes is fancy."
— Shakespeare

Scholars tell us that there are five basic shapes in the art of all cultures — the *circle*, *square*, *triangle*, *cross* and *spiral*. All of these can be found in the megalithic architecture of our Northern European ancestors.

We find the square, an image of man-made stability, in Neolithic tombs like Maes Howe in the Orkneys, where the form is also mirrored in the nearby houses of the tomb's builders (PLATE 16). The circle, and by extension the spiral, is a symbol of wholeness and dominates the design of Bronze Age tombs. Some circular barrows, focused on a single burial, may have been built over the remains of similarly shaped huts.

The basic interior form of the megalithic mound is the cross, an image we find sacred to many cultures. We have the Egyptian ankh, the Maori symbol for the moon goddess, the Mayan Tree of Life and the Christian crucifix. The triangle reaches for the Divine or channels cosmic energy. The pyramid-like shape of many standing stones may have served the same purpose as our church steeples do today.

Something else we find at work in megalithic architecture is the layout of the structures themselves. Could the long barrow's design be a method of imitating a return to the womb, a Cave of the Dead into which the human soul passes on its journey to the underworld to await rebirth in the central chamber? Did mounds and pillars (tombs and standing stones) represent the duality of the universe, those contrasts in our lives behind which spiritual thought perceives a unifying force? In juxtaposing them, we recreate the unity of Beginning, the primordial Oneness so colorfully recorded in our cosmologies.

Mounds and pillars may have been raised side by side to celebrate and re-establish the natural order of things, symbolizing the dynamic male/female duality that first constructed the universe. We balance the standing stone, a masculine celestial principle (PLATE 17), with the tomb, which being of the Earth, is feminine (PLATES 18 and 19). When our prehistoric ancestors left their nomadic wanderings to focus on the natural seasonal manifestations of the Earth, was there a need to pin down that force, to control and direct the natural flow of power between the Earth and the sky?

THE CIRCLE AND THE SPIRAL

"GOD IS A CIRCLE WHOSE CENTER IS EVERYWHERE,
AND WHOSE CIRCUMFERENCE IS NOWHERE."
— Metaphysical principle

As in all art, the purest, simplest and most all-encompassing form in megalithic architecture is the circle (PLATES 20 and 21). With no beginning and no end, the circle is a power spot of non-ordinary reality that is the center of all things, everything and nothing all in a moment. We see the circle as wholeness and unity, which, by extension, represents to us a divine connection.

Our natural world, dynamic and full of curves, uses the circle almost as a source of comfort. The sky touches the earth on every side, the circle of the horizon wrapping around us. This circular horizon, along with the perceived dome of the sky, gave rise to the early human model of the universe as a series of concentric shells. Trees grow in the concentric patterns of growth rings; rippled circles spread outward from pebbles dropped in water. The circle is the shape of celestial objects and their movements — the sun and the full moon, a circle from which portions are continually being removed and restored. The circle is the perfect image for our cycle of life, death and rebirth, the round of the seasons, day and night — even for the womb and the skull.

Connecting the beginning with the end, above with below, creation with death, the circle is full of meaning for many cultures, old and new. We have Navajo sand paintings, Aztec sun calendars and Tibetan mandalas. Four thousand years ago in ancient Sumer, we know that priests chanted prayers to establish a "Circle of Protection." Medieval magicians withdrew into the safety of an inscribed circle. One of our oldest and most basic forms of dance is the circle. No one comes first. No one comes last.

The spiral, one of our most ancient symbols, aspires to something even higher. Where the circle is wholeness and unity, the spiral is eternity, evolution and growth; the same place on a different level; a new perspective; circular movement carried into the fourth dimension; a path through time. As Jill Purce writes in her book *The Mystic Spiral*, "In the centre of any spiral is the calm core through which we pass to eternity. The spiral we travel round life is the means we have to compare ourselves with ourselves and discover how much we have changed since we were last in the city, met our brother or celebrated Christmas."

We find the spiral everywhere in the natural world, in the macrocosm of our solar system, in nebulae and galaxies, what we might call "the spiral of the stars." The spiral is prominent in the microcosm of fingerprints, hair growth and DNA strands. We see spirals in whirlpools, lotus blossoms, ammonite fossils, seashells, snail shells and the growth pattern of leafy vines such as honeysuckle and woodbine.

Whirlwinds are one of our most potent spiral forms. Irish peasants called them "fairy breezes." In the Gobi Desert, they are known as Kwei or "demons." In the nineteenth century, believing they were ghosts, Russian peasants threw axes at them. Some researchers believe that stone circles may mark hallowed ground where a spinning column of air first arose, stone avenues tracing its paths.

The earliest man-made spiral motif we've found appears on an Upper Paleolithic ivory medallion from a ritual cave burial in Siberia that dates to about 16,000 BCE. The spiral there emerges from a center-cut hole. Since then, we've placed spirals on objects of stone, ceramic, wood and metal. We've put them on Hopi artwork, Egyptian scarabs, Bronze Age Greek jewelry, Japanese paintings, medieval cathedrals and much more. The Celts clearly used the spirals and lozenges of Neolithic stone art in their own work, just as they copied the corbelled roofing and capstones of ancient tombs like Newgrange.

In Austria, the double spiral brooch that represents the jewelry of Celtic Iron Age Hallstatt is a direct descendant of the Neolithic double spiral, exactly like the one etched on the entrance stone at Newgrange. Christians took the spiral and placed it on crosses, gravestones and illuminated manuscripts — even on the hook of a Bishop's staff, where it gives ecclesiastical guidance to a soul on its spiraling life's journey.

As an artistic motif, we have countless theories about the spiral's intent and meaning. It may have been copied from natural forms. Spiral-shelled snails, for instance, have horns that resemble a phase of the moon. Many cultures have revered these gastropods, associating them with both the miracle of birth and the magic of the moon. For good fortune, nineteenth century Cornish miners fed small bits of food to the snails they happened upon on the way to work. As the snails emerged from their shells, so, too, would the miners return from the womb of the Earth.

European folklore is filled with the healing power of snails, especially in easing childbirth. The snail embodies the universe in miniature — male/female, sun/moon, life/death. Large quantities of snail shells have been found in Mayan crypts in the Yucatan, in burials in Pompeii, in post-holes at Avebury, in the core of Silbury Hill and in ditches at Stonehenge. Nine hundred and twenty-two large snail shells were discovered in a pit at Rainsborough Hill Fort. Almost all were still intact.

We've found other spiral seashells in burials like the nineteenth century BCE interment in Glamorgan, now in the National Museum of Wales in Cardiff, where the deceased wore a necklace of marine shells. The bones had been smeared with red ochre. Perhaps our ancestors based the spiral in their architecture, art and jewelry on the simple geometry of the curving line or on the ropes and cords of weaving. A clockwise spiral may have meant a beginning, a counterclockwise one, an end.

One of the most powerful constructs we have of the spiral is the concept of dynamic equilibrium, the wisdom that comes from the balance and reconciliation of opposites. Probably our most familiar example of this is the double spiral of Taoism known as Yin/Yang, a Chinese symbol of asymmetric polarity. The ancient meaning of Yin was literally "the shaded, north side of a hill;" Yang "the sunny, south side of a hill." Yin (negative, feminine, cool, moist, soft, dark, earth, water, nebulosity) must be balanced in life by Yang (positive, masculine, warm, dry, hard, light, heaven, fire, firmness). This is the unifying, primary principle we call the Tao, or Way.

We might therefore see the spiral carvings of megalithic tomb art as representing the expansion and contraction that is the nature of life. An unending and returning cycle, the spiral is our emblem of birth, life, death and rebirth. The spiral both comes from and returns to its source; its ends are opposite and yet they are the same. All things return to the root from which they sprang. The rhythms of the universe form a spiral of continuous creation and expansion, dissolution and contraction, as we see in the waxing and waning of the moon or in the changes of the seasons.

All the pillars, poles, mountain peaks, temples, spires and soul ladders of our various religious traditions and mythologies represent our search for this Axis Mundi, this "Navel of the Earth," the Unmoved Mover (God) from which all things extend, radiate and rotate in spiral form. The Muslim seven-fold path to Mecca around Ka'aba, for example, is called "Tawaf," meaning, "To attain the summit of a thing by spiraling around it."

Snakes, too, by shedding their skin, akin to continually dying and being reborn, show us the spiraling, oppositional energy currents of both the human body and the universe. In Yogic traditions, this Kundalini energy coils and spirals snake-like down the spine. Many healing systems like Tibetan mandalas and Navajo sand paintings identify the control and understanding of this energy as the function of healing.

Revealing and concealing, condensing and dissipating, protecting and destroying, coiling and uncoiling life, rolling and unrolling the universe, spiral oppositions are complimentary and have a certain unity. One could not exist without the other. Outward, upward, clockwise spiraling away from the center-point shows us birth, growth, creation, order, regeneration and the expansion of spring. Inward, downward, counter-clockwise spiraling (widdershins) toward the center-point shows us destruction, death, chaos, re-absorption and the contraction of autumn.

These two movements and their poles of birth and death define our very existence. Through birth, Heaven is brought down to Earth, at which point the process is reversed and we begin reaching back for the wholeness and enlightenment of Heaven. These polar opposites point out the importance of breathing in conscious meditation. Exhale and the spirit winds into matter, as the breath of God creates life. Inhale and matter unwinds into spirit; we become one with "All That Is."

We've found spiral barriers and carved spirals in passageways to inner chambers in Neolithic and Mesolithic cultures around the world, from Europe and Mexico to China and Egypt. Two spirals are sometimes juxtaposed (PLATE 22). We might see these as representing the balancing of opposing energies by which we reach wholeness, enlightenment or rebirth. They may also have meant something as straightforward as a simple depiction of life (birth and death) itself, or womb openings for the release of spirits, as we know springs and wells were to the Celts.

Corbelled roofing, spiral capstones like those at Newgrange and the Tomb of the Eagles (PLATE 23) and the carved spiral motifs in megalithic tombs might have symbolized the cosmic journey of the soul of the departed from birth through death to find rest in the central chamber, the womb of the Earth. We could call this the walk through the valley of the shadow of death, the descent into the underworld or the dark night of the soul, by which the dead — in body or spirit — are reborn into a new world.

In the labyrinth — a series of symmetrical pathways leading to a central spot and back out again — we see a more literal form of the spiral as a passage through time. The earliest known labyrinth dates to nineteenth century BCE Egypt, but for many of us, the most famous comes from Minoan Crete, where the Athenian hero Theseus slew the Minotaur (Mino's Bull). Such a legend is probably connected to Minoan bull worship, but it's just as easy to see Theseus' encounter with this fabulous beast as the classic hero/soul journey to the underworld.

In the center of the labyrinth, at the still axis around which the universe revolves, we overcome death by a direct encounter with Divinity, and we are reborn. Circular labyrinths and turf mazes still survive in the English countryside. Walking these narrow, winding paths can clear the mind, helping us reach a contemplative state.

SPIRITUAL FITNESS

"THE POWER OF THE WORLD ALWAYS WORKS IN CIRCLES." — BLACK ELK

One simple and powerful way we can use the circle — the dominant form of megalithic art and architecture

— is to draw or paint a mandala, a visual representation of inner or cosmic wholeness and unity. The word comes from Sanskrit and means "circle" or "magic circle," though mandalas can be square or even rectangular. Their interior space is divided into sections called courts. The Eastern concept of the mandala probably originated in India or China and moved into Tibet, altered by the cultures through which it passed.

In the simplest terms, a mandala is a series of concentric forms that depict the connections between different dimensions. The mandala's center is the "Beginning" or the "Eternal," the divine center of the Self, or the divine center of the Cosmos. By creating colorful and symmetrical mandala diagrams, we're depicting symbolic or abstract states of consciousness; we're representing figuratively the collected forces of the universe. Sanskrit Mandalas consist of a square — the earth or the man-made world —placed inside a circle, the image of the cosmos. The basic framework of the Tibetan Mandala is similar, though here we have three protective circles around the square, portraying different levels of consciousness.

Buddhist and Hindu monks meditate on mandala drawings to help them reach a state of inner awareness of their own spiritual progress. In Hindu or Buddhist Tantrism, a mandala is sometimes prepared to honor a Buddha or some other divinity or to be used in the performance of some sacred rite or healing ritual.

A well-recognized Western form of the mandala is the Navajo sand painting, constructed for healing ceremonies. The patient sits in the center, an image of the awareness of the Eternal. The healer then connects the individual to the cosmos with designs in colored sand, healing a specific rift in the web of time and eternity.

All beings, all objects and all of our experiences are organic wholes arising from and returning to one source, everything an equal manifestation of the one divine whole. Here again we see dynamic equilibrium, oppositions that are part of the same totality. At one time, humanity probably understood this simple truth. Our modern thinking, however, tends to polarize things — left and right, black and white, east and west, man and woman, good and bad. We are too often unaware of the common ground of the center; that place between the bark and the tree, between the foam and the water. With a mandala, we can harmonize polarities. We reconstruct and bring ourselves back to an ancient existential unity, and we recognize that all experiences are equal. All goes forth, all returns. Our past and our future are held together by the singular moment of the present. Like the labyrinth, the mandala helps us to create order, wholeness and balance.

The psychiatrist Carl Jung re-introduced the concept of the mandala into our Western world as a therapeutic tool. Beyond this, we have used mandalas for healing and initiation, for guarding against disease or evil and for focusing on birth, peace, prayer and the passage through death. Creation of and meditation on our own personal mandalas attunes us to life, the divine order of the universe and the relatedness of all things.

To make your own mandala, begin with the outer form, which can be a circle, a square, a rectangle or some other shape. For instance, you might want to use a diamond, which contains all colors and yet is colorless, as an image of order and clarity. You may find it helpful to meditate on a variety of shapes before choosing your own.

Place a symbol of the Self — *your* Self — as a central image, a representation of "the All reflected in the ego." This helps you realize that you must function from the same still Center no matter how things around you may change. "Be still and know that I am God," the Bible says. If you like, you can work next into the four cardinal points, representing each with pertinent symbols — elements of personality, for example; your own emotional, physical, mental and spiritual states of mind. These may or may not be placed inside a square within your primary form, to denote an Earth-bound incarnation.

A personal mandala is a purely creative expression. There are no rules, no right, and no wrong. You can include or exclude whatever representations you want. You can use illustrations of the round of life and death. You can choose emblems of cosmic creative forces, of seasons, or even of galactic cycles. Color is usually an important part of your personal mandala, but the only firm necessity is mindful construction. As you meditate on the unique mandala you have fashioned, you will absorb the energy and power of the symbols you've chosen, carrying them with you into your everyday life.

The ancient spiritual practice of walking a labyrinth is another way to access the spirit, and truth-seekers have taken this spiritual journey in meditation and prayer for thousands of years. Few of us have room in our homes for a full-sized maze. But we can find hand-held labyrinths painted or etched on stone or paper. *Labyrinths from the Outside In* by Donna Schaper and Carole Ann Camp is an excellent place to look for further labyrinth inspiration.

CHAPTER 4

HONORING THE EARTH
SACRED SPACE

"THE SPIRIT OF PLACE IS A GREAT REALITY."
– D. H. LAWRENCE

"WHO SHALL DWELL IN THY HOLY HILL?"
– PSALM 15:1

F OR MOST OF US, SACRED SITES – both
natural and man-made – have their own unique
presence, a sense of power, peace, harmony and
transcendence. They may be places of singular beauty, or
we may associate them with a specific individual, moment
or event. As places where physical and spiritual worlds
converge, holy places allow us to achieve, if only for a
moment, a cosmic wholeness or a renewal of spirit.

Our oldest and deepest religious inclination appears
to be a reverence for the spirit or spirits of the Earth, the
impression of an Earth Mother whose aspects of virgin,
bride, matron and crone correspond to the seasons. The
Earth sustains us all, providing us with food, water, clothing,
shelter, air to breathe and inspiration. Ancient wisdom
traditions celebrated our relationship to the land. Sadly, only
rarely does modern culture honor the Earth.

In days when ancient societies perceived the natural
landscape to be spiritually alive, the Divine spoke to
humanity through plants and animals, weather patterns,
landforms and the spirits that lived in them. The most holy
places were natural ones. Waterfalls like Niagara and Angel
Falls. Rivers like the Nile, the Ganges and the Amazon.
Islands such as Lindisfarne, Iona, Easter Island and the
Galapagos. Rocky outcrops like Machu Picchu, Ayres Rock
in the Australian Outback and Cathedral Rock in Sedona,
Arizona. Hills such as the Mount of Olives in Jerusalem
and Menez Bré in Brittany. Lakes of stillness or depth like
Superior. Healing springs, trees, mountains, moors, caves
and forests. All of these were suffused with the Divine.

For our Stone Age ancestors, the richly painted caves of
Southern France and Northern Spain probably played a
similar role to today's cathedrals. Such an ancient tradition

99

of worship continued through millennia, manifesting in such power spots as The Cave of a Thousand Buddhas in China, the grotto on Mount St. Michael in France, the Eluru and Anjanta caves in India, St. Ninian's Cave on Wigtown Bay in Scotland (PLATE 24) and the burial caves of the New Caledonian Islands, among many others.

With their inherent grandeur, mountains and high places also elevate the human spirit above the plane of everyday existence. On such hallowed ground, the material and spiritual are one. Whether it's Mt. Fuji in Japan, Shasta in California, Benbulben in Ireland or the Haleakala Crater in Hawaii, we have undertaken sacred pilgrimages to sacred mountains for thousands of years. Greek gods dwelt on Olympus; the Kachinas of the Hopi live on the San Francisco Peaks near Flagstaff, Arizona; Buddhist and Hindu deities reside on Kailas.

Some researchers speculate that when the ancestral agricultural cults of the Sun God – a deity removed from the Earth – overcame the more widespread cult of the Earth Goddess, humanity lost a great deal of its reverence for the land. A formal "Paradise" of shrines and altars took its place, developed with sanctioned attendants and solemnized with ritual and magic at specific times. The *whole* Earth was no longer holy. Instead, we contained our holy spirits. We locked them away so we could break the earth for planting, for building, for mining. Many of us still spend our holy days confined, so that "God has to go out and praise the mountains" (Paul Roche).

Our Neolithic and Bronze Age ancestors seem to have understood that the whole Earth was holy ground, including hills and springs, caverns and forests. And yet, their restricted access and intricate approaches to many stone circles and burial chambers created a sacred inner precinct similarly set apart from the outside world, an inner sanctum that was dangerous to anyone not authorized or properly prepared.

Informed observation and specific and timely ritual were essential as burials continued to be performed at Neolithic and Bronze Age sites for hundreds, and in some cases thousands, of years. These places, together with standing stones (alone or in patterns) appear to have reached the particular state of holiness we now give to temples, cathedrals and churches. As with other sacred sites, those of our Neolithic and Bronze Age past must have each had their own unique appeal and power. It's possible that our ancestors first built chambered tombs in imitation of caves like Lascaux, as a means of reconnecting to the Earth (PLATE 25). The sacred rites and dances performed in those caves were probably repeated in later tumuli, facilitating similar visionary experiences resulting in spiritual or even physical transformation. (PLATE 26)

The Earth as holy ground is a concept that has generally not traveled well through time, though there are exceptions. Sacred groves and woodland clearings were revered by the Celts, who believed the ancient and expansive forests of Europe were enchanted. Druid initiates retreated to the silence and solitude of the forest to shut out ordinary reality, just as Christian ascetic monks and hermits did.

For the Australian Aborigine, every element of the landscape relates to a segment from the histories of the gods. Ritual imitation and the symbolic portrayal on stone of the creative forces active at any given site perpetuate life cycles. At a time when those forces were likely the sun, the moon and the stars, the same might be said of the artwork of our prehistoric ancestors.

Unfortunately, Christianity generally took a dim view of our prehistoric holy places. In many cases, they were eradicated altogether. A papal edict in CE 658 instructed bishops to "dig up and remove and hide to places where they cannot be found, those stones which . . . are still worshiped."

The subsequent invention of gunpowder made this task ever so much easier.

Still, the old places exuded a powerful aura and Christian authorities often chose to suppress ancient belief by claiming venerated "pagan" sites as their own, by baptizing or otherwise transforming the stones. The grit-stone Rudston Monolith in the churchyard of All Saints, Rudston (PLATE 27) – Great Britain's tallest monolith at twenty-five feet, nine inches – is one example, as is the Preacher's Stone at St. Gwrthwl's Church in Wales. Christian burials were likewise placed around the ancient stones at Plas Godendden, also in Wales.

In Brittany, the early eighteenth century Chapel of the Seven Sleepers near Plouaret (PLATE 28) incorporated a Neolithic burial chamber, the Dolmen of Stivel, in an outside crypt. The dolmen is behind bars these days, as I saw on a brief visit back in the late 1990s, and a model ship had been placed inside, ringed with votive candles.

The chapel is a quaint old stone building made up of large, lichen-covered granite blocks. Built between 1703 and 1714 in the form of a Latin cross, it has two raised side chapels, a rare and unusual feature. This is because the south chapel is built directly on top of the dolmen, its two capstones forming the floor. Oriented east and west, the dolmen is made up of four uprights, along with those two hefty capstones. The dolmen crypt is dedicated to the Seven Sleepers or the Seven Saints of Ephesus, seven young men who were said to have been walled up alive in a cave near the grave of Mary Magdalene in the third century for refusing to deny Christ. Statues of these martyrs line a niche above the altar of the main chapel. The Koran also records their story, which is still regularly recited in Islamic mosques.

Using rituals of sensory deprivation, Christian retreat houses continued the fantastical practices of our ancestors' prehistoric holy caves and tombs. In time, the monasteries of great teachers and the caves of hermits became sacred spaces themselves. As repositories of ancestral wisdom, these sacred sites in the landscape transcend both time and the physical universe, reaching for eternity.

SPIRITUAL FITNESS

"Sacred space and sacred time
and something joyous to do are all we need."
– Joseph Campbell

Many of our own recognized holy places are severely overcrowded. Nevertheless, it's still possible for us to experience their sacredness, if they're approached with respect, reverence and a sincere desire to connect with a higher power.

But why not create your own sacred space? What we need to remember is that the whole Earth is sacred, and each separate part is therefore hallowed. Places of positive and deliberate solitude, where we can achieve balance in our lives, can be designated both inside and outside of our homes. The Benedictine Monk, John Main, writes that, "The Kingdom is not a place we are going to but rather an experience we carry with us on every breath." Sanctuaries reflect our individual search for inner peace. Sacred space can therefore be experienced by anyone, anywhere. As Siberian shamans say, "We live in an ensouled universe." The creative powers and uplifting qualities of that universe manifest everywhere. We can find the Divine in the everyday moment.

It's easy to create your own sacred space, whether it's a small altar in a corner of your home, an ordered and secure retreat in the back garden or a place of quiet meditation, prayer, contemplation or relaxation on a nearby hill or mountain; in a woodland, canyon, beach, garden or public park. In our homes, a sacred space can be furnished with comforting objects, with incense, candles, sacred images or icons or natural objects such as stones, seeds, leaves or seasonal flowers.

The primary purpose of creating a sacred space is to experience the sense of being in a place we can visit regularly, alone, that has something powerful to say to us — even if it's in our own backyard. As Shirley Toulson writes in her book *The Celtic Year*, "All places are holy if we keep ourselves aware of where we are."

PART II:

FANCY

BECAUSE OF THE HUMAN REMAINS frequently found in them, we can assume that many prehistoric stone monuments were primarily burial chambers. Beyond that, we have absolutely no idea what other purposes they might have fulfilled.

Traditional studies of the prehistoric past mirrored the intellectual climate in which they developed. In the early Middle Ages, for example, monks looked on Stonehenge as the work of the great Arthurian magician, Merlin. In the classical Renaissance, Stonehenge was ascribed a Roman ancestry. During the romanticism of the Victorian era, it was assigned to the Druids. "Every age gets the Stonehenge it desires or deserves," archeologist Jacquetta Hawkes has written. The same can be said for all such monuments.

The seventeenth century antiquarian and gentleman-scholar John Aubrey was the first to think about megalithic sites as being prehistoric. The amiably romantic William Stukely, a Lincolnshire antiquarian and physician who surveyed the stone circles of Avebury and Stonehenge in the 1720s, concluded that they were built by gentle, proto-Christian, Druid philosophers. What we've made of them since has been influenced to a large degree by the scientific trends of the twentieth century. With the architectural interests of the 1920s, we looked at *how* they were built. The geological sciences of the 1930s had us asking *where* the stone had come from. *Who* built them occupied the cultural theorists of the 1940s.

Apart from being burial places for the dead, the best evidence we have from the structures themselves suggests that some may have been used as observatories, a theory that first arose in the late nineteenth century. It wasn't until the last half of the twentieth century, with the birth of space exploration and computer technology, however, that we took a closer look at the idea that some structures, perhaps operated by astronomer/priests, were aligned to aspects of the sun, the moon or the stars. The work of Alexander Thom, a Professor of Engineering at the University of Oxford, was at the forefront of this now popular idea.

For the most part, any theory we now have for the use of stone monuments depends on the personal beliefs of their observers, the imaginative explanations given by the people who lived — and, in many cases, still live — among them. We can't possibly consider every impression, every possibility or every fanciful notion, and no interpretation is binding, but in the following pages we're going to contemplate four major areas— *Life and Death*, *Heaven and Earth*, *Secular and Sacred* and *Body and Soul*. We need to remember, of course, that in any concept of their world and the sacred way in which it functioned, our prehistoric ancestors probably looked on all of these aspects as one.

LET'S START AT THE BEGINNING.

LIFE AND DEATH

"WE DIE WITH THE DYING; SEE THEY DEPART
AND WE GO WITH THEM.
WE ARE BORN WITH THE DEAD; SEE THEY RETURN
AND BRING US WITH THEM."

– T. S. ELIOT

The possibility of a stone ring being an observatory, a marketplace or a ceremonial center is a matter of conjecture. A stone ring's connection with human remains is not. Throughout time, humanity has erected the tomb, the pyramid, the monument, the mausoleum, to remind the generations that followed that *we were here*. Many, if not all, prehistoric megalithic structures — apart from stone houses — probably related to death and burial.

Because the meaning we give to death depends on the meaning we give to life, our discussion will separate life and death only in the interest of clarity. *Earth Goddesses* and *fertility* — including birth, marriage and the expression of male and female principles in stone — will be explored under *Life*.

Under *Death*, we're going to talk about *ancestor and relic cults*, *the dead*, *burial* and *sacrifice*. All of these elements, to varying degrees and in varied mixtures, most likely figured in the building and maintenance of megalithic architecture.

CHAPTER 5

LIFE

"WE CAN NEVER BE BORN ENOUGH."

— E.E. CUMMINGS

WE FIND AN EARTH GODDESS — embodying the essence of life, the fruitfulness of the soil, marriage and procreation — in many ancient cultures. We've called her by many names, Ga-Tum-Dug in Mesopotamia; Gaea in Greece; Tellus Mater in Rome; Nut in Egypt; Devi-Shakti in India; Pachamama in Peru; Inanna in Sumer; and Ishtar in Babylon.

These are, of course, epithets that the Western world associates with mythology, a word we now use to describe someone else's religion. Our Paleolithic ancestors, however, lived literally in the body of the Earth. Her flesh was the soil, her hair the vegetation; the rocks were her bones and the wind, her breath.

We can find these Earth/Mother Goddesses, sources of birth, life, death and rebirth, in all aspects of prehistoric art. Figurines and drawings depict pregnancy or feature exaggerated breasts, buttocks and genitalia. Where the dark quartz veins petered out in the prehistoric flint mines of Grimes Grave in the north of England, a sculpted pregnant woman and a chalk phallus were found, as if these sexual symbols could induce the Earth to produce more flint.

Earth Goddesses represent the great mystery of life. Plutarch, the early Greek historian, quotes an inscription in the temple of Nut in Sais on the Nile Delta that reads, "I am all that has been, that is, and that will be. No mortal has been able to lift the veil which covers me." The Indian Earth Goddess Devi-Shakti is seen as the very essence of being, the single source of the energy of the cosmos, the embodiment of the Earth.

It seems that our Neolithic ancestors may well have had a goddess-centered religion focused on the sacredness of the Earth and of life. When a father's connection to pregnancy and birth is not scientifically understood, the female principle – whether Hecate, Artemis, Isis, Brigid, Diana, Proserpina, Luna, Cybele, Selene or any other Earth Goddess – is seen as a sacred unifying force.

Later, European Celtic society set aside Midsummer's Eve as the holy day of the Earth Goddess Ma (Matu in Sumer; Matuta in Rome; Mat among the Hittites). The Sumerian word "ma" means "that without which life is not possible." Ma evolved into Danu among the Irish, becoming one of Celtic Ireland's trinity goddesses, the others being Madb (Maeve) and Macha.

Some researchers theorize that the economic changes, population shifts and warrior societies we've seen in the late Neolithic and Bronze Ages undermined earlier goddess-centered religions, replacing them with male deities of the sky, light or thunder. In some cases, the dichotomy of Earth Mothers left us with battle goddesses like the Irish Maeve, Welsh Rhiannon and Norse Freya or destroyers such as Pele of Hawaii or the Indian, Kali.

More often though, Earth-Mother religions, believed to be steeped in the dark and the mysterious, were opposed by the evolving Indo-Aryan gods of Light. Humanity thus began to fear, repress and belittle both women and the natural world, the departure from previous beliefs becoming increasingly evident. Under Mesopotamian Sumer law, for example, a rapist would be executed. Later, under Hebrew law, the married *victim* of rape was killed. Virility superseded fertility and perhaps reason. Light and life were no longer part of the same unity with darkness and death, and female power began to be associated with the negative, with sirens and witches – a force to be feared and/or controlled.

With an implied male ownership, virginity became the dominant concept of "the female." The tale of Pandora's Box may be our best illustration of this fundamental change in spiritual belief. Just as the serpent – another ancient symbol of fertility — became a source of evil (Yahweh slew "the Leviathan of the deep;" a snake tempted Eve in the Garden; St. Patrick drove the snakes out of Ireland; St. George killed the dragon), so Pandora, "The All-Giver," the life-producing womb, became the source of all evil.

One of the aspects of the Celtic Earth Goddess Bride, also known as Brigid, was fertility. Her holy day, Imbolc, roughly the first of February, celebrated the renewal of life in spring. Imbolc derives from Early Irish "imbolg," meaning "sheep's milk," and falls at the time of year when ewes come into milk for the coming season. It was later appropriated as the Christian festival of Easter; a name the eighth century theologian and historian Bede tells us was taken from yet another Earth Mother, the Anglo-Saxon goddess of spring, Eostre. Brigid herself became immortalized as St. Bridget, midwife to Mary at Jesus' birth.

Well into the nineteenth century, even Mary, the "Motherhood of God," was known in the Highlands and Islands of Scotland as "The Corn of the Land" and "The Treasure of the Sea," both Earth Mother epithets and fertility descriptions. We can easily see the present-day "Marian, Queen of Heaven" theology in Roman Catholicism, as an attempt to rescue and acknowledge the female Divine.

One of the most powerful personal representations of this came about for me as the result of a visit to the Cathar country of Southern France in 2006. On a deep-blue summer's day buzzing with cicadas, I had the pleasure of staying in the ancient hilltop village of Quarante, near Beziers. The church there, the Abbaye de Santa Maria, was heavily influenced by the Cathars. Their distinctive crosses decorate the nave's inner columns, with life-of-Mary depictions filling the stained glass windows and a gilded Mary, arms outstretched, gracing the altar. The crucified Christ has been reduced to a small, minor statue off to the side. Similarly, the popularity of Dan Brown's *Da Vinci Code* clearly mirrors an age-old impulse to recognize the female Divine after centuries of neglect or suppression.

When the male role in fertility and birth was unknown, our ancestors saw pregnancy as the result of very specific, albeit inaccurate, actions — of eating or drinking certain foods or coming into close contact with magical substances, practices or practitioners. In different times and in different places, people have believed that pregnancy could result from rain, wind, bathing, a sprinkling of sacred water, sunshine, moonlight, a glance, a wish, fire, an amulet, a talisman or another sacred image.

Even after the male role in conception *was* more clearly understood, women continued to employ the magical practices common in folktales and mythology. The Druids used the powder of mistletoe to render women fruitful; the Welsh used rosemary.

Until recently, many fertility rituals involved prehistoric monoliths and ancient burial chambers. On the Isle of Man, for example, women about to marry filled their mouths with water from St. Patrick's Well, walked three times around a nearby standing stone and then swallowed this "child-giving" water. At Nohant-Vic in Brittany, barren women sucked on a fragment of red sandstone chipped from a nearby dolmen. Other standing stones of Brittany were likewise believed to cure infertility.

Until a hundred years ago or so, newly married couples passed naked through the Tovan Holed Stone in Great Britain to ensure fertility. Clasping hands through the Holed Stone of Odin while reciting Wodden Prayers did the same. Pits filled with deposits of dark brown chalk-free soil — pockets of rich earth in an otherwise barren landscape — have been found at the great stone circle of Avebury. Could this, too, have been part of some fertility ritual? The possibility is not unlikely.

Humankind once considered marriage and sex, the

components of new life, symbols of the life-giving oneness of an Earth Mother's union with a Sky God. Among our prehistoric ancestors, this sacred alliance may have taken place first between a local female earth spirit and a tribal totem animal, the male partner evolving into a horned warrior god — suggested in megalithic art by axes, crooks, bows and daggers — and later into a sky deity and a male priesthood. Celtic kingship rituals, in which a claimant was married to the Earth, included consummation with the spirit of the land, represented by a young woman chosen from the tribe.

We can easily see many megalithic structures as expressions of male and female principles. Tall standing stones concentrate the male fertilizing power of the cosmos. Many of the huge monoliths we see scattered around the countryside in Brittany were quite possibly phallic symbols promoting fertility, health and male virility.

One of the most impressive of these is the Kerloas Menhir near Plouarzel (PLATE 29) in Brittany. My husband and I picnicked once, in early July, at the base of this great stone, in the sole company of, fittingly enough, the birds and the bees. The 150-ton, lichen-topped monolith graced a countryside overflowing with lilac hydrangeas, pale purple artichoke fields and cool green summer woodlands hazy with morning mist. According to legend, newlywed couples used to rub their naked bellies against the two carved knobs on opposite sides of this menhir, in hopes that their union would be fruitful.

In contrast with standing stones, womb-like burial mounds, dark chambers of female power and rebirth, convey receptive female energy. The stone circle, another possible symbol of the life-generating womb, may have been a means of generating and conserving these forces. Pairing squat stones with tall pillars or stones of differing color, between which processions could move, our ancestors may have sought to reproduce these male and female principles. Based on suppositions related to Stonehenge — from the excavations at Durrington Wells — the avenues they created, many of which lead from circles to funerary monuments, linked life with death; a ritual center and a place of death fused into one.

In the British Isles, villagers used to skip atop prehistoric burial mounds on Good Friday to help raise the spring crops. Young women in France straddled a number of conical shaped stones in the interest of fertility; the Pierre-de-Chantecoq stone, the pillar of La Roche-Marie and the leaning menhir of La Tremblais at St. Samson-sur-Rance among them. They rubbed their abdomens against others like the Giant of Kerderff standing stone near the Ménic rows at Carnac.

In some areas of megalithic architecture, we can clearly see a distinct representation of the sacred union between the Earth and the Sky. If we could stand in the interior of Newgrange at Midwinter — not that any of us is likely to get the chance, the waiting list being always more than ten years long — we'd see sunlight enter and penetrate the dark passageway, integrating lightness and dark, male and female, Heaven and Earth. One Stonehenge theory suggests that light from the Midsummer sunrise throws the long phallic shadow of the Heel Stone into the center of the circle, as though entering a womb.

If we look at more recent tradition, we can be easily convinced that male and female, as expressions of life itself, were celebrated at many of the stone structures of our prehistoric past. Well into the nineteenth century in the Orkney Islands of Scotland, men and women who intended to marry visited the islands' two great stone circles in a ritual of mutual dependence. At the Stones of Stenness (The Temple of the Moon PLATE 30) — of which only four of twelve stones now remain — the bride-to-be gave an oath to her betrothed asking the Norse god Woden to bless her marriage. At the Ring of Brodgar (The Temple of the Sun PLATE 31) – of which thirty-six stones still stand – the husband-to-be offered his own oath and repeated the Woden prayers.

We know that Christian processions and the performance of sacred rites took place regularly in and around prehistoric stone monuments at least until the Reformation, and in some cases well beyond. How anciently rooted and deeply ingrained our contemporary religious beliefs have been.

SPIRITUAL FITNESS

"Just to be is a blessing.
Just to live is holy."
– Rabbi Abraham Heschel

It's easy to believe that the purpose of life for our Neolithic and Bronze Age ancestors, if they contemplated any purpose at all, was simply to celebrate life – sunrise and sunset, seedtime and harvest, childbirth, water and fire. Our contemporary world leans toward pursuing financial success or some other individual achievement, when our life's most meaningful work may actually be more spiritual, the simple appreciation of life's beauty. "See if you notice the rose in the vase instead of the dust on the table," as Kay McConaughey, mother of Irish actor Matthew McConaughey, has said.

Only the birth of something new can conquer death. Or as Bob Dylan put it, "He who is not busy being born is busy dying." Let's try something we've never done before, discover another side of ourselves, some unexplored interest, ability or talent. When we give birth to anything on the physical plane, we recreate the universe; and anything we create — a painting, a garden, a song, a poem, a family, a home — survives us. Manifest the glory of God within. Everyone has a measure of creativity. What's yours? Make finite the infinite. Express the Divine.

Our physical birth separated our consciousness into "I" and "Other." Through meditation, we can rediscover our innate unity, the dynamic force in all things that makes us whole again. "Man is a god in ruins," the poet Emerson wrote. Aspire to wholeness. Meditate on the four ancient elements of life — fire, earth, water and air. When we appreciate that all things are connected to the Universe, we know with certainty that all things evolve into something else, something sacred.

Chapter 6

DEATH

"There is a deep longing in us
that we too
will not die on the day we die."
– Kevin Crossley-Holland

"How very simple death and
burial are,
just as easy as the falling of
an autumn leaf."
– Vincent Van Gogh

"İF YOU WANT TO CONSIDER LIFE,

START WITH DEATH."
– DALAI LAMA

"THOSE WHO DIE GO NO FURTHER

FROM US

THAN GOD, AND GOD IS VERY NEAR."
– ANONYMOUS

D EATH IS UNIVERSAL. EVERYTHING DIES. The only other sure thing we can say about death is that it relates to life, since life depends on death and decay for sustenance. "In nature nothing dies. From each sad remnant of decay, some forms of life arise" (Charles Mackay).

No doubt, as soon as humanity realized that death was inevitable, we devised ways to try to avoid it — or at least to minimize our associated fear. Death has made us behave in ethereal, macabre and even joyful ways. Emotional reactions to death run from qualms about our own mortality and feelings of separation, sadness, shock and anger, to a backlog of terrors aroused from the simple nearness of death. We experience fear of decay, fear of what happens after death and the possibility of suffering or punishment. We fear the possible pain of dying, fear of supernatural "pollution" from the corpse, fear of the rift left in society when a powerful person passes on. Death accentuates whatever we most value, making it common for the funerals of "primitive" people to be dominated by celebration, sexuality or fertility.

It would be hard to find a culture, past or present, that did not respect its dead, however fearfully. Ancient Greeks put coins on the tongues of corpses to pay Charon, the ferryman of Hades, to carry them to their final rest. The keening during Irish wakes placates the spirit of the deceased and ensures its safe passage to the next world. Such vigils might also shield them from any harmful intervention, like possession by an evil spirit.

Today, jazz funerals in New Orleans celebrate death in a largely joyful way. On the Hispanic Día de los Muertos (The Day of the Dead), believers honor the souls of the dead by offering a sweet bread called Pan de Muerto (The Bread of the Dead) on visits to family graves.

Archeology can uncover only hints about the prehistoric past's core cultural beliefs surrounding death. If we focus on the survival of grave goods and stone monuments, we assume that death and its rituals were of supreme importance to Neolithic and Bronze Age cultures; yet we have no real context in which to place these elements. Do we see a cist grave at a single stone, for example, as a respectful burial or as a ritual deposit that augmented the stone? Did the change from inhumation to cremation represent an act of love — the freeing of a spirit from a body — or an act of fear meant to shield the living? We have only a persistent historical association of prehistoric stone monuments with death, together with a nearly uninterrupted tradition of their being revered, to go by.

Even here, there is room for skepticism. A simple grave in the flank of the rich pre-Christian Saxon burial at Sutton Hoo in England may be just the hasty interment of the unconverted in a "pagan" place, where they would lie forever in the eternal darkness of unconsecrated ground. Without written records, we can never know whether death and burial were of as paramount importance to Bronze Age and Neolithic societies as they were to, say, the Egyptians.

It's unlikely that humans ever held any single definitive body of belief about death and its meaning. Throughout the ages, we've burned and we've buried our dead, quickly or within a prescribed period of time, with or without animal or human sacrifice. We've eaten them — raw, rotten or cooked; preserved them with pickling, smoking or embalming; dismembered them, abandoned them or purposefully left them exposed to carrion. When we grieve, we might choose to avoid people altogether, or we might throw a party; we might fight, laugh, cry or celebrate, with sexual excesses, with feasts or with festivals.

We often underscore death with a great deal of noise, during fixed rituals that preserve and elevate society over the individual. Loud rhythmic sounds are believed not only to scare away unwanted spirits, but they're also natural symbols of change, like the beating of a heart. They also suggest power and communication with the Divine. "Make a joyful noise unto the Lord," Psalm 100 tells us. Through countless generations, we've venerated our dead and marked their transition from life to death with fireworks, gunshots, horns, sirens, drums, gongs, bells or wailing chants.

Legend and mythology are no less varied. In Brittany, Death, (the Ankou), appeared as the ghost of the last man to die each year. He was tall and gaunt, with a wide-brimmed hat and empty eye sockets, and he carried a scythe, a sword or a club. Driving about at night, in a cart drawn by horses or oxen, the Ankou would carry off the dead. England, Scotland, Wales, Germany and Scandinavia all have legends of Death mounted on a huge horse, attended by a posse of huntsmen seen as clouds or as shadows on the moon, all racing on the wind across the night sky.

As we further examine the *Dead*, *Burial* and the *Afterlife*; *Ancestor and Relic Cults*; and *Sacrifice*, we recognize once again that the components of death do not stand alone in any culture.

THE DEAD, BURIAL AND THE AFTERLIFE

One of our distinguishing traits as humans is that we dispose of our dead ceremoniously. In fact, the success with which we channel the power associated with the dead may even have helped determine the longevity of some societies.

The first people we know to have buried their dead did so about 125,000 BCE, in Europe about 80,000 years ago. Even in these earliest of times, mourners sometimes placed stone tools and other objects with the dead, suggesting a belief in an afterlife in which the items could be used and an immortal, invisible something that could use them. We now call this entity "the soul." For Zulu tribes it's a shadow, as it was for the Ancient Greeks who called it a Shade and for the Egyptians, who knew it as Ka or the Double. Australian aborigines recognize this "something" as fog or smoke. Some of us find the soul essence in an echo, a reflection or even in the breath, which ceases at death.

Many of us believe that the dead exist on some other plane, in some other dimension — in "heaven" or in dreams, for example. With their unknown powers, we've sometimes seen them as dangerous spirits who might come back to harm us out of envy, jealousy or revenge, and so we've taken steps to appease them or otherwise render them harmless. The eyes of the deceased may be shut in order to discourage them from choosing someone to accompany them to the grave. In some cultures, the deceased's home might be burned to prevent a return, or doors and windows might be thrown open the better to ensure the soul's escape. In nineteenth century Dublin, the corpse was taken from the home feet first to prevent the spirit from looking back into the house and perhaps enticing some other household member to follow. Stopped clocks also allowed spirits to move on. This may have been the motive behind our prehistoric ancestors' penchant for flexing or breaking the legs of a corpse, the better to discourage any undue lurking about.

Ghosts are considered entities that survive a body's death and return to or remain with the living. Sources and circumstances vary, but we most often see them as having died violently or from hunger or thirst. In ancient Egypt and Mesopotamia, ghosts were spirits who had not received sufficient offerings for the afterlife and were thus compelled to scavenge.

A vengeful infant ghost called an Ulburd ("child carried outside") haunted the Old Norse. The Ulburd was the spirit of a child born sickly, malformed or into a household that already had too many mouths to feed. The child was laid in an outside grave to freeze to death, a sadly all too common world practice in hard times. For the Finns, the ghosts of such children, buried in the forest, would appear as the luminescence on bogs or water meadows. We now call this eerie glow Will o' the Wisp, Jack-o-Lantern, foxfire, elf-fire or corpse candles. Encountering it was long considered an ill omen.

Cultural rituals of burial help move the dead from this world into the next, while in some cases keeping the living from being hauled along after them or harassed by their spirits. The form of these rituals was, and is, endlessly diverse. One of our most prominent motifs is that of a journey. In the early twentieth century, the Berawan tribe of Borneo recognized a point at which mortals were neither dead nor alive. This transition between one state and another lasted until the deceased's bones were hard, dry and clean.

While the Berawan corpse rotted, the soul, too, was in a sort of limbo, a homeless object capable of bringing illness or other malicious damage to the living. When the soul's passage was complete, a great feast honored the dry bones, which were then recovered and moved to a new location. The soul had reached and been accepted into the land of ancestors, and the survivors could resume their normal lives. When the Berawan converted to Christianity, the purgatory of Roman Catholicism became the place where souls went "until their bones [were] dry." Members of the Bara tribe of Madagascar called their own ceremonies of reburial "doing the corpse" or "moving the dried one out."

The shaman, as a link to the spirit world in traditional societies, not only performs rites of renewal on behalf of the living, but also conducts the ceremonies that guide the dead safely into the next world. For the Celts, Neolithic communal tombs were the source of such power, channels through which knowledge flowed to those who had the right skills and authority. Hinduism's *Tibetan Book of the Dead* and the *Egyptian Book of the Dead* have both been seen as Shamanic journeys, records of the preparation required for safe passage into the next world.

Moving to and from the land of the dead is a common element in many myths. The journey may be long and arduous, adventurous and full of danger, like that of Odysseus. Our hero may need both physical skill and supernatural aid. He or she breaches a barrier into the realm of the dead and comes up with some material profit. In other accounts, like Jesus Christ's, the journey may be shorter, culminating in wisdom and non-material gain. From long before Christianity, great wisdom was won from the time-honored belief that certain individuals among us could access the potency of another world.

Icelandic Sagas tell of journeys to the land of the dead that began with the entry into a prehistoric burial mound surrounded by fire. Such stories may be based on memories of ancestral raids into ancient graves; their robbery was common, for example, in the Viking Age.

The idea of a journey from life to death is clearly behind our lore about purgatory, if not behind the concept itself. St. Patrick's Purgatory — a cavern on a small island in Loch Derg in Ireland — is now a place of Catholic pilgrimage, though the cave itself was long ago demolished as being "pagan." The cave began as a sacred site our pre-Christian ancestors seem to have used for lengthy and mystic initiations.

We can see the same spiritual journey in the mythologies surrounding Proserpina, Osiris, Theseus, and others; in Semitic teachings about heaven and hell; in the Christian resurrection as an extension of pre-Christian and Jewish rebirth doctrines; in subterranean dedications to the Sun-God Mithras, preserved as ancient ruins throughout Southern Europe; and in the legends associated with other underground sites like the Neolithic tombs of Newgrange and Gavrinis.

We've brought forms of this journey with us into modern times. In Joseph Pennell's *Highways and Byways in Yorkshire*, written in the late nineteenth century, Pennell quotes the lengthy and, at that time, well-known Lykewake Dirge, "splendid and memorable verses, throbbing with the passionate faith of Christian conviction, yet lurid with the somber glow of Pagan fancies dying hard among these hills."

"Lyke" is an ancient British word for corpse. The root word is "lych," from which we have the lych-gate of a church, which often had seats and a bench on which a coffin and coffin bearers could rest before entering the church or the cemetery. Wake is, of course, the watching over of a corpse.

In the Middle Ages, churches with consecrated ground were few, and so the dead had to be carried many miles to the nearest church on the shoulders of mourners. These trails became known as Coffin Roads. Some of them have Coffin Stones on their steeper hillsides. The Lyke Wake Dirge describes the journey of the dead across the great unknown to a final resting place. An old manuscript in the Cotton Library in England contains an account of another such dirge. "When any dieth, certayne women sing a song to the dead body, recyting the journey that the partye deceased must goe."

An afterlife, with far too many variations to be included here, is the obvious reward of such a journey. The afterlife beliefs of the early Hebrews, Romans, Greeks, Etruscans and others were generally of a dreary, glum and indifferent locale, replete with dank marshes and inky black hollows. "Down into the pit," the Old Testament says. "All are of the dust and all turn to dust again," The Preacher writes in Ecclesiastes, adding, "Whatsoever thy hand findeth to do, do it with thy might, for there is no work, nor device nor knowledge, nor wisdom in the grave whither thou goest."

Norse sagas place little emphasis on a concrete and specific hereafter, preferring to focus on a future life fraught with the dangers and glories of the road, so to speak, rather than on any ultimate destination of permanent joy or grief. Valhalla, the Hall of the Slain, was for the gods. For Celtic society, eternal youth was a companion to the belief in immortality.

In our prehistoric past, lives were short, and epidemics and starvation were all too common. How those who came before us perceived death and the dead, what burial rituals they devised and what beliefs they had in an afterlife can only be guessed at from incomplete physical evidence. Our ancestors passed through many generations living in extended families. Members were born and died in homes where few children of the many that were born survived. Death was a constant and intimate presence for them, never very far off. Under these circumstances, even the presence of grave goods becomes a riddle. Do these remnants illustrate an ancient belief in an afterlife? Do they indicate the deceased's status during mortality? Or were they simply something that, being too painful for survivors to keep, was buried with the remains of a loved one?

All we really have left is the empty stillness of ancient ruins, yet there are tantalizing hints of their significance. We find Paleolithic remains sprinkled with red ochre interred in crouched positions, as though returning to the womb. A third millennium BCE Neolithic mass inhumation north of the Black Sea shows us bodies stretched out on a bed of red ochre, the color of lifeblood. A bowl of food remnants that may have been offered to sustain the departed was uncovered at a Bronze Age tomb.

Though our knowledge of Neolithic and Bronze Age culture is restricted to rock carvings, megalithic monuments, burials, implements and artwork, we can hazard a guess as to these artifacts' use and meaning based on archeology, literature and the continuity of countless centuries in which humanity lived in much the same way as they did.

In most Paleolithic burials, the dead were isolated from the community in graves cut out of rock and sealed with a large boulder, or placed in hollows with a scatter of stones arranged to cover the body. In the Neolithic mass grave at Pontcharaud in France, the remains of about ten men, women and children were discovered together, buried face down and weighted by heavy rock slabs; their heads were turned to one side, with hands and feet removed. The Germanic Saxons of the Middle Ages were similarly known to cut off the feet of their dead to prevent unsettled corpses from walking.

Behavior like this among our ancestors gives us some idea of their possible beliefs about death and the afterlife. Tombs sealed with boulders not only protected the dead from predators, they might also keep departed souls from stalking the living. Tools and ornaments in a prehistoric grave suggest that they may have been meant for use in some future existence.

Both the forecourts and enclosures at megalithic tombs and the henges constructed nearby suggest the presence of charnel houses, depositories for human remains unearthed during subsequent burials. When the body of the newly deceased was laid out in the open air, accompanied by feasting and fires of purification – the forecourt of Cairn Holy I in Scotland (PLATE 32), among others, has evidence of hearths – the burial chamber would be opened; the bones of a previous occupant would be removed to make room for the new. The skeletal remains of the more recently departed could then be carefully arranged inside the tomb. The sepulcher would then be sealed again until the next auspicious death.

Until the 1940s, St. Kilda, an island off the west coast of Scotland, had been inhabited continuously for more than 2000 years. To make room for the newly dead, bones of the long since departed were regularly taken from the graveyard to a fenced-off area west of the village. We still move remains about regularly in the raised graveyards of New Orleans, where the process is called the "year and a day rule." Any time after a year has passed, buried remains can be put in a small bag, which is then placed in a corner of a tomb, on a shelf or even on top of the new casket for which the burial was disturbed in the first place. The old coffin is then destroyed.

In Austria, we see the same consolidation in the eleventh century parish church of St. Michael, in the steep hillside village of Hallstatt. The church was locked when Dan and I visited in the fall of 2001, but not so the charnel house. With bodies continuing to accumulate, arm and leg bones were neatly stacked three to four feet high on the floor. Several rows of skulls lined the upper shelves, some 2500 in all; each beautifully painted with a name and a floral decoration (PLATE 33).

Megalithic monuments, for the most part, were clearly

designed to be seen from a great distance in the rural landscapes of our farming ancestors. Again, we have only to glimpse the awesome portal dolmen of Poulnabrone, on the Burren in Ireland, to realize their significance. They must have played a substantial role in the societies that built them. Tombs in which great masses of bones have been found may have been central repositories for several nearby monuments. As the "hole of the soul," we can envision the passageway of these graves resuscitating the spirits of our departed ancestors as they entered and were reabsorbed into the earth to be reborn.

Some houses of the ancient dead echo those of the living. In Northern Scotland, as already mentioned, the burial chamber of Maes Howe on the main island of the Orkneys was fashioned as a square with side cells, exactly like the contemporary houses in the nearby settlement of Skara Brae. In the very same way, people have constructed elaborate monuments in Victorian cemeteries like Père La Chaise in Paris (PLATE 34), Highgate Cemetery in London and the sunken burial grounds of New Orleans, where the houses of the dead reflect the buildings in which our more recent ancestors once lived.

ANCESTOR AND RELIC CULTS

Though generally not as common as the attention we pay to death itself, the veneration of ancestors deepens our relationship between the living and the dead. We replace the disagreeable aspects of the departed with respect and reverence, as repositories of traditional wisdom or as elders or early rulers.

Most of our ancient predecessors in the Mediterranean

area, in Europe, Asia and Africa developed some form of ancestor worship, either individual cults or communal ones. In communal worship by a family, a clan, a tribe or a nation, we most often focus on a life force, such as the old Roman "Genius," celebrated on Lemuria, the third of May. This traditional festival of family feasting was similar to the Hispanic Día de Los Muertos.

Individual ancestor worship often turns communal, as did the cult of the Roman Emperor. We further distinguish ancestor cults by the age of the deceased or by a family's founder; and some of our ancestors reach the status of gods themselves. The Ndengei, a being of great power among Fijian tribes, began simply as the representative of tribal ancestors. He was eventually transformed into a symbol of eternity and creation, the supreme Fijian god. The ancestral rulers of Egypt were similarly looked on as incarnations of the Sky God, Horus. An analogous idea was applied in the European Divine Right of Kings, a concept ostentatiously overdone by the Sun Kings of France.

The ancient rulers of Ireland thought of themselves as the descendants of old gods known as the Dé Dannan. Newgrange became the home of these deities, a sacred place from which ancestral power could be sought. Celtic society as a whole considered gods and goddesses as the ancestors of men, rather than as creators. At other times, our ancestors have become vague, removed, anonymous and largely benign influences called upon in times of sickness or crop failure.

The labor involved in clearing land for cultivation must have created a bond between our first farming ancestors and those who came after them. In the kinship-based agricultural societies of our Neolithic past, the ability of one family line or another to produce a surplus for feasting and monumental construction signaled to the rest that some supernatural patronage was at work, some genealogical proximity to a founding spirit or ancestor. It was then allowed, and expected, that the elders of that family – in a direct line from some revered ancestor – would control the community's ritual practice, labor force and valued items, such as ceremonial axes. Interred in large tombs that overlooked the fields their descendants still worked, these ancestors were honored with rituals to encourage their attention and were available, through sufficient appeasement, as advisors and protectors. Their holiness lay *in* them, not *through* them, and they were revered simply *because* they were dead. Central cult monuments like chambered tombs could protect and evoke the most renowned of the ancestral dead.

Entrances to Neolithic tombs were often blocked in the Bronze Age. This may have been reverential, though it may equally suggest that deteriorating farming conditions led to once hallowed ancestors being accused of failing to keep up their end of the bargain, and so they were consequently neglected. Veneration of ancestors often goes hand in hand with success, agricultural or otherwise. Nevertheless, as sacred burial spaces for chieftains who would later merit single graves, people of lesser rank continued to be entombed in the flanks of these long-venerated mounds for some time to come.

In the nineteenth century, cemeteries were separated from places of worship, and the living were no longer literally surrounded by the dead. In today's mobile society, we likewise travel, sometimes great distances, to visit ancestral graves. For our prehistoric forbearers, however, ancestors were the psychic cohesion, the literal spirit that held a group or a family together. If kept nearby, they could be invoked, exalted or consulted as oracles. They could continue to instruct their descendants through dreams or visions, guiding them through life's journey. Powerful and potentially dangerous forces that they were, they might well have been ritually confined within the magical rings of earth or stone that make up those dramatic megalithic monuments we still see scattered throughout the landscapes of Western Europe. And even when those tombs were emptied in preparation for a new occupant, they may still have imparted spiritual guidance to their community in the form of relics.

Relics are objects we now associate with saints or martyrs. We venerate them for any number of reasons. Mere possession of a relic honors the person from whom it came, while we often see the relic itself as a protector, a conduit for spiritual merit or divine blessing, a means for working miracles or a purveyor of power. The sacredness of relics is an ancient belief in which the "soul-stuff" of a person infuses certain body parts —especially teeth, hair, blood and fingernails — and by extension, clothing or personal belongings; anything directly associated with a revered person. The spiritual power of that individual is then available to the person or place possessing the relic.

Most contemporary religions have relic cults, with the exception of Hinduism, which has no founder and teaches the illusion of reality. The first Christian reference to a relic is found in the Acts of the Apostles, where the author writes, "God did extraordinary miracles through Paul, so that even handkerchiefs and aprons that had touched him were taken to the sick, and their illnesses were cured and the evil spirits left them." In CE 156, contact with the bones of one Christian bishop was described as "more valuable than precious stones."

Not surprisingly, we find a good many Christian relics in Italy. One of those, with the most opulent of settings, is the reliquary of St. Mark, housed in the spectacular St. Mark's Basilica in Venice. A few years ago when our family visited, we drifted from our hotel along the Grand Canal through Venice's narrow, romantic pedestrian alleyways to St. Mark's Square and joined a lengthy line for the Basilica tour. It was fast moving, and within a few minutes, we were inside.

St. Mark's was the Doge's chapel until the end of the eighteenth century, when it became Venice's cathedral. The first church was designed as a sepulcher for St. Mark after CE 828, when his body was stolen from Alexandria, where he had settled. Alexandria was being plundered by Muslims at the time, so two enterprising Christian businessmen shipped out the saint's remains hidden in baskets of vegetables and pork. (His gospel was supposedly written in Rome about CE 50, and legend has it that he preached in the Venice lagoon area.)

The first church was destroyed by fire in 976 in an uprising against the duke. Rebuilding began in 1063, and St. Mark's bones were given their final burial in 1094. They are contained in an urn on the high altar, which is covered in a canopy of green marble supported by four sculpted alabaster columns. We found the entire complex — with its extensive gold-backed mosaics, raised cupolas, Byzantine carvings, bronze portals, columns, statues and marbles — a giant, stunning reliquary.

Of the tidal wave of relics that flooded into Europe with the crusades, most were of doubtful authenticity and questionable procurement. The "hawking about of limbs," as St. Augustine would later write. As late as the end of the fifteenth century, an inventory of the relics in Canterbury Cathedral included "Aaron's rod. . . Some of the stone upon which the Lord stood when he ascended into heaven. Some of the Lord's table upon which He made the Supper. Some of the prison whence the Angel of the Lord snatched the blessed Apostle Peter. Some wool which Mary the Virgin had woven. Some of the oak upon which Abraham climbed to see the Lord. And [the most fanciful of an already delusory list] some of the clay out of which God fashioned Adam."

Islamic relics include items associated with the Prophet Mohammed — hair, teeth, the hilt of his sword, his prayer mat. For Buddhists, the cremated remains of the Buddha were distributed equally among eight tribes in India, with relics such as teeth, collarbones and an alms bowl going to various monasteries.

Interred in the massive burial chambers of our prehistoric past, the bones of the special dead may have served a similar function. A collection of skulls might mean the periodic clearing out of accumulated bones, or it might mean that our ancestors had turned the tomb into a reliquary itself. In other tombs, heads are missing entirely. Skeletal remains in many sites have other missing or severed bones that may have been carried off as relics.

In early Celtic society, the skull, as the source of wisdom, truth and healing, was believed to be the seat of the soul. Possession of a head – much like the eating of brains or hearts in other cultures – gave the bearer of the head access to the departed *owner's* soul or personal power. For the Huichol Indians of Northern Mexico, the skull contained Ncircka, the opening through which a spirit passed into the next world. As late as the early twentieth century in the Balkan Peninsula, soul matter was transferred from an enemy by the taking of his head. The tenth century Anglo-Saxon abbot, Aelfric, writes in *St. Oswald* that "after the killing of Oswald, his brother, Osiu, succeeded to the kingdom of Northumbria and rode with a host to where his brother's head stood fastened to a stake and took that head and his right hand and carried them with honor to the church at Lindisfarne."

Skull caps or complete skulls have also been placed at sacred wells. The use of the body part of an auspicious person, a saint perhaps, for drinking or washing, is believed to impart some specific benefit to the water. Few body parts lend themselves so well to such a belief than a skull or skullcap.

Our past beliefs leave severed heads and skulls very much alive after death –talking and singing, even moving about on their own. The head of the Teutonic god Mimir, for instance, guarded the well at the base of the world tree Yggdrasil. Welsh legend claims that the severed head of Bran the Blessed, "King of the Mighty," was buried on Tower Hill in London as a talisman against invasion.

Even after martyrdom, legend says, various Medieval Christian saints continued to walk around with their heads tucked under their arms. In *St. Dionysius*, Aelfric writes, "And the body of the bishop arose with that light, and he took his own head that had been cut off onto that hill and went with it away from there for over two miles, with the people looking on, praising his Lord with holy songs of praise."

SACRIFICE

The word sacrifice derives from the Latin "sacrificare," meaning "to make holy" (sacer – holy; facere – to make). The *act* of offering to the Divine is not itself a sacrifice, only the means by which something consecrated is presented to a deity or returned to its godly source. Through sacrifice, we established a beneficial relationship with the Sacred.

Throughout history – and presumably prehistory – our sacrifices have come in all shapes and sizes. In times of illness, drought, famine or other misfortune, sacrifices of propitiation have been offered individually or from entire communities in order to repair the imbalance between the human and the Divine. The sin offerings of early Judaism, for example, transferred sin to a chosen victim with the "laying on of hands" or the sprinkling of blood. We might call these sacrifices bribes, and they are offered for many purposes. With gift sacrifices, we propose an exchange – a votive offering for victory in battle or restored health, for example. Thank offerings give back to the Divine the first fruits of the earth, symbolically removing their sanctified nature. Crops can then be eaten, and the Earth can be replenished. With communion offerings, part of a sacramental meal is available to worshipers. In the past, we likewise presented a portion as a burnt offering to a deity who received it by the sense of smell.

The sacred presence in a foundation sacrifice neutralizes any harmful forces and redresses the Earth for human interference. Worshippers have long used humans, animals and objects to consecrate important buildings such as shrines or houses, and sometimes entire villages. The cornerstone containing valued items that we often still put in place on erecting a public building is essentially the remnant of a foundation sacrifice.

Humanity's sacrificial tactics have also included burnt offerings for celestial deities, burial for Earth divinities and libations. A likely element of the burial culture of our Neolithic and Bronze Age past is the ritual pit, probably begun as part of an open-air shrine. These pits were dug in circles or sets of lines that may have originally been marked with upright posts or stones, which in turn may have been the precursors of some stone circles and alignments. One of these pits, dug thirty meters deep in Wiltshire chalk in England about 1600 BCE, held Roman pottery in its topmost layers.

The most profound element of sacrifice is the division between bloodless offerings and those that require blood. Milk, honey, oil, fruit, grains, beer, flowers and especially water and wine — the blood of the earth — have traditionally made up our bloodless sacrifices. These may also be ingested by priests or by animals connected with particular gods. Discoveries of grains, burnt or otherwise, have been associated with the prehistoric burial mounds of the

continued on page 173

136

Plate 1 Callanish Stone Circle, Isle of Lewis, Outer Hebrides, the most exceptional and impressive prehistoric monument in the west of Scotland.

Plate 2 The eight-foot monolith inside Callanish Stone Circle.

Plate 3 The Ring of Brodgar, Orkney Islands, Scotland, contains a stone etched by the Viking Bjorn in the twelfth century CE, at least 5000 years after the circle was raised.

Plate 4 La Table du Marchand, Lochmariaquer, Brittany. Neolithic long-mound with decorated menhir erected on the rich coastal plains of Brittany.

Plate 5 Entrance, Ile de Gavrinis, Brittany.

Plate 6 The massive restored mid-Neolithic passage grave of Newgrange, in the Boyne Valley, Republic of Ireland, dates to 3200-3300 BCE. It is one of the primary fairy palaces of the Tuatha de Dannan.

Plate 7   Gleninsheen Wedge Tomb, on the Burren, Republic of Ireland, dates to about 3000 BCE. Wedge tombs were still being raised in Counties Cork and Kerry over 13 centuries later and were possibly still in use as late as 900 BCE.

Plate 8   Cairn Holy II, Scotland. The final ceremonies here involved the breaking of Beaker pottery.

Plate 9 The recumbant Neolithic stone circle of Loanhead of Daviot, Scotland, showing the recumbant with flankers.

Plate 10 The sculptural portal dolmen of Poulnabrone on the Burren in the Republic of Ireland with its dramatic capstone of slender limestone.

Plate 11 Long Meg's Daughters (Cumbria, England) are all of igneous granite, while Long Meg herself is red sandstone.

Plate 12 The undressed sedimentary sandstone monoliths of the Ring of Brodgar, Orkney Islands, Scotland.

Plate 13 Metamorphic Lewisian Gneiss monolith in the Callanish complex on the Isle of Lewis, Scotland.

Plate 14 This foot depression at the Dark Age Celtic hillfort of Dunadd, Scotland probably played an important part in inauguration rituals of the Dalriadic kings.

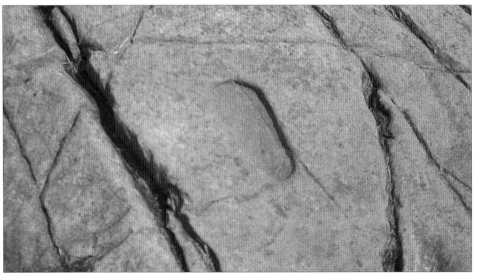

Plate 15 Decorated passageway stone at Gavrinis, Brittany. U-shaped lines may have been a counting mechanism, a symbol of the vault of heaven, even the horns of sacred cattle.

Plate 16 Corner of the squared chamber of Cuween Cairn in the Orkneys, a form that echoes, along with Maes Howe and others, the dwellings of the people who built the tomb.

Plate 17 Standing stones like Doonfeeny in Ireland express the male principle.

Plate 18 Mounds like Bryn Celli Dhu in Wales, express the female Earth Mother principle.

Plate 19 The entrance passage of Maes Howe imitates the return to the womb.

Plate 20 The nearly perfect circle of Drombeg, in Ireland.

Plate 21 Swinside Stone Circle in the Lake District of England. The circle is a symbol of wholeness and unity. Swinside is sited to sunrise in early November and may have anticipated the Celtic celebration of Samhain by more than two thousand years.

Plate 22 The double spiral of the entrance stone at Newgrange, showing the roof-box above, through which rays of the rising sun filter on the Winter Solstice.

Plate 23 The spiraled corbel roofing in the Tomb of the Eagles, Orkneys. The spiral represents eternity, evolution and growth.

Plate 24 St. Ninian's Cave, Scotland. Sacred caves are an ancient worshipping tradition.

Plate 25 The entrance to Le Roche au Bono, Brittany. Chambered tombs were perhaps built in imitation of caves, as a means of reconnecting to the earth.

Plate 26 As repositories of ancient ancestral wisdom, sacred sites in the landscape transcend both time and the physical universe. Recent excavations at the Stones of Stenness in the Orkneys uncovered a small pit inside the circle dated to the sixth century CE, containing burnt grain.

149

Plate 27 The author at the ancient Rudston Monolith, in the churchyard of All Saints, Rudston, England. Rudston is the tallest standing stone in Britain.

Plate 28 The early eighteenth century Chapel of the Seven Sleepers near Plouaret in Brittany, incorporates the Dolmen of Stivel, a megalithic burial chamber now used as a chapel. The dolmen's capstone forms the floor of the south chapel. The black arc near the center of the following photo is the entrance to the dolmen.

Plate 29 The author at the Kerloas Menhir, Plouarzel, Brittany. Newlywed couples rubbed their naked bellies – each to a side – against the two carved knobs on the stone to ensure fertility.

Plate 30 In the nineteenth century, at the Stones of Stenness ("The Temple of the Moon") in the Orkneys, a bride-to-be gave an oath to her betrothed asking the Norse god Woden to bless her marriage.

Plate 31 At the Ring of Brodgar ("The Temple of the Sun"), the husband-to-be offered his own oath and repeated the Woden prayers.

151

Plate 32 The forecourt of Cairn Holy I in Scotland – the probable scene of feasting and fires of purification – has shown evidence of prehistoric hearths.

Plate 33 Painted skulls stacked in the eleventh century ossuary of the parish church of St. Michael, Hallstatt, Austria. The same consolidation likely took place in megalithic tombs.

Plate 34 The elaborate monuments in the Victorian cemetery of Père la Chaise in Paris, reflect the houses their inhabitants once lived in, just as the Neolithic burial chambers of the Orkneys reflect the squared houses found in the nearby contemporary settlement of Skara Brae.

Plate 35 One of the most prominent examples of probable prehistoric animal sacrifice can be found in the Neolithic chambered tomb of Isbister – the Tomb of the Eagles, on South Ronaldsay in the Orkneys. Among the bones interred was a collection of skulls with the remains of white-tailed eagles.

Plate 36 Recumbant circles from the third and second millennia BCE, such as Loanhead of Daviot, Scotland, have in their southwest sectors horizontal slabs. Guardian pillars that frame the moon as it passes over, flank these recumbants.

Plate 37 Castlerigg in the Lake District of England has a gap at precise north.

154

Plate 38 The Callanish Complex. A detailed examination of forty-six possible sight lines failed to find even one accurate alignment, except for a row of stones two miles away.

Plate 39 Little Callanish. Callanish can be seen faintly on the horizon at the center of the photo.

Plate 40 The Menec Alignment at Carnac. Carnac's fan settings have been interpreted as a kind of lunar observatory grid system on which eclipses could be plotted and forecast, though they have also been viewed as three thousand Roman legionnaires turned to stone for pursuing St. Cornelius.

Plate 41 Flowers offered at Long Meg on the Fall Equinox.

Plate 42 The Fairy Spring of Barenton, also known as Merlin's Well, in the Forest of Brocéliande in Brittany. "Colder than marble," water tossed over the shoulder or sprinkled over the Perron de Merlin (Merlin's Stone), a standing stone near the basin into which the water flows, calls up a storm.

Plate 43 The holy well of St. Clether's, Bodmin Moor, Devonshire, England. Well dressings and offerings serve as gifts to the Divine or the medium through which ailments can be addressed.

Plate 44 An arm of Callanish Stone Circle, one of the many megalithic monuments of prehistory associated with water. The avenue of Callanish appears to link with Loch Roag.

Plate 45 The Farndale Stone serves as a marker for routes across the Yorkshire Moors in the north of England.

Plate 46 Clach Mhicleoid (The MacLeod Stone) on the Isle of Harris may have indicated a primary landfall.

Plate 47 Penloic Menhir, Brittany may have marked a former estuary. The water level has risen since it was raised.

Plate 48 Barpa Langais Neolithic Chambered Tomb, North Uist, Outer Hebrides, Scotland was possibly used as a tribal boundary marker expressing a community's right to the surrounding lands.

Plate 49 Merryvale Stone Row, Dartmoor, Devon, England. Lines of uprights four or five feet apart are just wide enough for a single-file procession.

Plate 50 The Merry Maids, Cornwall are nineteen women turned to stone for dancing on the Sabbath.

Plate 51 The holed stone at Glencolmcille, Donegal, Ireland. Holed stones have been deemed particularly effective in matters of virility, fertility and childbirth, and in the treatment of bone disorders.

Plate 52 The Druid Spring in Brittany, Christianized with a stone cross.

Plate 53 The prehistoric burial chamber called Queen Maeve's Tomb is seen atop Knocknarea in Ireland, from the prehistoric cemetery of Carrowmore. Its actual construction was much before Queen Maeve's actual Celtic Iron Age days.

Plate 54 The 25-ton capstone of the Neolithic burial chamber of Arthur's Stone on the Gower Peninsula in Wales was legendarily removed from King Arthur's boot and tossed over his shoulder to land on Cefn Bryn Common as he traveled to the battle of Camlann in 539 CE.

Plate 55 King Arthur's Stone in Wales.

Plate 56 The Dwarfie Stane on the Isle of Hoy, Orkney. The devil hurled a boulder into which a local troll later moved.

Plate 57 The Fir Bhreige or "Falsemen" of Callanish, converted into stone by "ane Inchanter."

164

Plate 58 The Hurlers of Bodmin Moor, Devonshire, England, were turned to stone for gaming on a Sunday.

Plate 59 Long Meg and her daughters were petrified as a coven of witches.

Plate 60   Pobull Fhinn Stone Circle above Langass Loch in North Uist in the Outer Hebrides of Scotland.

Plate 61   Swyn-y-Don Stone Circle, Wales.

Plate 62   Lligwy Neolithic Tomb, Anglesey, Wales.

Plate 63 Chun Quoit, Cornwall, England.

Plate 64 Roc'Hou Bras Dolmen, Brittany.

Plate 65   Castlerigg Stone Circle, Cumbria, England.

Plate 66   Dyffrin Burial Chambers, Wales.

Plate 67 Castlerigg Stone Circle, Cumbria, England.

Plate 68 Lanyon Quoit, Cornwall, Engand.

Plate 69   Carreg Coetan Burial Chamber, Wales.

Plate 70   Castlerigg Stone Circle, Cumbria, England.

Plate 71   The Llanfechell Stones, Wales.

Plate 72   Dolmen de Keriaval, Brittany.

Plate 73   Castlerigg Stone Circle, Cumbria, England.

Plate 74 Vizar Roc'h, Brittany.

Plate 75 The Great Cairn, Gower, Wales.

continued on page 136

Neolithic and Bronze Ages. In fact, some if not all of the grave goods of prehistory — buttons, shells, stones, jewelry, hammers, scrapers, axes, etc. — might have been intended as sacrifices, just as were the weapons and ornaments left as votive offerings at the sacred water sites of the Iron Age Celts. When the dead partake of the life of the gods, sacrifice to the dead is equivalent to sacrifice to the gods, expanding the power of the deceased.

An impulse common to almost all religions, blood sacrifices were endemic in the ancient world. As the sacred life force in man and animal, blood was the most powerful sacrifice imaginable. Through blood offerings, the gods lived — and mortals along with them. For far too long, humankind has believed that life must be fed by life, bringing power to the supplicant. Over time, we've offered up different species in different parts of the world. But whether goat, ram, bull, ox, lamb, horse or bird of prey, all have required regulations and formulas. "And he shall put his hand upon the head of the burnt offering," it's written in the Book of Leviticus, a catalog of sacrificial instruction. "And it shall be accepted for him to make atonement for him. And he shall kill the bullock before the Lord: and the priests, Aaron's sons, shall bring the blood, and sprinkle the blood round about upon the altar."

We've most often chosen the victim of our blood sacrifice because of some direct bearing on a particular deity, pregnant cows for the Earth Mother Demeter, for instance, or a ram, a boar or a bull to a fertility god. And blood sacrifice has hardly been restricted to the ancient world. In CE 601, discussing the Christian conversion of the Saxons of south England, Pope Gregory the Great wrote to St. Augustine that ". . . they have a custom of sacrificing many oxen to devils." The "Bull Feast" (Tarbhfheis) of early Celtic society involved a Druid priest who ritually ate the flesh and blood of a slaughtered bull. Bundled up in the hide, the priest then dreamed the name of a new king. In

173

some parts of Ireland, as late as the nineteenth century, a sick villager would be wrapped in the skin of a newly slaughtered sheep and then placed inside a circle of friends, family and neighbors who consumed the mutton. Until the early twentieth century, English farmers sprinkled the blood of a Martinmas pig over their fields to increase fertility, and on May Day, for the same reason, they slit the throat of a ram tied to the granite menhir at Holne, Devonshire, letting the blood flow over the stone. The animal was then roasted and eaten.

One of the most prominent examples of a probable animal sacrifice among our prehistoric ancestors can be found in the Neolithic chambered tomb of Isbister — The Tomb of the Eagles — on the island of South Ronaldsay in the Orkneys (PLATE 35). In a field of buttercups and fleabanes, Isbister stands just back from lofty sea cliffs covered with the white specks of nesting gulls. Seabirds soar above and, in the water below, large white-bellied seals with big brown eyes bob and dive, their portly black bodies paling in the dark water.

Isbister is on private property, and a visit there, I found, is a unique experience. The passageway is low and rock-walled, traversed by a small, wheeled contraption the farmer/owner/discoverer, Ronald Simison, calls a "trolley." With his permission, I laid face up on the device, and wheeled myself backward into the tomb. The central chamber is lit by small windows Mr. Simison has placed in the ceiling, and there are two end chambers and several side ones. In one of these, Mr. Simison has restored a long line of thirty human skulls exactly as he found them. Alone in the main chamber, with a view to the row of skulls, their eye-sockets staring out from the darkened recess, I confess to a fleeting but eerie sense of uneasiness.

Sixteen thousand bones belonging to 342 people were found buried in Isbister, none a complete set. Significantly,

Mr. Simison's collection of human skulls rested with the disarticulated remains of over ten white-tailed sea eagles. As a probable tribal center for more than a thousand years, Isbister had further evidence of past animal sacrifice – cattle bones outside, lamb bones inside and a heap of shallow-water fish bones at the entrance.

The chief power of our Neolithic farming ancestors was the ox, which was used as a draft animal as well as for milk, hides and meat. If it's true that sacrifice requires offering what we deem most valuable, oxen may have been the primary blood sacrifice of the Neolithic Age. We have many remnants of this in our own contemporary folk traditions. In Ireland in the nineteenth century, cattle were driven through May-Fire embers, and in Elizabethan England, young girls would lead a beribboned and flower-festooned cow into an enclosure before the Maypole.

The offering of wealth and the destruction of animal life obviously have great significance in human history, even power. How much more dramatic and potent then, as a religious expression, must be the blood sacrifice of a human? In the name of devotion to *whatever cause*, people throughout the ages have been buried alive, burned, drowned in sacred lakes, wells or waterfalls, tossed over cliffs and slung up in sacred groves. In a particularly barbaric form of blood sacrifice, more than 700,000 people lost their lives in the coliseum in Rome. Three thousand animals were slaughtered on the first day of its "grand opening;" a gruesome prelude to future bloodshed.

With some probable exaggeration, Roman and Greek writers tell us that the Celts burned criminals or prisoners of war in large wicker effigies, and Druids predicted the future from the writhing of dying stabbing victims. Irish tales describe similar customs, and there is archeological evidence that in the Iron Age, both men and women were buried under Celtic forts as probable foundation sacrifices to strengthen the walls.

We also have Lackcrom, an ancient by-gone forest near Donegal. The name is taken from Leac Crom, "leac" being a particular flagstone associated with Celtic worship; "Crom" being Crom Dubh (Black Crom), a powerful fertility deity who, according to Celtic mythology, received human sacrifices in the interest of a bountiful harvest.

Of course, the shedding of blood for the renewal of life is the very essence of Christianity, an echo of the blood sacrifice of a pre-Christian past. Isn't it possible that the passion of Christ can be interpreted, in part at least, as a divine appeal to end all such slaughters?

We have some hint from our Neolithic and Bronze Age past that buried human bones conferred sanctity on a site. Their presence, along with pockets of fertile earth, red ochre or some other distinctive stone, suggests prehistoric sacrifice. Henges with human burials at their entrances may have been ritual foundation offerings that blessed these areas as sacred space and doubled as their guardians.

The human sacrifices of our past may have involved the disabled or other "expendable" members of a community, or they may have included strangers whose spirits were unfamiliar with the local landscape. There's been some speculation that a burial uncovered near one of the sockets of the Neolithic stone circle of Avebury may have been just such a consecration, as the lone remains were of an unusually short adult woman. And at the causewayed camp of Hambledon Hill in Dorset, broken pottery and animal bones indicate food and/or blood offerings. But, just as the later Celts fastened skulls to gates and ramparts in dedication to various deities, there were also fragments of human skulls set upright at regular intervals along the ditches at Hambledon Hill. These too may have been meant as ritual deposits.

Most round barrow burials in the Bronze Age were cremations of powerful men. It may be that their communities sacrificed women and/or slaves to accompany them into the afterlife, as was later seen in the massive ship burials of Norse chieftains or in the burial of an early Balinese queen to whom twenty-two female slaves were sacrificed.

A series of Bronze Age burials in the Brenig Valley of Wales points to another, more disturbing element of our penchant for human sacrifice — the offering of children. One secondary burial in the side of one of these barrows consisted of the ear bones and molars of a baby. Three cist burials in the center of The Druid's Circle in Wales contained the cremated remains of several children buried with a Bronze Age knife and several food bowls. Bones from newborns and the ear bones of a six-year-old child were also discovered at two different prehistoric sites on the Isle of Anglesey.

As our world has grown ever smaller — and we've ostensibly become more compassionate and empathetic toward our neighbors — human sacrifice has been eliminated. Unfortunately, this enlightened attitude has not yet been extended to animal sacrifices, leaving our modern societies just short of being truly civilized.

SPIRITUAL FITNESS

"WE ALL SHARE THE ONE HUMAN JOURNEY
FROM LIFE TO DEATH."
– KEVIN CROSSLEY-HOLLAND

"THE MEANING OF DEATH IS LIFE, AND HE ALONE
TRULY LIVES WHO KNOWS HOW TO DIE.
ONLY IF WE FEEL DEATH WITHIN US CAN WE ALSO
FEEL THE LIFE TO WHICH IT OPENS US."
– KARLFRIED GRAF DURCKHEIM

Megalithic sites suggest a system of veneration that transformed the dead into relics, propitiated departed ancestors and the Divine with ritual and sacrifice and acknowledged the sacred journey from life to death to renewal. Every aspect of our contemporary society reflects an effort and a will to continue our existence beyond the grave. Few people living do not ask, "What will happen after my death?"

Why, then, do we so often think of life as a straight line from birth to death? If we speak of death at all, it's usually in hushed tones, and we fail to appreciate life's circle. Our observable world demonstrates that life and death move in the round, the one following the other as spring follows winter, or as a new moon follows a full one. So, too, do our own lives flow in an eternal round.

The great gift of life, therefore, is to be lived in the present. To live in the moment is to live in eternity. As it was for the Old Norse, it's our journey that's important, not our destination. We can all celebrate the present, both the grand moments and the small.

And yet, as the inspirational writer Roger Housden has said, "We are never more alive than when we know our end is near." In *The Everyday Meditator*, the contemporary mystic Osho elaborates on this when he writes that "stopping the world is the whole art of meditation." Included in the book is a fifteen-minute meditation on death. Before going to sleep, Osha instructs, totally relax and create the feeling of your spirit disappearing from the body entirely. In this moment, know that the mystery, surety and energizing power of your life will continue without your *physical* presence. Death is a transition.

Is there something in our lives, living or attitude that needs altering or needs to be sacrificed altogether? If there is, we can work to change that. We can allow something new and hopeful to rise up in its place. And we must all learn to be aware of emotional or psychic deadening, of a psychological or spiritual death, which can result in habitual behavior, like taking a partner or friend for granted.

Each of us can keep a journal of personal history for ourselves or our children, letting them hear our stories in our own words. In each family, there's usually one member who is called to find the ancestors, to put flesh on their bones. Are you that storyteller? Genealogy should go beyond just documenting the facts. When we bring our ancestors to life, we somehow find ourselves. We learn who we are and why we do the things we do. We respect their hardships and their losses. We find pride in what our ancestors accomplished, in the contributions they made to what we are today.

Honor your ancestors, because we are them and they are us.

HEAVEN AND EARTH

"BEHOLD THE HEAVEN AND THE EARTH AND
ALL THE ELEMENTS;
FOR OF THESE ARE ALL THINGS CREATED."

– THOMAS À KEMPIS

Clearly, much of the stone building of our Neolithic and Bronze Age ancestors focused primarily on burial monuments, though in exactly what context we can never know. The strong possibility also exists that some structures, especially stone circles and stone alignments, may have been rudimentary observatories; attempts by our ancestors to regulate or hallow earthly pursuits by heavenly means.

For the most part, our modern cultures, especially from a theological point of view, separate Heaven from Earth. Nature as a boundless spiritual entity is something too few of us consider. Instead, we fill Heaven with the pure and the Divine, with goodness, light and spirit, while we too often look on the Earth and the things of the Earth as mundane and mediocre. We view it as lowly, dark, vulgar, godless and impure, with the added irony of being considered polluted.

The religions of sky-based deities that dominate our world today emphasize this dichotomy. The Oxford Bodleian Library, for example, contains a manuscript known as MS Bodley 343, a large collection of late tenth/early eleventh century Anglo-Saxon sermons copied at the end of the twelfth century, most of them in Old English. One of these, *The Transfiguration of Christ* (based on chapter seventeen of the New Testament's book of Matthew), is filled with heavenly light, so to speak. "Faithful people shine as brightly as the sun in their Father's Kingdom." And "Faithful people will be led into the kingdom of heaven . . . and they will ever live there and shine in brightness." Sin, the sermon says, replaced "that great joy" of Heaven with a mortal life "here in middle earth," where even the stars are deprived of a great deal of their brightness.

By contrast, another sermon in MS Bodley 343, *The Transience of Earthly Delights*, includes a fearsome and graphic description of Hell, long believed to be located deep down in the bowels of the Earth. Hell writhes and seethes with worms, toothy dragons and eternal burning. "And the black night will never end together with the dim darkness. Nor will a beam of light ever appear."

For farming cultures, Heaven and Earth seem thoroughly bound up in one another, the Earth responding directly to Heaven's sunlight as manifested in growth cycles and changing seasons. Heavenly light, whether from the moon, the sun or the stars, was a strong component in the shape and function of the buildings of prehistory. Though the unanswerable question will always be "why," we can speculate and shed a little light on "how."

In this section, *Heaven* will include a discussion of *Light* itself; its manifestation in the *Sun*, the *Moon* and *Fire*; its effect on the Earth through *Seasons*, *Natural Cycles* and *Calendar*s; and its physical application in *Archeoastronomy*. Under *Earth*, we'll look at *Water* and the magical art of *Geomancy*, both of which may well have been features in the megalithic building of our Neolithic and Bronze Age ancestors. Once again, we recognize that these components rarely stand alone in any culture.

Chapter 7

Heaven

"All the way to Heaven is Heaven."
– Catherine of Siena

"Somewhere in the distance lies the soft spread of heaven."
– Kenneth Paul Kramer

OUR CONTEMPORARY RELIGIONS HAVE long emphasized a heavenly home of deity somewhere above the Earth, splendid with eternal light and opposed by primordial and earthly darkness. Early interpretations of an afterlife, however, did not often include such hopeful or comforting expectations. In the earliest traditions of the Hebrews, we see that Heaven was the home of Yahweh, the tribal warrior/creator/Sky God of the Old Testament, who directed the destiny of Earth and its inhabitants from a lofty perspective. At the same time, a Jewish afterlife called Sheol existed under the earth. When, through death, a person's breath of life returned to Yahweh and the body had decayed, the *essence* settled in Sheol. Good and bad, saint and sinner, rich and poor, the faithful and the infidel, all men, women and children who passed from mortality were believed to be sheltered in Sheol together in a nebulous, lifeless existence; unaware and unconscious, feeling neither pain nor pleasure.

Only in the centuries immediately preceding Christianity did Jewish thought begin to look on Heaven as the destination of the righteous dead, delineating a system of resurrection where all humankind would be judged; being either rewarded in Heaven or punished in Hell for their actions on Earth. At about the same time, the Greeks determined that their gods, and those entitled to share their life of bliss, were housed somewhere in the western ocean or in the lower world.

For Confucius, Heaven was equal to Divine Will. Both Hinduism and Islam have varied and numerous conceptions of the concept of Heaven. For the worshippers of Vishnu, for example, Heaven is the place or condition in which suffering, fear and death are eliminated and eternal light reflects the glory of Vishnu, something like the Christian Heaven. By contrast, Buddhism's ultimate goal of emancipation from *any* existence precludes a belief in Heaven in any traditional sense.

As defined in this book, Heaven is both the home of a deity who encourages us to direct our attention/intentions upward and the expansive and divine vault of space that encompasses the Earth, the great expanse through which the sun, moon, planets and stars move. In this context, light has a key role.

LIGHT

"Light is the secret presence of the Divine."

– John O'Donahue

We humans have a fascination with light that is timeless. "For the rest of my life I will reflect on what light is," Albert Einstein wrote in 1917. The Northern Lights and the Milky Way, both rivers of light in the sky, have fascinated us for countless generations. Europeans saw demons in the streamers of the Aurora Borealis; the Chinese saw dragons; the Inuit, spirits; Teutonic tribes, flashes of Valkyrie armor.

In my own experience, there was the unmistakable sense of a sentient being in the shimmer of the Northern Lights I witnessed one blistering cold November night at Chena Hot Springs in Alaska. The gorgeous but eerie lights, dipping and flowing like bottle-green draperies, were mesmerizing.

We are, all of us, constantly in the midst of light; surrounded, bathed and energized by it. We most often see light as merely the means by which form and color are made visible; when in fact, color *is* light. An object projects color only because light is reflected from its surface. Green leaves reflect green light, though the shade of that light varies by hue, value and intensity.

Light is made up of electromagnetic waves we can measure by frequency. Long light waves allow for things like radio communication, heat induction and photography. Short light waves provide us with gamma rays and X-rays. People and animals radiate a light known as "kirlian."

The hormone melatonin, manufactured in our pineal gland — located in the center of our brain between the two hemispheres and behind and above the pituitary gland — is our body's light meter. Light suppresses the secretion of melatonin, allowing us to stay awake and alert. Sunlight received through the eyes regulates the circadian rhythms and functions of our bodies, those functions pertaining to vital processes in plants, animals and humans, most of which recur every twenty-four hours. Without light on our bodies, these rhythmic functions would be erratic.

Night and day have profound effects on us. We've seen the positive effects of light from light therapy. In one study in Sarasota, Florida, identical windowless first-grade classrooms were subjected to different light sources. Students working under full-spectrum, radiation-shielded fluorescent light fixtures showed academic improvement and positive changes in behavior within a month. Students working under standard cool-white fluorescent light fixtures showed hyperactivity, fatigue, irritability and attention deficit behavior.

Studies like this have led us to better understand Seasonal Affective Disorder (SAD), a form of depression found in one to five percent of people living in middle and northern latitudes. As much as fifteen percent of the population of some countries suffers from the sub-syndrome of SAD we call "winter blues," and every university hospital in Canada now has a SAD clinic to address its prevalence.

SAD itself is most common in young adult women. The treatment of choice, according to the *Journal of the American Medical Association*, is light therapy — timed exposure to daylight-intensity light. Light may produce antidepressant benefits within one week of treatment.

Light therapy found early acceptance in Europe, a population already accustomed to herbal remedies and other natural treatments for depression. Light therapy is also being investigated for insomnia and immune disorders. As a treatment for circadian disruptions, such as jet lag and shift work, bright light theoretically speeds up our body's adaptation to different time zones or schedules. As lighting devices become portable, less expensive and more powerful, some hotels have offered them to jet-lagged guests. Typically, a dawn-simulating alarm clock replicates outdoor light near dawn or dusk, light increasing gradually starting thirty minutes before a desired wake-up time; a far gentler way for us to start the day than with a traditional alarm clock.

Just as we may speak of someone's birth as "seeing the light of day," light, both literal and symbolic, is today often equated with life itself. Those of us who live in the natural world have a strong innate sense of light and darkness. Religious symbolism has persuaded most of us to associate light and warmth with happiness, health and contentment; darkness and cold with fear and discomfort. The essence of our environment is defined in terms of both literal and symbolic *light*, expressed as an integral part of wellbeing.

Early Anglo-Saxon Christian poetry celebrated morning and the coming of spring, connecting light with goodness and life. The darkness of deep forests or desolate fens and moors embodied evil and death. Christian hermits battled evil in lone sea caves, in dim forests or dark mountain huts. For early Celtic societies, smith-craft was associated with the magic of alchemy, and metalwork — sparks flying in dark caverns — was looked on as a manifestation from another world. The darkness of an ancient burial chamber was a fitting home for the sídhe, the sometimes "fierce and horrible" Celtic fairies.

But in the same way that Heaven and Earth were likely considered intrinsically connected for the agricultural societies of our prehistoric past, so, too, were light and darkness. Ireland's Newgrange is certainly one of the most dramatic examples of this. Facing southeast on the summit of a low hill, this magnificent passage tomb looks out on the lush Boyne Valley. Anyone fortunate enough to be inside on the morning of the Winter Solstice (December 21) will see the first rays of the rising sun filter through a gap in a roofbox above the entrance, gradually moving down the passageway to illuminate the dark central chamber. Well before the rediscovery of this roofbox, it was said that sunlight penetrated the passage on certain occasions and focused on the tri-spiral stone in the end chamber.

On December 21, 1967, Professor M. J. O'Kelly of the University College of Cork was the first known person in thousands of years to witness this phenomenon. Two years later, he did so again and described the experience. "At exactly 09.54 hours BST, the top edge of the ball of the sun appeared above the local horizon, and at 09.58 hours the first pencil of direct sunlight shone through the roofbox and along the passage to reach across the tomb chamber floor as far as the front edge of the basin stone in the end chamber. As the thin line of light widened to a 17 cm band and swung across the chamber floor, the tomb was dramatically illuminated and various details of the side and end chambers could be clearly seen in the light reflected from the floor. At 10.07 hours, the 17 cm band began to narrow again, and at exactly 10.15 hours, the direct beam was cut off from the tomb. For seventeen minutes therefore, at sunrise on the shortest day of the year, direct sunlight can enter Newgrange, not through the doorway, but through the specially contrived narrow slit which lies under the roof at the outer end of the passage roof."

This stunning representation of springtime rebirth at the ebbing of winter demonstrates for us a maxim from the thirteenth century German mystic Meister Eckhart, "God shines in the darkness where every now and again we get a glimpse of him."

Light symbolism, as a spiritual concept, is a cross-cultural phenomenon. For the Celts, light produced a battle aura around warriors and represented the frenzied sacred/ supernatural heat of battle. The Christian halo is much the same, considered the "flame of thought in the mind," an image of the sacred quality of light.

Christmas, based originally on an ancient celebration of light, is an oasis in the dark of the year, as is Hanukkah, the Jewish festival of religious freedom and light. Those of us who have had a near-death experience, or the privilege of a mystical encounter with Divinity, almost always describe the experience in terms of light. We've extended the spiritual depth of light, its metaphorical perception, to other substances that shine, among them fire, the sun and the moon.

THE SUN

"Spirit of the rising sun, lift me up.
Hold me there and never let me go."

– Bono

The awesome, eye-bedazzling sun was probably among the first objects the world's earliest populations named. Daily, we see the sun, an independent and visually prominent power, appear to rise of its own accord, swing through the heavens and drop down again into the west.

To the Egyptians, this was the Sun God Ra (Re), sailing across the sky in a boat. For the Greeks, Helios drove his chariot through the firmament. In the fifth century BCE, Apollo – originally a god of light and a relative newcomer to the Greek pantheon – came to represent the sun. Among the Aztecs, Huitzilopochtli did battle in the sky each day with the moon and the stars. At the center of the Indian zodiac, the Sun God Surya rode a chariot pulled by seven horses, representing the seven days of the week.

Attributes of the sun, like warmth and light, also have a dark side. We see that the sun can bestow life through germination and growth, but we also see that it can destroy life with drought and excessive heat. In the past, most inhabitants of hot, dry lands feared the sun for this reason. In the ancient Valley of Mexico, the Aztec god Huitzilopochtli was considered a voracious spoiler who required regular penance and sacrifice. In Egypt, however – a hot, dry land moderated by the Nile – the Sun God Ra had a more humane and benign disposition. In places like Northern Europe, where winters are often long, bleak, dark and cold, our forbearers deemed the sun especially bright with a positive divinity.

Up to the third century CE, the dominant religion of the Roman Empire was Mithraism, which saw the rise and fall of the sun as a metaphor for humanity and included a glorious resurrection after death. The sun was worshiped as the "Unconquered Sun," a concept that grew in time to encompass the conflict between good and evil, light and darkness, life and death, summer and winter and so on, especially among Romano-Celts.

The birth of Mithra, the symbolic representation of the sun's light, was celebrated on December 25, the day following the end of Saturnalia (December 17-24), a festival of the Winter Solstice honoring Saturn, the Roman god of spring planting. In the middle of the fourth century, unable to suppress this thoroughly entrenched "pagan" festival, the Christian church chose December 25 as the birth date of Jesus, in an effort to displace Mithraism. A celebration in which the old sun died to be restored by the birth of a child "son" that gave mankind victory over darkness had an obvious appeal for Christianity. Nonetheless, the Winter Solstice is still celebrated in Northern Europe in anticipation of brighter, longer and warmer days.

One example of the sun as creator and nourisher of the Earth is found in the Celtic Sun God, Lugh, "The Shining One," whose festival of Lughnasadh traditionally fell in August. Lugh developed out of pre-Celtic Indo-European gods, one of whom, Lugh Lamhfada, had a fairly clear connection to rays of sunlight, as his name translates as "Long-Armed Lugh". Lughnasadh observances included massive bonfires, as earthly reflections of the sun. Julius Caesar writes that the Teutonic tribes of Gaul likewise worshiped the sun with fire festivals at times of the year when the sun's appearance was of particular importance.

Evidence of probable sun worship among our Neolithic and Bronze Age ancestors first appears in the fourth to third millennia BCE. From Neolithic times through Romanized Europe — roughly 2000 BCE to CE 400 — reverence for the sun as a divine and supernatural phenomenon was apparently a dominant notion. Although we can't fully understand them or their origins, prehistoric artwork gives us tantalizing clues to these ancient beliefs.

I was privileged to see one of the most beautiful such representations in the Danish National Museum in Copenhagen during a Christmastime visit in 2004. The Sun Chariot from Trundholm peat bog in Odsherred, Denmark, is an exquisite figure discovered by a farmer's plow in the late summer of 1902. The image represents the sun — a disc made of two bronze plates, one side of which is covered in gold – pulled across the sky by a bronze horse, both sun and horse set on a six-wheeled chariot. This Sun Chariot dates to around 1400 BCE and is an astounding piece of craftsmanship.

As we've already seen, people of the Neolithic and Bronze Ages drew symbols of the sun, built shrines and constructed images and complexes that appear to acknowledge both daily and seasonal celestial behavior, as well as to express gratitude to the sun for its heat and light. Our farming ancestors needed to symbolically harness and propitiate forces like the sun over which they had no actual control. The sun could bring about crop failure through drought or flood. How could its power of destruction be tempered? To implore the Divine for sympathetic intervention, our prehistoric forbearers probably honored the sun with fire festivals, along with making images on and raising stones. Likewise, farmers need to measure time, and their carefully built megalithic arrangements may have been used to help track the sun's movements.

In those ancient times, humanity no doubt saw the sun as life itself, firmly linked to their own fertility and that of their crops and livestock. Wheat, the principal harvest of the time, even ripened to the golden color of the sun. With the sun's creative might, our ancestors awakened, seeds sprouted, plants bloomed and flourished and diurnal animals set out to hunt. Crops grew only where and when they received enough sunlight, so it seemed clear that the sun's rays must penetrate and fertilize the Earth. The rising and setting of the sun was equated with life, death and regeneration – the "coming of dawn after the death of night."

But when we see the sun vanish at night, where does it go? With no concept of the world as a sphere, the most compelling answer in our prehistory was probably the Underworld. This might be one reason why solar symbols were carved so regularly on prehistoric burial monuments and why passage graves were so often aligned toward the sun. In darkness, the sun lights the way for the dead. Sun-signs in tombs would shine through the gloom of death to rekindle life in another world.

The eighteenth century antiquarian, Charles Vallancy, once referred to Newgrange as the "Cave of the Sun," and he may have been accurate. The connection of solar power with death is one of humanity's most ancient beliefs. As late as the mid-twentieth century, the islanders of St. Kilda off the west coast of Scotland waited for the sun's shadow to reach a designated spot before beginning a funeral service.

As we have seen, the sun, depicted as a simple radiated circle, a wheel, a spiral, an eye or an antlered stag, was a dominant motif in Neolithic megalithic architecture. The growth and shedding of antlers, which radiate outward like rays of sunlight, is seasonal, just as the intensity of the sun changes from winter to summer. In this context, it's interesting that the Hebrew word for "horn" – "shofar" – comes from the root word "shafar" meaning "bright, glistening, radiant or shining." The eye, too, is a mirror of the world, a receptor that reflects both sunlight and human personality. Like the divine sun, the eye penetrates in search of truth.

As the climate deteriorated during the Bronze Age, Europe became colder and wetter, farmland was abandoned, and populations shifted with the erratic movements of ruptured civilizations. In response, our ancestors may have been even more vigorous and desperate in their dealings with the sun, while still revering it as a beacon of hope. With metalworking, sun imagery could be further enhanced with gold and bronze, bringing still greater attention to this powerful manifestation of the Divine. Such efforts may also have included an ever-broadening calendar of ritual and ceremony.

The material culture of our Bronze Age ancestors hints

at complex rites and observances associated with sun cults, with magical attempts to warm the earth after each dark night and each cold winter. Bronze Age interest in cremation may even have sprung from a desire to waft the souls of our loved ones back to Heaven's dazzling creator/destroyer, from the darkness of death back into the light.

As Bronze Age societies became increasingly belligerent, sun symbols turned to hunting, warfare and fire – lions with golden manes; horses and sharp-eyed eagles; the stags and brightly bristled boars of Bronze Age burial urns. In Scandinavia, both the solar discs in horse-drawn carts and their spoked wheels were buried with the dead. The sun's rays were embodied in the arrows of subjugation, and the sun as ruler of the heavens — an all-seeing, all-knowing judge — evolved into kingships, lawgivers and other representatives of authority.

By the Iron Age, the sun had fully bonded with warfare. Warriors decorated their armor with sun symbols to prevent injury, and solar amulets were placed in graves for protection in the afterlife. The sun cult reached its height in the Romano-Celtic phase of Western European culture, likely during the first century CE, when sun gods were depicted in full human form.

The sun has had a long, impressive and tumultuous reign over humanity as a deity, spirit or power. In general, our ancestors were hesitant to alter such an ancient belief system, and for untold eons, they looked on the sun as a force to be placated, invoked and glorified. The sun depicted with a water bird was first found on items dated to the Urnfield period, about 1300 BCE. We find that identical motif still viable in Iron Age Gaul, more than a thousand years later.

FIRE

"Bright-flaming, heat-full fire."
– Guillaume de Salluste

Like the sun, fire can be a miraculous gift or a fearsome enemy. In civilization's early days, when loss of personal property was of minor concern because there was so little of it, fire was relished simply for its light and heat. Myths like that of Prometheus, who stole fire from the gods, tell us of the civilizing influence of fire. Learning to *control* fire, which first separated and protected us from other animals, was a form of cultural refinement, as was preserving and transporting fire. Placing hot coals in the hollow of a horn or using slow-burning wood is behavior exclusive and universal to human society. Without the *active* use of fire, its influence on the natural environment is a simple matter of awed observation.

Beyond providing us with light and heat, fire can cook our food; clear our lands of underbrush so our animals can graze and our crops can be sown; flush prey out of hiding for hunting; eradicate insect infestations; and provide us with protection from wild animals. When our agricultural ancestors first appeared in the Near East about 7000 BCE, they cleared their fields with slash-and-burn cultivation, resulting in ash that could be used as a fertilizer.

Over the past 10,000 years, the history of science and technology has depended on the constant increase in available energy through our control of fire. This includes the specialists of prehistory — the potters and the metal smiths who armed the warriors of the Bronze Age.

Aristotle, in sixth century BCE Greece, numbered fire among the four essential elements, the others being water, earth and air. Fire was perhaps the most potent of these, since its application brought about changes in the others — in solids (earth), liquids (water) and gases (air). Alexandrian

Greeks would later plant the seeds of alchemy, the precursor of chemistry, by combining this primal-substance philosophy with oriental technology and religious mysticism.

Because of its similar attributes and effects, fire is often considered the earthly equivalent of the sacred sun. Zoroastrians in ancient Iran worshiped fire as the most sacred, powerful and ethereal principle of all. References to Fire Gods and holy fires akin to the sun are prevalent throughout history. In Vedic scriptures from ancient India, for example, Agni, a messenger god of fire, received offerings and brought the "sweet smelling savor" of burnt sacrifice into the presence of celestial deities. The Romans, Greeks and Aztecs all honored Fire Gods with sacred flames. The Incas ignited their sacred fires by concentrating the sun's rays with a mirror.

Celtic Druids considered all things as comprised of three mystical elements — fire, water and earth, all of which had to be in balance. Fire was to be worshiped and carefully tended. Beltane fires — probably originally relating to the worship of the ancient Sun God Bel or Baal — were lit by Druid priests on the first of May. All domestic hearths would then be relit from them. Well into the nineteenth century, country people in Celtic regions waited for smoke to drift up from the priest's chimney on Beltane before lighting their own fires. For many centuries, animals kept alive through the winter were taken out to summer pastures on Beltane. In Scotland, these summer farmsteads were called shielings. The Hill of Uisneach, the "Center of Ireland," where a great stone marked the meeting place of all five ancient Irish provinces, was for many years the focus of a Feast of Bel.

Fire was also a symbol of the Celtic Mother Goddess Brigid, whose festival of Imbolc, celebrated on the first of February, became the Catholic St. Bridget's Day.

Another Celtic fire festival took place during Samhain, a Gaelic observance held on the first of November. With insufficient feed for all animals, those that could not be wintered over were slaughtered on Samhain with great feasting. Bonfires — a word that may have its root in "bone-fire" — consumed the inedible waste parts of animal carcasses. Animals were also driven between great fires for purification and fertility. Christian houses of worship lit fires on Samhain as well, though they called it All Soul's Day. The Cistercian "White Monks" of Fountains Abbey in North Yorkshire, England, for example, kindled two huge fires in their warming house on the first of November. These warming fires, the only fires allowed other than those in the kitchen and the infirmary, burned until Easter. In Britain, the ceremonial flames that now mark Guy Fawkes Day on the sixth of November were no doubt first lit for Samhain.

Midsummer (June 21) bonfires — called in Breton the "tan heol" or "the Fire of the Sun" — were lit on the tumulus of St. Michel in Brittany into the nineteenth century. Christianity transformed Midsummer's Fire Festivals into the Feast of St. John the Baptist. In the nineteenth century, a ceremony in Basse Kontz, France, celebrated the birth of St. John by rolling a wheel of fire down Stromberg Mountain to the Moselle River, imitating the sun's gradual decline. An unimpeded roll signaled a good wine harvest. In the fourth century, St. Vincent observed a similar rite in the Aquitaine. Midwinter (December 21) fires to encourage the sun's return are often lit in the colder parts of Northern Europe like Scotland, where winter days are especially short.

Flints, pyrites and fire drills found in Neolithic sites demonstrate the control of fire among our prehistoric ancestors. And there's evidence that fire rituals were connected to a variety of their stone monuments, from Carnac — where the bases of two cromlechs (one aligned to Midwinter sunrise and the other to Midsummer sunset) contained charcoal and ashes — to burial chambers in Scotland that have evidence of hearths in their forecourts. In the prehistoric settlements of Skara Brae and Barnhouse on the mainland of the Orkney Islands, central hearths, as the first stage in the laying out of a building, were placed in line with a Solstice sunrise or sunset.

Our ancestors in Northern Europe had a high tolerance for cold. A Versailles dinner in the Hall of Mirrors in the winter of CE 1695-96 featured frozen wine and water on the table. Yet no hellfire could compete with the agony of eternal frost. We still seasonally light celebratory and protective fires throughout Western Europe. As mentioned earlier, I have witnessed Midsummer fires on the hilltop of Menez Bré in Brittany and in the center of Pobull Fhinn, a remote stone circle in the Outer Hebrides. I've also seen a Samhain/Guy Fawkes fire outside of Portree, on the Isle of Skye.

The Christian Church perpetuated the sacred flame with altar fires, which we have now reduced to symbolic representations with lamps or candles.

THE MOON

"... it's a touch of the moon."

— Wilfred Grenfell

Our fascination with the moon, the largest body in the night sky, encompasses fear, awe and adoration and must be as old as civilization. Stars blaze in a deep, dark sky only until the moon rises. Even today, after we've witnessed astronauts walking on its surface, the moon is still a symbol of romance, intrigue and enchantment. We are beguiled by its constantly changing shape, its size and its brightness. It affects our tides and our dispositions and correlates with the stages of life and death. At least seventeen nations currently have a crescent moon symbol on their flags.

Of the eight phases of the moon — new moon, waxing crescent, first quarter, waxing gibbous, full moon, waning gibbous, last quarter and waning crescent — the full moon has probably influenced us most throughout history. A full moon, reflecting seven percent of the sunlight that strikes it, graces the Earth every twenty-nine days, twelve hours, forty-four minutes and three seconds.

Along with the full moon, we see an apparent increase in incidence of madness and violence. Myths and legends connecting insanity to the moon are archaic and very common. The words "lunacy" and "lunatic" are both related to "luna," the Latin word for moon. The Gleann na Gealt, or "Valley of the Mad," in Ireland was a glen where the mentally disturbed could go to be cured. The word "gealt" has its root in "gealach," meaning "moon."

Today, studies hint at the possibility that the phases of the moon cue changes in the Earth's magnetic field, causing us to experience headaches, fatigue, memory loss, irritability and insomnia. This may be why we see an increase in activity in psychiatric hospitals, crisis centers, emergency rooms and 911 hotlines on nights with a full moon. On the other hand, a full moon, with the luminance it creates, may simply make it *easier* for miscreants to create mayhem.

Along with emotional disturbances, we've also associated the moon with other illnesses. The same lunar forces that produce tides were long thought to be the cause of epilepsy, once known as "water on the brain." Disorders as vague as feeling "under the weather" were often attributed to the moon as well.

In the early twentieth century, Wilfred Grenfell, a Newfoundland physician, told of a boat-building friend who'd lost his appetite and scarcely slept. "Jake Rumford says he thinks it's a touch of the moon," Grenfell writes in his autobiography. "They had worked a bit by moonlight." In the Middle Ages, anyone falling asleep in moonlight on open ground on a Friday night was believed to run the risk of becoming a werewolf. Such convictions not only reflect the weighty influence we've given to the moon, but also our fear of wolves, which were nearly exterminated in Europe during the Middle Ages and in North America by the late nineteenth century.

We've also given the moon a role in healing. "Going out to the new moon" is a frequent suggestion in metaphysical circles to promote new beginnings — a marriage, the gathering of herbs or the start of some new construction, business or other enterprise.

Birth and mating cycles in animals are affected by a full moon, as are violent rainfall patterns such as hurricanes and tropical storms. In Nova Scotia, the largest catches of North Atlantic herring were taken at the full moon. Sea turtles lay their eggs at the margin of a full moon's high tide so they will be protected from wave action until they hatch.

In an average lifetime, each of us will see about a thousand full moons. When the moon reaches its fullness during the day, it will be nearly full both the night before and the night after.

We often call the full moon of July the "Hay Moon" because it gives farmers extra time to gather in their hay before a rain. The full moon of May is the "Planting Moon," signifying the beginning of the growing season. The full moon nearest the Autumn Equinox is the "Harvest Moon," and the full moon that follows that is called the "Hunter's Moon." With fields bared and clean, hunters can more easily scope their prey. In the north of Scotland, the Midwinter rising of a full moon is called the "Midnight Moon," a moon that just brushes along the horizon in its passing. A full moon in September is cause for Japanese moon-viewing parties. When there are two full moons in a single month, the second is called a "Blue Moon." The phrase "once in a Blue Moon" refers to the fact that this phenomenon occurs only very rarely, during only 41 months in a century.

We have also used the moon to predict our weather. Irish farmers say that a bright, clear moon in winter will bring frost; a certainty if the sky is cloudless on a deep winter night and the day's heat can radiate back into space. An Italian proverb, "Ring near, water far; ring far, water near," predicts the rainfall probability from a halo around the moon. Science and folklore have used different methods and reasoning, but they very often reach the same conclusions.

The moon is a dynamic object that we see rise, set and move across the sky just a little bit differently each day. Its light is dramatic and impressive in spite of the artificial heavily lit night skies of our modern cities. For our ancient ancestors, who had none of the explanatory knowledge of contemporary science, the moon must have been an even more captivating and active participant in daily life. "The moon may have been the first creation to be seen dying and rising three days later," says author Kathleen Cain in her book *Luna*. Especially for nomadic people and early farmers, the coming and going of the moon mirrored the cycles of human life and the passage of time — birth, death and rebirth; the maiden, the mother and the crone.

It's no wonder, then, that the moon has figured so prominently as a living being in the songs, poems and stories of our ancestors' earliest days. In the late nineteenth and early twentieth centuries, Scottish Highlanders welcomed the moon with a curtsey or a bow, turned coins in their pockets, made a wish or uttered a short greeting.

We frequently associate the moon with fertility, both in plant and animal life. Vegetation has always responded to the phases of the moon. Pinto beans, for example, absorb water fastest four times a month, at lunar quarters. Flowers like the lily, the poppy and the lotus have been connected with the moon, the poppy possibly for its "dream state" qualities.

Menstrual cycles also correspond to a lunar cycle, a phase of twenty-eight days; though this is a mystical connection and not a literal one. In one New Guinea tribe, the name for the moon — "Ganumi" — also meant menstrual blood. In Pre-Columbian Peru, the moon, the sea and woman were all known by the same word.

In Australia and India, the moon was traditionally viewed as a male spirit, the light of a full moon having the power to impregnate women. To the Maori tribe of New Zealand, the moon was looked on as "the husband of all women." In ancient Brittany, women were careful to shield their torsos for fear of being "mooned" — made pregnant — by the full moon.

Another prominent male moon deity is Sin, the Babylonian/Sumerian Moon God, sometimes also called Nanna, who was known as the "Lord of Wisdom." Ancient Palestine was first called "Sinim," the Land of the Moon. Mount Sinai also takes its name from this ancient deity.

In the older cultures of the Scottish Highlands, a full moon was considered a prime time for marriage, as it represented the fullness of passion and fertility. Brides in the Orkney Islands conducted fertility rites at the Stones of Stenness, the remains of the megalithic circle they called "The Temple of the Moon." Young married couples danced naked in the moonlight around the stones at Carnac in Brittany. The connection humanity has made between the moon and women even extends to the widespread custom of putting a crescent moon on an outhouse. Originally, if one of our forbearers could afford more than one latrine, a crescent moon marked the women's.

Culturally, some researchers have theorized that the position we place the moon in is identical to the one we have historically given women. The Neolithic farming societies of our prehistoric past may have looked on women as somewhat akin to magical lunar deities. A woman has a monthly cycle and changed shape with pregnancy. So does the moon change shape during its lunar phases. Menstruation, like other cycles of nature, was believed to function on a lunar rhythm. Fertility appeared as connected to a woman's cycle as it was to the moon's, and our Neolithic ancestors may thus have revered women on many levels, unlike most ensuing patriarchal societies.

Patriarchies often arise when personal property is prized and accumulated in place of communal property. When compared with a woman, a man's physical strength makes it easier for him to increase his personal material assets, a process that results in masculine power structures. Perhaps the resultant subordination of women can likewise be compared to the disparity in reverence often exhibited toward the moon when contrasted with that afforded the "more powerful" sun.

Many of our most ancient agricultural societies identified the moon with a great Mother/Earth Goddess known by many names — Anu, Isis, Cybele, Ceres and Demeter among them. Current evidence suggests that this deity preceded sun worship and may have been most prominent from about 7000 to about 3500 BCE, through the Neolithic Age. The moon was also a chief deity of both the Basques and the Iron Age Celts, whose Druid priests adorned their hands with a crescent moon. Fleachta temples in County Meath were also sacred to the moon. For the Celts, the "male day," ruled by the sun, was enclosed by two "female nights," ruled by the moon. Time was reckoned from nightfall to nightfall, without our contemporary focus on daybreak.

One of our ancestors' earliest representations of the Mother/Moon Goddess was a triad of female deities, in imitation of the phases of the moon. In Greece, these were Persephone, the maiden or new moon; Demeter, the waxing Mother; and Hecate, the waning Crone. For the Celts, they were known as Danu, Madb and Macha. The Romans had

202

Diana Triformis, "The Bright One." Her name probably originated as a combination of the word "di," meaning to shine, with a reference to the Moon Goddess Anu. A Greek name, "Selene," denoted both the Greek Moon Goddess and the name given to the moon itself. The Moon Goddess Selene was worshiped at both new and full moons.

The Latin word for moon is "mensis," though the Celtic/Teutonic Mother Goddess, Mona, likely gave us both the word month and the word moon; "mona" being the Old English word for moon. A month began when those who were entrusted with watching for the moon first sighted it. The German Valkyries, prominent in Norse mythology, were essentially Moon/Mother Goddesses, who survived the course of history to some degree as the Weird Sisters of *Macbeth*. In the Middle Ages, the moon was essentially worshiped by Christians in the form of the Virgin Mary, who exhibits many aspects of a Moon Goddess; though, with the exception of sorrow, Mary is not consigned the darker aspects of the moon.

Boanda, "The White Cow Goddess," was a Celtic water deity who was also connected with the moon, the different phases of which were represented by different colored cattle. Horns and horned animals have long been associated with the moon. We can easily see that the growth and shedding of "horns" are common to both; the "horns," or tips, of the crescent moon waxing and waning with the lunar cycle much as the horns of animals change seasonally.

Sometimes, our nomadic ancestors considered the moon a bull shepherding the stars across the sky. The great masculine bull cults, like that of Minoan Crete, may have arisen from this notion. Minoan civilization placed bull heads and bull horns as powerful architectural elements of its great palace in Knossos. Frescos and ceramics of Minoan origin often depict a bull-leaping ritual in which both men and women grasped the horns of a bull and hurled themselves over the bull's body.

In ancient days, when our ancestors most frequently traveled by water, tides must have been of great importance in many places. (With the nearly tide-free Mediterranean Sea, it's not surprising that tides are rarely mentioned in Greek and Roman writings.) As the moon passes over the Earth, it draws water up into a high tide. At the same time, there is also a high tide on the opposite side of the Earth. High tides have a worldwide average of about two-and-a-half feet.

In general, there are two high tides and two low tides in a lunar day. Tides are highest twice a month, at the new moon and at the full moon. At these times, the sun and the moon are aligned and are pulling together. During a full moon, they are in line on opposite sides of the Earth. With a new moon, they are in line on the same side of the Earth. Though they occur throughout the year, these tides are called Spring Tides. Quarter Tides, on the first and third quarter moons, arise when the sun and moon are at right angles relative to each other, and the sun's influence is diminished. These lowest tides are called Neap Tides.

The pull of the moon has been extended to many areas of our lives. My father, who grew up in the Annapolis Valley of Nova Scotia, shared a great many stories of moon lore with me. The one I remember most clearly is his grandparents' penchant for making sauerkraut. Prepared cabbage was set outside in a stone crock so that the force of the full moon could "draw out the water."

There are, of course, other moon cycles that must have played some part in our prehistoric past. Few events were more fraught with portent to our ancestors than an eclipse of the sun or the moon, a horrifying time when either godlike celestial presence hid its face.

The word "eclipse" comes from the Greek word "ekleipsis," meaning "forsaking." When the moon passes between the Earth and the sun, its shadow sweeps over the Earth. If we are lucky enough to be standing within the shadow of a total eclipse, the sun is completely covered by the disk of the moon. The resulting eerie darkness, in which bright stars appear, must have been terrifying for our ancestors, who had no scientific understanding of such a phenomenon.

Total solar eclipses are visible only from a very limited portion of the Earth, a narrow band only about fifty miles wide. On the other hand, we can see a lunar eclipse in its entirety from a whole hemisphere – anywhere on the Earth, in fact, where the moon is above the horizon. At any specific point, the Earth can experience an average of forty lunar eclipses in fifty years, but only one total solar eclipse in about 400 years.

When the moon moves through the shadow of the Earth, it loses its direct illumination from the sun and is eclipsed. Lunar eclipses can only occur at the time of a full moon. The surface of the moon is never completely darkened, but retains a dull reddish color caused by refracted light traveling through the Earth's atmosphere; the same process that produces red-hued sunsets. In many cultures, this "bloody moon" was considered an ill omen. The Roman historian, Polybius, tells us that an eclipse of the moon (that we now know to have taken place on June 12, 168 BCE) was interpreted as an omen of the eclipse of a king. As Rome was then a republic, this sign gave encouragement to the Romans, who were at war with the kingdom of Macedonia at the time.

After an interval of eighteen years and eleven days – a "saros cycle" – the moon and the sun come nearly to the same relative positions, and eclipses will repeat themselves, though a little farther to the west. The saros cycle, which allows eclipses to be predicted both forward and backward, was well known to the ancient Babylonians.

The saros cycle encompasses the amount of time it takes

for the moon, the sun and the Earth to return to the same position in the sky relative to each other, whether or not eclipses are involved. In the early twentieth century, farmers in the southwest of Ireland used the word "Duibhre," a word related to darkness, to indicate the time of year every eighteen or nineteen years when the moon did not rise above the nearby mountains. When another Roman historian, Diodorus Siculus, reported that "the Hyperboreans had a temple to Apollo where the god visited every nineteen years," he may have been referring to this cycle. Whether the "temple" was located at Stonehenge, Callanish or some other megalithic complex, we can only guess.

Like fire and the sun, the moon also has a dark side, which has been greatly feared throughout history and has often been associated with death, sickness and evil influences. The notion that the moon retires to the underworld in its dark phase has been the model for countless myths and legends, the story of Christ among them. The Sumerian/Babylonian Moon God, Sin; the Greek Moon Goddess, Selene; and the goddess Ishtar, known as the Queen of Heaven and Earth, all made this significant journey. Early Hindu writings call it "the road of the soul after death," "the road of flame" or "the road of smoke," and by it, we naturally link the moon with our ancestors and rebirth. On Babylonian funeral carvings, we see representations of the moon marking the place where the souls of the dead repose. Egyptians, Greeks and Romans did the same, using the crescent moon.

As a reflection and recognition of the connection between the moon and their ancestors' place of rest, many cultures ceased activity of any sort at the dark of the moon. The Sumerians called this time "the days of lying down." The Assyrians knew it as "Sabbatu," a "day of rest for the heart." The Christian Sabbath, then, began as a day of rest at the dark of the moon. Some Christian churches still forbid work of any kind on the Sabbath. Traveling in Scotland some years ago, I stayed at a flowery bed and breakfast in a stalwart grey-stone Highlands cottage. My hostess told me that she would have to duck down behind the stone wall of her property, compelled to crawl about on her hands and knees, should she choose to do a wee bit of gardening on a Sunday. If discovered, her Church of Scotland neighbors would see to it that she was roundly denounced from the pulpit the following week.

CALENDARS (SEASONS AND CYCLES)

"AND GOD SAID, 'LET THERE BE LIGHTS IN
THE FIRMAMENT OF THE HEAVENS TO SEPARATE
THE DAY FROM THE NIGHT; AND LET THEM BE FOR SIGNS
AND FOR SEASONS AND FOR DAYS AND YEARS."

– GENESIS 1:14

"TO EVERYTHING THERE IS A SEASON,
AND A TIME TO EVERY PURPOSE UNDER HEAVEN."

– ECCLESIASTES 3:4

A sense of the passage of time must have developed very early in our human consciousness, with time flowing continuously for us as a notion that can delineate the occurrence of specific events. In humanity's earliest times, civilizations expressed dates in terms of generations, wars, plagues, famines or migrations. Later, they did so by the reign of a new chieftain, king or other ruling official. Such ancient dating systems can only be accepted with any certainty if we can identify some other known phenomenon, such as an eclipse, in the ancient record.

In this way, we have confirmed Chinese chronology from

the Shang Dynasty (1766-1123 BCE) onward. Ptolemy's list of Babylonian, Persian, Alexandrian and Roman rulers can be confirmed back to 893 BCE. Identifiable eclipses recorded under named Roman consuls extend back to 217 BCE. These however, are the official, public reckonings of powerful and expansive societies.

By contrast, our Neolithic and Bronze Age ancestors, being loose-knit agriculturists, probably first viewed time as a seasonal change correlated with weather patterns or the habits of plants or animals — the migration of certain birds, the birth of animals, budding leaves, rainy seasons or flooding rivers, for example. Just as they do for farmers today, natural occurrences signaled to small farming enclaves the best time to plant or to harvest, no doubt according to some local tradition or natural lore. On farmsteads from prehistory to the early twentieth century, farmers have gathered sheaves into stooks or shocks to ripen, carted them away for storage in stacks or ricks, separated straw and chaff from the grain with flails and winnowed with sieves and shovels. All of these things have been accomplished according to local customs and timetables, area-to-area and sometimes even farm-to-farm.

One of the simplest ways to structure time into predictable patterns is to watch the daily movements of the sun and the moon. What happens in the sky repeats itself. Through all ages and in all epochs, we've been dazzled and enchanted by celestial phenomenon that we've looked on as both the origin of and the symbols of powerful forces that regulate our world. We've described the passage of time by the number of suns, moons, nights, sleeps, dawns, snows and harvests; by intervals of daylight such as daybreak or sunrise, twilight or sunset; by the sun's position in relation to some well-known feature, such as a mountain or a standing stone; or by some daily event like the crowing of a rooster.

Especially among nomads, the moon, with its cycle

of twenty-nine or thirty days between full moons or new moons, has been one of the simplest objects used to mark the passage of time. Months in the Islamic, Jewish and Chinese calendars still begin with a new moon, though the Chinese one also uses the sun to describe a year. Celts and Hindus have similar solar and lunar calendars, as do the Kwakiutl and Haida tribes of the American Northwest. Though it doesn't coincide with a solar cycle or the seasons, the moon is still a useful clock if its phases are visible at night.

The position of stars or constellations on the horizon at sunrise or sunset can also be used to denote the passage of time. In ancient Egypt, the New Year began with the rising of the star Sirius, a time that originally corresponded to the flooding of the Nile. In about 750 BCE, the Greek poet Hesiod described a season in this way:

> "WHEN ORION AND THE DOG STAR MOVE
> INTO THE MID-SKY, AND ARCTURUS SEES
> THE ROSY-FINGERED DAWN, THEN PERSES,
> PLUCK THE CLUSTERED GRAPES, AND BRING
> YOUR HARVEST HOME."

The Bafioti tribe of Angola and the Blackfoot of North America both had calendars that were a mix of stellar and lunar observations, the stellar observations being constellations. The Pawnee tribe of the American High Plains had extensive star charts. The Thonga of South Africa, the Mandaya of the Philippines and some native Brazilian tribes farmed by the movements of the Pleiades, by whose dawn setting the ancient Greeks also determined the most auspicious time to sow their winter fields and prepare for autumn's storms.

Lunations are useful if our full reckoning of time is based solely on months. But the moon changes shape.

Its movements are complicated, requiring years, possibly generations, of observation to more fully understand. And it often disappears altogether. Eventually, the stars get out of sync with the seasons, as Sirius did, rising later and later as the centuries passed.

For most of us, the sun is more predictable. The sun's motion produces seasonal changes that mirror our rhythms of life, like the growth cycle of vegetation. To sedentary, agricultural people, sun worship superseding the moon seems a natural evolution.

When we link the movements of the sun, the moon and the stars to our planting, our harvesting and the festivals that accompany them, the logical result is a calendar. A calendar divides time into long and short units, which were at first purely practical — time for plowing, sowing, harvesting, propitiating gods and other religious observances.

The word "calendar" comes from the Latin word "kalendae," meaning "the day on which the accounts are due." Our earliest and most technologically primitive calendars were no doubt predominantly local — ancient Egyptian sundials; water clocks; etched spirals in Arizona's Chaco Canyon, where a beam of light announces the Summer Solstice; and Mayan pyramids in Yucatan, where a snake of light on the steps marks the Spring Equinox.

Twelve lunar months are eleven-and-one-quarter days shorter than the solar year that determines our growth seasons. Thirteen lunations are too long by eighteen-and-one –quarter days. This discrepancy explains the development of leap year in our present-day calendar, an extra day being added every four years to make up the difference. In the case of lunisolar calendars — like those in Hindu, Burmese and Tibetan cultures — an extra month is added.

Lunar calendars marking religious observances developed first among our wandering ancestors. Solar calendars marked seasonal changes for sedentary agricultural societies.

As trade increased, people saw the advantage and the necessity of reconciling these two, to correlate the "seasons" of one locale with the "seasons" of its neighbors. Sometimes, a number of month-less days were added to the end of the year. Sometimes, an artificial value was added to each month. Religious festivals associated with a lunar calendar, like Easter, for example, became "moveable feasts," their dates variable from year to year. The Sumerians of ancient Mesopotamia had a twelve-month solar calendar and a 364-day lunar calendar, which had an extra month added every eight years to keep up with the seasons.

The Egyptian calendar, the first calendar known to be based on 365 days, divided days into twelve months of thirty days each, with an additional five days set aside for festivals. The year began when the rising of Sirius, the Dog Star, was in direct line with the sun. Inscriptions on ancient pyramids show us that this calendar was in existence at the time they were built. Egyptologists, however, still debate precisely what that date may have been. The introduction of the Egyptian calendar is thus recognized as taking place in either 4241 BCE or 2781 BCE, according to which date one believes the pyramids may have been raised.

The Babylonians, for whom the rising and setting of the sun defined the day as the basic unit of time, divided the day into twenty-four hours, the hour into sixty minutes and the minute into sixty seconds. In ancient Rome, priests controlled the calendar, adding extra months arbitrarily, often in response to a bribe. The Julian calendar, with one year of 365 days followed by one year of 366 days, was introduced in Rome under Julius Caesar. As a result of changes to correlate with the seasons, the year 46 BCE had 445 days, making it the longest year on record. Our present world civil calendar is the Gregorian calendar, introduced by Pope Gregory XIII in the sixteenth century. It compensates for "extra time" as previously described.

Calendars have not always arrived at the same seasonal divisions for the year. The Teutonic year, for example, had just three seasons – winter, spring and summer. Researchers speculate that the Celts may have adapted the cycles of the moon to a tree calendar created by the Druids. Each of the thirteen lunar months corresponded to a certain species of tree, linked to a letter of the ancient Ogham alphabet. But we have no reliable evidence to prove this.

Each month of the Celtic lunar calendar had a bright half, the fifteen days of a waxing moon, and a dark half, the fifteen days of a waning moon. As with the Jewish reckoning of time, a day was defined as from sunset to sunset. A concurrent solar calendar marked important Celtic junctures in farming and pastoral cycles and divided the year into two equal parts, the bright half beginning with Beltane, and the dark half with Samhain. These lunar and solar calendars were reconciled by the addition of an extra thirty-day month at two-and-a-half to three-year intervals.

Of the four great feast days in the Celtic year, Imbolc, a word translated as either "purification" or "budding," marked the coming of spring on or near the first of February and was a celebration of the lambing season. Beltane, occurring on or near the first of May, welcomed summer, when livestock were moved to summer pastures after having first been driven between two great fires for protection, purification and fertility. An important Celtic assembly took place in Ireland on the royal hill of Tara at Beltane.

The third festival, Lughnasadh, or the "Feast of Lug," celebrated the autumn harvest and took place on or near the first of August. It was celebrated for two weeks, both before and after the actual date, with feasting, games and the disposition of political and legal affairs. Samhain, the final annual ritual, marked the beginning of the dark half of the year and was celebrated between October 31, and the first of November. Samhain was likely the time designated to round up free-ranging animals, choose which among them would be wintered over for breeding and subsistence, and slaughter the rest for food. Samhain, sometimes believed to be the beginning of the Celtic New Year, was a particularly dangerous time. Passages to the Otherworld were open then, and mortals and immortals could mingle freely.

Imbolc, Beltane, Lughnasadh and Samhain — known as cross-quarter days — were especially important to sedentary herding people like the Iron Age Celts, but these cultures also recognized the more agriculturally-oriented Solstices (December 21 and June 21) and Equinoxes (March 20 and September 23).

If we look at Celtic mythology, we see the distinct possibility that the Celtic reckoning of time was carried forward from prehistory. The Celtic hero Conn, for example, was said to have made sunrise observations at an ancient burial mound. Much of Celtic mythology, with its warrior/heroes and magic cauldrons and weaponry, seems to have been derived from Bronze Age memories.

Moreover, the recent discovery in Germany of the 3600-year-old Bronze Age Sky Disc of Nebra (a twelve-and-a-half-inch wide bronze disc with gold-leaf appliqués representing the sun, the moon and the Pleiades) appears to demonstrate that our Bronze Age ancestors had learned to harmonize the solar and lunar years at least a thousand years before the Babylonians. According to Babylonian astronomical knowledge, a thirteenth month must be added to the lunar calendar every two to three years to keep it in sync with the seasons. Scholars have theorized that the time to add that thirteenth month was reckoned much earlier by our Bronze Age ancestors, by holding the Nebra Sky Disc to the heavens and finding that the position of the moon and the Pleiades in the sky matched their representations on the disc.

Nonetheless, claims that the stone circles, standing stones and burial chambers of our Neolithic and Bronze Age ancestors show an elaborate and sophisticated knowledge of mathematics and advanced astronomy are probably exaggerated.

Given what we've since learned about astrophysics, it seems safe to say that the megalithic architecture of the Neolithic Era and Bronze Age was probably not contrived by an elite group of astronomer/priests; though early stargazers may have exerted some control over a population through their "magical ability" to predict eclipses and so forth. Leaders of the growing chiefdoms of the Bronze Age may also have used their knowledge of the sun's movement to enhance their power.

A much more likely explanation for the raising of stones in this regard was to use them as a meeting place for ceremonies and rituals at specific times of the year, as plotted by simple astronomical observations. The longer the sun takes to move from east to west, the warmer the season. All of us can easily detect and use such a day-by-day sunrise pattern, especially when our life's work is connected to the land.

Farming provides the food necessary for life. Having recognized this, our ancestors naturally bound feasts, sacrifices and other rituals to the seasons. Stone alignments often mark a celestial object's presence – a sunrise or a sunset – at a specific time of the year; in Midwinter or Midsummer, for example. Solstices are times when the sun appears to stand still; Equinoxes a time when day and night are of equal duration. In that sense, our prehistoric ancestors may well have used stone structures, with or without connections to local landmarks, as simple local calendars. We see, for example, that the Wren's Egg stone in Wigtownshire, Scotland, marks the Equinoxes. A quarter mile away, a pair of stones at Milton Hall represents the sunset at Midwinter Solstice. One-half mile from there, at Drumtroddan, Midsummer's sunrise is featured.

As we've already seen, abstract design in megalithic tombs might refer to any number of objects or ideas, though their strong connection with death makes their most probable use religious. When we keep a close watch on the sky, we measure time not only for agricultural activity, but also for the prescribed performance of religious rites specific to a given time of the agricultural year. We can see, then, that the mounds and stones erected by our ancestors — and the symbols that decorated them — may likely have been sacred tributes to the sun and/or moon. Because light from one or the other features so prominently in their design and orientation, we can speculate that their significance was probably quite profound.

This is especially evident at the Knowth monument in Ireland, where we find a sundial divided into eight equal parts, separating the interior wall space of the tomb with the geometric projection of light or shadow. As communities grew, these rudimentary calendars also allowed growing populations to organize time for the exchange of goods, services and farming surpluses.

Some researchers have called the Neolithic and Bronze Age use of megalithic structures a "practical astronomy." In the end, this is a good description. Their system may have tallied days and nights, eclipses and other astronomical events by marking them on wood or carving them in stone, just as later societies would use the abacus or the written word. The lives of our Neolithic and Bronze Age ancestors were most likely governed by the use of these simple sacred calendars as they related to local topography, mythology and custom.

ARCHEOASTRONOMY

In simplest terms, archeoastronomy is the study of the astronomical methods and observations of ancient and prehistoric societies. At its best, it brings together such varied disciplines as astronomy, archeology, ethnography, mathematics and engineering in order to rediscover how ancient minds may have thought about and used the cycles of the sun, the moon and the stars.

Alexander Thom, a Professor of Engineering at Oxford University, pioneered the field of archeoastronomy in the middle of the last century, surveying more than 300 sites in Western Europe in more than fifty years of study. Professor Thom believed that most of the non-funerary monuments erected by our Neolithic and Bronze Age ancestors were lunar or solar observatories or "star-clocks." He took elaborate measurements in an attempt to prove this theory, identifying a unit of measurement he found common to many prehistoric sites. He called this unit of 2.72 feet a "megalithic yard."

Some of our relatively recent folklore traditions support Thom's basic idea. Alexander Carmichael, who published two collections of songs, poems and stories from the Highlands in the late nineteenth and early twentieth centuries, found that a number of Scottish megalithic sites were described by nearby residents as "moon temples." Likewise, the Piper's Stones, a collection representing a piper and dancers said to have been turned to stone for profaning the Sabbath, are found at Athgreany in Ireland. Athgreany means "Field of the Sun," suggesting some past solar connection. We've already talked about the Ring of Brodgar and the Stones of Stenness in the Orkneys being referred to as the "Temple of the Sun" and the "Temple of the Moon," respectively. Similarly, The Three Brothers at Lisglass, three stones in County Antrim, Ireland, stand near the hamlet of Greenan, a name that derives from "gianan," meaning "the place of the sun."

We find more ancient evidence of the connection between megalithic architecture and elements of early sky watching in the first century BCE, when Diodorus Siculus of Sicily described a place to the west where priests "worship in a circular temple . . ." "When the god visits the island every nineteen years," he wrote, he would "dance continuously the night through from the Vernal Equinox to the rising of the Pleiades." This god is most often presumed to be the embodiment of the moon in its saros cycle.

In the world of megalithic architecture, we have many other examples of how this connection worked. The Temple of Amon-Ra in Egypt is oriented to Midsummer sunset, with light passing down its axis into an inner sanctuary. In 1979, Alastair and Nicholas Service measured the direction faced by the openings of thirty-three passage graves near Carnac. Fifteen of these, including the oldest, Kercado, which dates to 4700 BCE, pointed generally toward the position of the sun at Midwinter sunrise.

We find many similar examples among the ancient stones of Western Europe. As we've already seen in the tomb of Newgrange, in the space of seventeen minutes, the light of Midwinter sunrise enters through a roofbox and inches its way down the primary passageway. The door slab at Maes Howe in the Orkneys is oriented to Midwinter sunset. Of the three pillars of mica schist by Ballachroy farm in Ireland, the central and highest is aligned to the Winter Solstice sunset, another to the sunset at Summer Solstice. Many of the recumbent circles from the third and second millennia

BCE in Grampian, Scotland (PLATE 36), and later in the southwest of Ireland, include, in their southwest sectors, horizontal slabs of stone. Guardian pillars that frame the moon as it passes over these recumbents flank these stones, the remaining stones of these circles gradually decreasing in height as they move away from the recumbent. The interior of a passage tomb at Loughcrew in Ireland is illuminated by Spring Equinox sunrise, when a beam of light frames a large radial solar disc. The northeast avenue at Stonehenge is oriented to Summer Solstice sunrise, its light rising over the Heel Stone, a twenty-foot sarsen monolith that aligns with an observer standing in the middle of the circle. Astrophysicist Gerald Hawkins sought to demonstrate that Stonehenge may have charted both solar and lunar movements, its intersecting cycles predicting eclipses.

As we've seen, the sky is familiar to country people everywhere, including, no doubt, our farming ancestors of Neolithic and Bronze Age Western Europe. We can easily see that some Neolithic chambered tombs and stone circles seem purposely built with their passages or entrances aligned in some approximate direction or based on some specific astronomical event. The beautifully situated Castlerigg stone circle in the Lake District of England has a gap, for example, at precise north (PLATE 37).

This entrenches our thought that the sky, sun, moon and stars were considered conscious and living beings by our agricultural ancestors, whose lives were regulated by the seasons. Their societies were certainly more aware of the activity in the sky, both night and day, than most of us are today.

It requires little of us, however, to recognize that by noting where the sun rises and sets, we can detect the patterns of the year. The longer the sun takes to cross the sky, the warmer the season. At the Vernal Equinox and the Autumnal Equinox, when the sun rises directly east and sets directly west, night and day are of equal length. At Midsummer and Midwinter, there are several days when the sun appears to stand still, rising and setting in the same place each day. These Solstices, winter and summer — the times when the sun reaches farthest north and farthest south — take their name from the Latin "solstitium," with "sol" meaning "sun" and "sistere," "to stand still."

As previously emphasized, however, recognizing our ancestors' awareness of the movements of the sun and moon is a long way from the argument that in our prehistory elite astronomer/priests with sophisticated observatories studied the night sky, as some archeoastronomers have claimed.

We can speculate from the easterly orientation of many burial mounds that our Neolithic forbearers must have drawn some conclusions about the relationship between the sun and the concept of life and death. Without scientific proof, however, we can't take that concept any further. The claim by some researchers that the southern row of stones at Callanish was purposefully aligned to the Pole Star is pure fabrication by those interested in advancing the theory of ancient proto-astronomers at any cost. Four thousand years ago, at the time Callanish was built, that star, Ursa Minor, rose twenty degrees from true north, more than five miles along the horizon from its present north-south alignment.

Based solely on the orientation of megalithic monuments to specific astronomical events like Solstices and Equinoxes, Midwinter and Midsummer, we have no definitive proof of the presence of any broad-based and formalized ancient astronomers' cult that may have erected rudimentary observatories. Some barrows in Dorset were placed parallel along ridge tops. Others in the Yorkshire Wolds faced neighboring tombs. At least one mound on the Isle of Arran faces Midsummer sunrise, but nineteen others on the same island are randomly set. And though fifteen of the thirty-three surveyed Carnac dolmens pointed generally to

Midwinter sunrise, nine others were aligned to a spot where the sun never set. Many other megalithic constructs appear to have no orientation whatsoever to any astronomical event; single stones only rarely align with distant menhirs or prominent hills, mountains or other features keyed to the rising or setting of the moon, the sun or major stars.

Moreover, many circles and solitary stones stand in featureless flat moorland or in deep valleys, or they may overlook a barren sea with no possible alignment in view. In any case, many such stones are too small to have been used for sighting lines. And consider the odds of simple probability. In any circle of twelve stones, there are sixty-six possible connecting lines, 132 if sighting is carried in both directions. We would expect that our ancestors incorporated one good alignment just by chance. Megalithic structures in hills or mountains have literally hundreds of features that *could* coincide with astronomical movements, especially those of the moon. Many supposed sightlines, however, are too short for accurate observations. A detailed examination of forty-six possible lines at the Callanish complex, for example (PLATE 38 and 39), failed to support even one accurate alignment, except for a row of stones two miles away that could just as easily have occurred by chance. Stonehenge, too, has many purported alignments – 112 to date. None of them has been agreed upon by scholars.

Some archeoastronomers have similarly claimed observatory status for the alignments of Brittany (PLATE 40), with Carnac's fan settings seen as a kind of lunar grid on which eclipses could be plotted and forecast. But were they really so complex? Many stone rows simply lead to burial cairns and were possibly processional ways. Also, some supposed alignments at circles, stone rows or burial chambers are often based on faulty evidence, as with an inaccurate re-erecting of a fallen stone, for example.

We might make another assumption about the

observatory status of stone monuments based on the fact that stone circle building stopped about the same time as the climate deteriorated. Perhaps, we might say, the skies were no longer clear enough for observations geared toward farming schedules and the raising of stones was no longer relevant. But as we've already demonstrated, farmers throughout the ages have harvested and sown according to natural signals from plants, soil and weather that are most often observed locally, year-to-year. "When the elm leaf is as big as a mouse's ear, then to sow barley never fear." Understanding their environment on such an elemental level, our stone-building ancestors quite likely had little time or need for the high-level contrivances suggested by any large-scale observatory.

Regardless of how much or how little we might choose to see a connection between megalithic architecture and ancient astronomy, we can clearly draw *some* conclusion about the skies and the stone-building activities of our Neolithic and Bronze Age predecessors. Some bona fide alignments *are* to be found, though the reason they were so carefully designed will always be a mystery.

Current evidence suggests that astronomical observation may have been one function of some stone circles. But we will likely never know exactly why and how they were used. Did our ancestors gather the strength of the reborn sun to the living or acknowledge the rebirth of the dead by orienting their burial chambers toward an auspicious Winter Solstice? Did they direct the light inching down the passageway of a tomb into basins of water made holy for healing or onto the remains of their revered dead? As the light of a full moon rolled across the surface of a recumbent stone, did that stone absorb its power? The possibilities are as endless, varied and intriguing as the human imagination.

SPIRITUAL FITNESS

"THE DARK NIGHT WAS THE FIRST BOOK OF POETRY,
AND THE CONSTELLATIONS WERE THE POEMS."

– CHET RAYMO

"I AM AWARE OF SOMETHING IN MYSELF
LIKE LIGHT DANCING BEFORE MY SOUL."

– ST. AUGUSTINE

"PRAISE TO THE PURE LIGHT."

– DAFYDD AP GWILYM

A chapter called *Heaven* might have been subtitled "A Celebration of Light." The sun, the moon, the seasons, fire and astronomy all bring to mind the existence of an awesome, primal creator/creation energy. "I am aware of something in myself whose shine is my reason," the thirteenth century German mystic, Meister Eckhart, wrote. Such is the power and the glory of light, a vibrant force of warmth and change that can banish our negativity and lift our minds to a higher plane.

One of the simplest ways we can honor light is to become more aware of it in all of its manifestations. Sun catchers hung in a window elevate the spirit, breaking sunlight into the miraculous colors of a rainbow. Something as effortless as a candlelit dinner can evoke the wonder of light. Candlelight or hearth fires focus our attention on the wonder of both light and fire. The point of a single living flame has been called "the spark in the heart of God." Richard D'Alton Williams put this idea in lyrical terms when he wrote in his poem *The Dying Girl*, "Descending swiftly from the skies her guardian angel came. He struck God's lightning from her eyes and bore Him back the flame." We can light a candle with the spiritual intention of focusing on that central presence, using colored candles to enhance our meditative experience.

"Sunrises are God's hit singles," Bono, lead singer of the Irish rock band U2, has said. Take time to watch and appreciate a sunset or a sunrise.

For most of us, ninety percent of our time is spent in artificial light. But our bodies need sunlight to make the most of the vitamins and minerals we get from our food. A brief protected exposure to the sun can brighten our mood. We can sunbathe by a sunny window in winter to take in the sun's healing light.

Many people see the moon's energy as even more spiritually potent than sunlight. Meditation on the full moon – "Drawing down the Moon" – allows us to bathe in moonlight, to mentally fill up with the moon's energy. Meditation is passive prayer. By focusing on an aspect of the full moon – prosperity, empowerment, completeness – we open ourselves to the guidance of the Universe. With new moon meditation – the auspicious manifestation of a new beginning – we recognize the cyclical nature of all things. Revel in a full moon. Remember, each of us has only about a thousand of them to appreciate in our lifetime.

An earthly reflection of the moon, a garden of silver foliage and white, night-scented flowers can keep us in touch with this most revered and ancient of sacred symbols. A circular opening in a garden wall can symbolize transition, completion or natural cycles. For some gardeners, planting is still done according to the phases of the moon. Root crops are planted on a waning moon to direct energy downward, with above-ground plants sown on a waxing moon to pull the Earth's energies upward.

We can even carry a part of the moon with us by wearing a pearl – produced mysteriously in darkness – or a small crescent moon.

The dark night is one of nature's most awesome gifts. Any of us can become acquainted with the whole of the night sky by learning about celestial patterns, beginning with constellations, visible planets and bright stars. We can witness an eclipse of the moon, a passing comet, a meteor shower or the bright stars of Orion. In the Northern Hemisphere, the Milky Way streams directly overhead in summer and winter, making them the best seasons for stargazing. Get out into nature as often as possible for evening barbecues, picnics or overnight camping.

Becoming aware of seasonal changes is one of the easiest ways we can honor light and appreciate the many natural cycles of life. Wherever we live, weather patterns announce periodic changes; vegetation blossoms and declines. People of many cultures around the world, past and present, celebrate Equinoxes and Solstices. As mentioned previously, I've seen cut flowers offered at the base of Long Meg in Cumbria on the Fall Equinox (PLATE 41). "Shine On 2000, Welcome Spring" showed up as a message to the Vernal Equinox on John Lennon's *Imagine* mosaic in New York City's Central Park. In Great Barrington, Massachusetts, author Laura Chester has built a small chapel of fieldstone, its altar aligned to the rising of the Summer Solstice sun. She calls it the Little Rose Chapel. We can each create our own small tribute to the sway of heaven, a simple thank-you note to the Universe.

CHAPTER 8

EARTH

"THE POETRY OF EARTH IS NEVER DEAD."

– JOHN KEATS

"NATURE IS SO COMPLEX AND
FASCINATING THAT IT'S AS CLOSE AS I'VE
COME TO UNDERSTANDING THE
NOTION OF DIVINITY."

– HARRISON FORD

Our modern industrial societies, by definition, exploit the Earth for material gain. We can never know for certain, but a look at so-called "primitive" contemporary societies tells us that our Neolithic and Bronze Age ancestors probably had a more intimate and powerful relationship with their environment than we do today. All natural objects — trees, hills, springs, stones — were manifestations of the same universal creative force that regulated seasons, shaped landscapes and granted fertility to crops, animals and people. The Earth was a sacred and living thing. A seed in the womb and a seed in the ground were considered equal, the same magical matrix from which all life springs.

The tombs and sanctuaries of our ancient megalithic forbearers may have been markers, generators or receptacles for Earth energy. Earth Mothers encourage us to venerate the land, strengthening our impulse to see the Divine in all things. The original purpose of the Greek Oracles of Dodona, Delphi and Delos may have been the same. The shrine of Gaia — the Earth — at Delphi, was taken over by Apollo the Sun God, only when his voice "became louder than hers." For Australian Aborigines, the "djang" — "the power of the land" — rules all of life.

From at least the thirteenth century CE, the Chinese have employed a geomantic science once called "Wind and Water." We now know this science as Feng Shui. Feng Shui uses those natural currents in the Earth followed by wind and water. Yin, or negative Feng Shui, dark, quiet and passive, is used extensively for funeral rites and for the correct alignment of tombs. By contrast, Yang Feng Shui energy is active and positive, bringing light and openness to homes and places of business. Feng Shui seeks to balance active and passive Earth energies in our living environment.

These concepts are reinforced by *geomancy*, an ancient system of architectural design that accounts for and takes advantage of the natural flow of the Earth's energies. *Water* is one of the most profound, living expressions of this energy.

GEOMANCY

The concept of the Earth having energy currents is a very ancient one. In the first century CE, Plutarch wrote that "some of these drive people crazy or cause disease or death; the effect of others is good, soothing and beneficial." The centuries-old Chinese art of Feng Shui harmonizes invisible currents called "lung-mei" or "dragon paths." Magnetic flows in the Earth's surface — male and female, positive and negative — are represented by a blue dragon and a white tiger respectively. A "luck-bringing site" occurs where these lines intersect. Like the Chinese concept of Ch'i (Japanese, Ki) — the energy in all living things — geodetic currents work on a planetary scale, representing the flow of this energy between power spots.

Geomancy, as it applies to the stone architecture of prehistory, is the art of designing and siting tombs, temples, shrines, wells and other structures to honor, acknowledge and capture natural geodetic currents at the places where we see them manifested most strongly. The word itself comes from the Greek "Ge" or "Gaia," — Mother Earth — and either "manteia," meaning "divination," or "magos," meaning "knowledge." Geomancy works through knowledge of how architecture is affected by earthly energy.

Alfred Watkins, (1855-1935) of Hereford in Wales, called the system of straight Earth-energy lines he saw in the British countryside, "ley lines," taking the name from the last syllable of many of the places through which these lines passed. The Saxon word "ley" means "a glade or clearing." Watkins believed ley lines connected standing stones, stone circles, burial chambers and mounds, holy wells and pools, earth works and other sacred sites where Earth energy accumulated. We have discovered a similar system of straight lines called "ceques" in Peru. These figurative "power lines" may have been as real to the societies of our prehistory as the invisible straight lines we know as longitude and latitude, Prime Meridian, Greenwich Mean and so on.

Geomancy adherents suggest that by incorporating this theory, our predecessors erected megaliths to mark, build up, channel or store geodetic electromagnetic energy for collective or individual use; the physical wellbeing of a clan, for example, or the building of harmony between the natural and human worlds. The specific shape of a standing stone — the pyramid was an especially active energy receptor — could better control or maximize the channeling of this energy.

A holed stone, or a stone whose shape mirrored a particularly potent nearby hilltop, might have been equally powerful. These stones acted as generators or storage batteries for energy that could then be tapped with the proper ceremonies, at the proper time, for a balanced flow of life energy. Rituals such as energetic dancing may have been first performed to "gather the power" that was to be stored in stones.

Channels of energy — spirit paths from the time of creation — were likely first taken up by wandering tribes whose sensitivity to the natural flow of the Earth's energy has since been lost. We can still find the memory of such spirit paths, however, in some of our contemporary religious processionals, festival routes or funeral paths. Traditionally, aborigines in many cultures have activated magical power centers by walking sacred paths.

Animals, too, seem to instinctively follow these lines and are often more keenly attuned to them than people. Horses at Scorhill on Dartmoor, for example, appear to be sound sensitive to some of the stone circles there. Many of our legends and folktales attribute the foundation of secular or sacred sites — a church, a hermitage or a castle — to following certain animals, white or dun cows being favorites. The fourteenth century Cawdor Castle in Scotland was built on a site traditionally believed to be chosen by a donkey. Likewise, the Celtic Saint Gobnat established her Irish monastery on the spot where she encountered nine white deer.

The theory behind a belief in Earth's energy lines and charged standing stones is not so far-fetched when we look at present research on the consequences of currents from cell phones, waterbeds or electrical lines. The same idea applies to our use of quartz crystals, which produce an electric current when under pressure or tension. Quartz vibrates when influenced by an electrical field, and, for that reason, we use it in the resonators and oscillators that control frequency in electronic communications equipment.

Granite, from which many Neolithic and Bronze Age stone structures were built, generally contains between twenty and forty percent quartz. The prehistoric tomb of Newgrange was apparently faced with quartz pebbles, stones that have long been placed in Irish tombs. In Inverary, in the Irish Republic, fishermen brought white pebbles to the graves of friends on Easter and Christmas.

Dowsers have found that many of the megaliths in stone circles alternate between exhibiting positive and negative charges. Some people have received shocks from standing stones or have felt a current or tingling sensation when they touched certain stones. Others claim to have been physically knocked back from a stone.

Aristotle thought of the four elements of earth, air, fire and water as the components of the Earth. But he also named a fifth — a solid crystalline substance that kept the sun, the moon and the planets in place. Scientists have since called the dark energy of the universe "quintessence," or "fifth element," and modern physics has shown us that every form has a crystalline pattern within its cells. Physics, the occult, metaphysics, the Kabbalah, mystical Christianity, Sufism and all the ancient Mystery Schools agree that there is something unseen in our universe, out of which the *seen* is formed.

Many of our local legends and folk traditions support Earth current memories or are at least open to that interpretation. White witches at Knowlton Henge used to dowse the henge with water in order to release "trapped energies." Ireland has a long tradition of the great trouble that can result from interfering with fairy paths — the invisible lines between prehistoric barrows called "fairy forts." According to legend, a child, temporarily stolen by fairies, becomes ill upon returning home. His or her parents consult a wise woman, who tells them that an extension of their house crosses a fairy path. The offending structure is removed, and the child improves.

Our legends of bottomless "milch" cows, treasure buried at a megalithic monument, stones that dance or walk at specific times — all of these — may be folk memories of an earlier age when Earth's energies were more active. We can say the same for single stones or local arrangements that are circled a prescribed number of times to "raise the devil;" find a suitable mate; or bring good luck. Well into the nineteenth century, parishioners in Manaton (in Devonshire) carried coffins three times around the churchyard cross until the vicar viciously hacked the cross to pieces and hid its remnants.

For centuries, Neolithic and Bronze Age stones have been ascribed qualities associated with an Earth spirit, performing functions to facilitate healing, fertility and productivity. With a standing stone, energies that formerly fluctuated could be balanced, increased or held in place. For example, the Greeks believed that the omphalos at the Temple of Apollo in Delphi possessed this ability.

Along with stone, various cultures have long used snakes to represent Earth energies. The Hopis of the American Southwest still use this metaphor. In Norse mythology, the serpent, Midgard, was believed to have encircled Yggdrasil, the Scandinavian world-tree, as the Earth's vital life force.

When we spear a serpent, legends say, we localize Earth energy and make it available year-round, instead of only at certain times. For example, Apollo increased the productivity of the Oracle at Delphi by spearing Python, the "earth dragon." What a potent way for a celestial/sky deity to supplant an Earth-centered religion! In fact, this could be the real impetus behind such legends as St. Patrick driving the snakes out of Ireland; St. George slaying the dragon; or Joseph of Arimathea founding Glastonbury by planting his staff in the earth. Settled people want their gods to settle with them.

The veneration of ancient stones — a reflection of a belief in the power and divinity of the Earth — was a clear threat to Christianity. The Decree of Nantes (CE 658) ordered the Church to "dig up and remove and hide to places where they cannot be found, those stones which in remote and woody places are still worshiped and where vows are still made." Condemned stones like Callanish — visited especially on May Day and Midsummer — were then visited in secret, as "it would not do to neglect the stones." We can be thankful that Callanish survived; allowed to quietly disappear under a steady accumulation of peat moss.

In nature, we do not normally see straight lines. This suggests that, in capturing Earth's energy lines at alignments or other standing stones — if that's what they were attempting to do — our ancestors may have believed they could manipulate these energy sources. Perhaps, in time, such energy was seen to revert to its own course, or it was believed an overuse, possibly during the fearsome weather changes of the late Bronze Age, had caused its decline. This eventuality gave us, perhaps, tales of witches milking into sieves or of milk cows drying up. The theory of ley lines was revived in the 1950s when their use was extended to magnetic landing runways for space ships!

Of course, there are serious problems with any theory of the containment and use of Earth energy lines by our prehistoric ancestors. To begin with, prehistoric worlds were intensely local. Even today, seemingly similar monuments and rituals operate differently from one society to another. And most prehistoric sites don't align at all, a fact that forced Watkins, in his exuberance to justify his theory, to include parish churches, hill forts and even notches on the horizon, claiming that these, too, were built on or naturally occurred at ancient sacred sites. Although Watkins' assertions might be a stretch, there can be little doubt that our prehistoric forbearers recognized something vital and vigorous in the landscape and may have represented this in the stone architecture they left behind.

WATER

"Towns may come and go but the well remains where it always was."
– I Ching

232

Do Earth energies follow watercourses? And did our Neolithic and Bronze Age ancestors acknowledge this power, as well, with their stone architecture? Guy Underwood, a dowser, has found complex systems of underground water at many megalithic sites. There may well be some underlying truth to the concept of the builders of prehistory exploiting this power with their architecture.

In Germany during the 1920s, it was discovered that the inhabitants of certain houses had been diagnosed with cancer generation after generation, even when the families living in those houses had changed. Neighbors, however, were not affected. Dowsers subsequently discovered underground currents of water crossing beneath these "cancer houses." All around the world, researchers claim to have similarly found an increased prevalence of colic in babies, sleeplessness and degenerative diseases like cancer and arthritis in places where underground veins of water intersect. Many megalithic monuments are among these places.

As with fire, humanity's worship of water is very ancient and powerful. Water, like fire, is both beneficial and destructive, allowing us to grow crops, yet threatening our lives with whirlpools, cresting rivers and raging seas. "Water touches the past and prepares the future," anthropologist Loren Eiseley has written. "It can assume forms of exquisite perfection in a snowflake or strip the living to a single shining bone cast up by the sea."

The Maori believe that everything in existence came from the "wai ora," or "the waters of life," which flowed from Nothingness into all things, including rocks and the crystals that comprise them. The Greek philosopher, Thales of Miletus, had a similar idea in the seventh century BCE. He thought that all matter, including the stars, came from one unifying essence — water — in which the Earth floated. Gnostics held water to be the original element. "Without water there is no life. But without life, there would still be water."

The Earth's first flickers of life probably arose about three-and-a-half billion years ago, when lightning delivered enough energy to primordial seawater to cause dissolved amino acids to gather and grow – a process we call organic evolution. Yet rain had already been falling, tides had been rising and rivers had been flowing for more than a billion years.

Seventy percent of the Earth's surface is water, given over to storage, transpiration, evaporation, precipitation and percolation. The human body is about ninety percent water. Sometimes bitter and sometimes sweet, water is magical. We see it arrange itself into rain, oceans, lakes, ice, rivers, pools, waterfalls, springs, snow, hail, mist, glaciers, clouds, dew, frost and fog. We can break it up, and it comes together again unchanged. It vanishes outright and then reappears.

We use clear bright water to wash away, cleanse and purify. Some objects float in water, others sink. Fresh water springs flow below salty tidal marks. And who can dismiss the mystical connection between water and the sun? Water glitters with reflected sunlight as if it had soaked up the sun itself. Both elements stir the regeneration of life when seeds are buried in earth, yet both have a dark side as well. With too much sun or too much water, the ensuing droughts and floods bring death and destruction.

The veneration of water as a source of life is most widespread within the precepts of animism, a philosophical belief that everything has a spirit. Many places are without a sacred mountain, hill or grove of trees, but we find water almost everywhere. There may once have been a single divine water spirit in our prehistoric past, but the vast differences in the sound of water – the soft murmur of a creek, the roar of a waterfall, the hiss of ocean spray – likely suggested varying personalities. As a result, our ancestors gave each spring, each well, each river, each tarn its own incarnation, representing some of them with animals like frogs, flies or fish.

Today, we still talk about seas and rivers as living beings — the force of the Atlantic or the North Sea, for example. Seamen on the Orkney and Shetland Islands were for many years hesitant to rescue anyone from drowning. In their minds, the sea was entitled to a certain number of sacrificial victims, and to interfere would be unwise. During the mid-nineteenth century, families living on the Isle of Lewis used seaweed as a fertilizer. On All Hallows Eve, an appointed messenger took ale into the sea as an offering to a god called "Shony," in hopes of a plentiful seaweed harvest. Some scholars believe that "Shony" is a corruption of the Cymric word for "sound." A god of noise, Shony represented the thundering Atlantic, whose fierce winter storms, it was hoped, would pile the beaches high with kelp.

As obstacles or passageways for travel and trade, we've often given rivers the same attention. The Seven Rivers of Ireland, for example, were believed by the Celts to originate from one sacred well. A river mirrors life — from the mystery of its birth, through the vibrant liveliness of its youth, to its sluggish ending in the sea.

During the eighteenth and nineteenth centuries, the River Ribble in Great Britain was believed to be endowed with a spirit known as Peg O'Nell, named for an abused servant who died at nearby Waddow Hall. A headless image of Peg remained on the grounds of the estate for many years, though this was likely an ancient spring marker. To avenge her death, Peg required a victim every seven years, on the last night of the last year. If some other creature had not been taken by then, a human would fall victim.

In Northern England, the River Tees was said to be inhabited by Peg Powler, a malicious spirit with long green hair and an appetite for human life. A chasm on the River Wharfe, known as "the Strid," was believed to send up the image of a white vaporous horse as a forewarning that another life was about to be lost to the river's black whirlpools. Several ancient rhymes echo this admonition. "Blood-thirsty Dee, Year needs three." "Wharfe is clear and the Aire lithe. Where Aire kills one, Wharfe kills five." "The shelving slimy river Don, Each year a daughter or a son."

Because we associate life with motion, ocean waves, waterfalls and rivers all have their mystic appeal. But there's something especially magical about a spring. We can clearly see that water falls from above, but it also wells from below; sometimes only seasonally. This phenomenon was inexplicable to early cultures, who explained the ebb and flow — especially of fresh running water — as the work of underground water spirits.

Over time, we have called our seasonal springs by many names, bournes, nailbournes, lavants, winterbournes and gypsies; and we often find them in areas where the calcium carbonate of limestone can easily be carved into fissures and joints. Surface streams move similarly underground. Water that disappears in the narrowest cleft can produce enormous, spectacular chasms called "swallow holes," where seasonal streams dissolve into a mist that freezes in winter. The same flow may then magically reappear on a hillside, in a streambed or, most mystically, from a cave.

Hot springs have always been of particular interest — waters "touched by the sun" while underground. Water, colored blood red from oxidized iron salts, has bubbled from a clay ridge in a bend of the River Avon at Bath in England for about 10,000 years, a marvel that must have both awed and terrified our prehistoric ancestors.

Until St. Patrick's Purgatory in Ireland was sealed up in CE 1497, gas escaped through the water regularly, manifesting in flames and sulfurous fumes. This is how the Roman poet Lucan described a similar spot in Gaul near Toulouse:

"A grove there was, untouched by men's hands from

*ancient times, whose interlacing boughs enclosed a space
of darkness and cold shade and banished the sunlight far
above. No rural Pan dwelt there, no Silvanus, ruler of the
woods, no Nymphs; but gods were worshipped there with
savage rites, the altars were heaped with hideous offerings,
and every tree was sprinkled with human gore. On those
boughs . . . birds feared to perch; in those coverts wild beasts
would not lie down; no wind ever bore down upon that
wood, nor thunderbolt hurled from black clouds; the trees,
even when they spread their leaves to no breeze, rustled
of themselves. Water also fell there in abundance from
dark springs. The images of the gods, grim and rude, were
uncouth blocks formed of felled tree trunks. Their mere
antiquity and the ghastly hue of their rotten timber struck
terror . . . Legend also told that often the subterranean
hollows quaked and bellowed, that yew trees fell down
and rose again, that the glare of conflagration came from
trees that were not on fire, and that serpents twined and
glided round the stems. The people never resorted thither to
worship at close quarters, but left the place to the gods."*

In the seventh century, Christianity banned all offerings
at wells, calling them devil worship. When their adulation
could not be eradicated, sacred springs were taken over by
the Church, some parishes enclosing them in their crypts.
Many a water spirit quickly became the patron saint of a
holy well. As a result, many such wells were not strictly
"sanctified," in that the abiding spirit remained "pagan" in
the minds of many of the well's devotees. Believers would
circle the well sun-wise — sometimes three times and often
on hands and knees — drink the water and then wet a piece
of cloth and tie it to a nearby tree or bush. As the fabric dried
whatever ailment the particular well was thought to address
would be dried up as well, healed by the well's spirit or saint.
Breton churches in what is now northwest France

almost always incorporated a sacred well in their precincts. "Pardons" were held there to cure ailments. This could be accomplished by bathing in the water, drinking from it or using it to wash sores. One of the most beautifully situated of these holy wells is that of St. They's Chapel on the Pointe du Van. Under the deep blue skies of high summer in 1995, I found the treeless, sandy peninsula blanketed with creamy white Queen Anne's lace and golden buttercups, its rustic landscape graced with thin mats of browning summer grasses and alive with the sound of a wild dark sea lashing at its roots. The well itself is sheltered in a miniature chapel, an exact replica of St. They's.

In the nineteenth century, a priest might lead his flock in times of drought to the Fairy Spring of Barenton in the Forest of Brocéliande in Brittany (PLATE 42). Tossing water over his shoulder or sprinkling drops over the Perron de Merlin (Merlin's Stone) — the large standing stone near the basin into which the water flows — he would call up a storm. It's also believed that a Druid seminary once stood near Barenton.

I had the great good fortune to wander through Brocéliande in mid-afternoon on a hot and humid July day, when a fellow Barenton seeker was there with a survey map. My husband and I followed this fellow deep into the woods, much of which had burned in 1990, though it was still restful and sylvan, full of bracken and lofty pines.

The twenty-seven square miles of the forest of Paimpont, of which Brocéliande is a part, are all that remains of the great eighty-five-mile deep woods that once covered the interior of Brittany. A mere two of these twenty-seven square miles now belong to the State. According to ancient lore, Merlin fell under the spell of Vivian, the Lady of the Lake, at Barenton, and she encased him forever inside the Merlin Stone. A knight named Ewein once poured water on Merlin's Stone and called up a great storm. The

Black Knight, the Keeper of the Fountain at the time, came out to complain about this and was killed by Ewein, who subsequently married the Black Knight's widow and became the well's present keeper.

In any case, my husband nonchalantly tossed a few flecks of Barenton water over his shoulder. Later that evening, a ferocious rainstorm was unleashed upon us. Like a living being, its thunder advanced and rattled over the roof of our bed and breakfast for well over an hour before passing on by slow degrees.

Most such holy wells are considered curative. We find over a thousand of them in Wales alone, most of them in ruins. More than 300 Welsh churches are built directly over, or very close to, a holy well. St. Winefride's Well, the oldest well in Britain, has a continuous pilgrimage tradition of more than 1400 years. The well sits at the edge of the Welsh town of Holywell. St. Winefride's annually welcomes thousands of visitors, seeking cures from their afflictions by immersion in the sacred pool. In the seventh century, legend says, St. Winefride literally lost her head to a drunken chieftain named Caradoc, who hacked off her head when she spurned his romantic overtures. Her quick-thinking uncle, St. Beuno, placed the severed head on her torso, bringing her back to life. A spring now known by her name gushes from the spot where St. Winefride's head fell.

Traditionally, visiting the appropriate well could cure rickets, stomach disorders, infertility, eye sores or headaches. In the Middle Ages, sulfur springs were considered particularly effective for skin problems. (We find the same medicinal property ascribed to water in the biblical New Testament, when Naaman dips himself seven times in the River Jordan to cure a skin ailment.) Many springs, especially in Brittany, are still considered cures for eye disease. The eye, like water, reflects sunlight. For the Celts, immersing in turbulent water, which represented divine frenzy, was thought to cure madness.

Not surprisingly, after each bout of bubonic plague in the Middle Ages, curative waters, both baths and infusions, grew in number. Today, spas are the descendants of these ancient healing wells. Lists of frequented spas of the nineteenth and early twentieth centuries included the mineral content of curing wells and hot springs – barium, iron, calcium – as well as descriptions of various treatments recommended to cure an illness or improve health.

A natural consequence of our ancestors' reverence for water was their need to placate the spirits believed to be living in or activating lakes, bogs, rivers, pools, springs and other water sources. Votive offerings can be traced from Neolithic times through to the Vikings and well into our own modern age. We've discovered Neolithic flints in some wells, and ritual deposits have been identified in shafts and pits dug during the Bronze Age. Five bone daggers found in the Thames date to about 1500 BCE. Daggers and swords offered to marshes, rivers, bogs and springs multiplied from the first millennium BCE, as metalworking increased among our prehistoric ancestors. Valuable weapons and ornaments were placed in east-flowing rivers like the Tyne, the Wear and the Humber. Today, we have wishing wells.

During a road trip through Great Britain with my mother, one of our objectives was to visit the holy well behind the church of St. Clether (PLATE 43). The well sits a short distance from the church itself. In its peaceful setting of cool serenity, among the brambles, bracken and stinging nettles at the edge of Bodmin Moor, I let the water soak into my skin. I even dropped a ten-pence piece into the crystal clear water and watched it vanish into the silty bottom. St. Clether's spring rises from a granite cliff well back of the chapel, flows underground to be gathered at the rear, flows under the building to a second collection point and then disappears underground again. You can hear the water gurgling below the hill; and yet the water of the well does not appear to move. Tiny ferns grow like small thin mats on the interior walls, and the water is clear, pure and sweet.

Spirits inhabiting peculiar waters, like deep, fast-flowing rivers or dangerous pools, required a special offering. Human sacrifice, as previously described by Lucan, eventually gave way to decorating wells with flowers and tying well foliage with rags, ribbons or clothing – a practice still common in Europe, the Middle East, Africa and India.

Tacitus writes of the clothed image of a German goddess being washed in a certain lake, along with her chariot. Her attendants were then "swallowed by the lake," probably in sacrificial drowning. On Midsummer Day, the Celts offered up prisoners of war as water sacrifices. Cattle were usually sacrificed in Europe, goats and buffalo in India. As late as the early twentieth century, roosters and goats were still being sacrificed in Bombay. Spirits of the drowned, known in Scotland as "Cups of the Fairies," were sometimes said to have haunted wells.

In contemporary Great Britain and Ireland, we regularly visit our holy wells, leaving nails, rags, ribbons, shells, buttons, pins, needles, coins and other trinkets as offerings, appeals for help or healing or even as a witness of our devotion. Offerings at a holy well in Ireland in the nineteenth century were left "in remembrance of us having made this holy station; and may they rise up in glory to prove it for us in the last days." Placing personal objects in the water or on tree limbs or bushes nearby, we can ostensibly make direct contact with the water's divinity. Pins force out a devil. Rags soak up an illness. It wasn't long, of course, before churches placed collection boxes for the coins.

Another aspect of our veneration of water is its ritual use. Holy wells have been used for divination, predicting both prosperity and misfortune. A nut thrown into a certain well in Kashmir, for example, portends success if it floats, failure if it sinks.

More widespread is our traditional use of water for ritual cleansing. The ancient Greeks, Romans, Babylonians, Egyptians and Chinese all used water to get rid of the negative energy associated with death, disease, menstruation, violence and childbirth — to clean away the filth, so to speak — or to sanctify, initiate or purify. Water for ritual cleansing may include salt, blood or urine, as in India, where cow's urine is added, cows being sacred to Hinduism. Similarly, a ceremony of purification through bath or baptism has been prevalent in religions of all times and places. It seems to be a universal element in the history of religion. Through baptism and bathing, we bring the "sinner" into direct contact with the Divine.

Despite its prevalence, what is definitively known about our ancient forms of water worship is tenuous, even in Western Europe's Iron Age. Holy wells, for example, are not specifically mentioned in early Celtic texts. In fact, we know of no specific well structure that can be dated earlier than the late Middle Ages, with its cult of healing and holy wells. A holy well, however, can mark an ancient spring, and — as we know from myth and legend — the Celts revered these waters. Their otherworldly properties, along with their movement from the underworld — the blood of Mother Earth from the womb of Mother Earth — gave them procreative or regenerative power.

During the Middle Ages, the Christianized Celts of Britain walked three times sun-wise around a holy well to ensure fertility. Water similarly brought clarity to and connected the three realms of Celtic cosmology — the Upper World of rain, clouds and storms; the Lower World of underground rivers and springs; and the human Middle World of flowing, earthbound rivers. Continuously cycling through these three spheres — rain falling into rivers and lakes, soaking into and springing from the ground and evaporating into mist and fog

— water traveled through the known universe and therefore contained all knowledge. Taliesin, the sixth century Welsh poet, acquired inspiration and wisdom from the water of the Cauldron of Ceridwen. King Arthur hunted for the Cauldron of Annwn, a gift of Bran the Blessed, in an adventure thought by some to be the model for the later Quest for the Holy Grail.

Relying on the instinct of animals to discover water, Celtic settlements were often founded where cattle stopped to graze or pigs rooted. Places where elements met were considered especially sacred, sites of mystical potency and wisdom like the water's edge of a riverbank or seashore, fog, mist and dew — those "in-between places" that are neither definitively one thing nor the other. Within the tenets of Christianity, nature was considered haunted, wild and full of darkness and could only *reflect* God's glory. But for the Celts, the forest was not just beautiful. It was divine.

The Celtic veneration of water integrated a Cult of the Head. In fact, some of the cauldrons of Celtic mythology were thought to be skulls. Skull caps, possibly representing spirit guardians, were often placed at wells to be used as drinking cups. They might also have been used for the preparation of mind altering or initiatory drugs, just as water from the Castalian Spring, one of several at Delphi, in Greece, was thought to have been used to mix the potent drugs given to the prophesying Sybil.

Of course, we will never know for certain exactly where the Celtic belief in the sacredness of water came from. Well worship, such as that in ancient Iran, is common in hot, dry areas where water is scarce. If Celtic culture is rooted in the Iberian Peninsula, as some Irish legends suggest, memories of an arid homeland may be the source. Another explanation for the Celtic emphasis on water, with votive offerings in lochs and bogs and springs, may reflect the importance of water in a deteriorating climate. It may have even represented one of the three cosmological realms in the "three-fold death" of Celtic sacrificial victims — stabbing, hanging and drowning.

Our cultures may flourish and fade, but our customs and concepts live on in people who are not necessarily directly descended from us. We don't know if water featured in the rituals of our Neolithic or Bronze Age ancestors, but we do have some intriguing clues.

The great megalithic monuments of our prehistory are often physically associated with water. Many stone circles and avenues appear to be links to water — Broomend of Crichie with the River Don; Callanish with Loch Roag (PLATE 44); and Stonehenge with the River Avon. These links may have given our forbearers processional access to water for purification and fertility, memories of which might be behind legends of walking, swimming or drinking stones. Well dressings and offerings at sacred springs could be folk memories of the same ancient rituals that included oaths under old oak trees or circled fertility stones.

In the British Isles, we find water deposits of ornate and valuable shields, vessels and swords increasing from the Late Bronze Age through the Early Iron Age, roughly 1400-600 BCE. They're in lakebeds, river bottoms and marshes. At about the same time, the building and use of old megalithic monuments — and presumably the initial burial customs that accompanied them — came to an end. A new water-centered religion, its funeral rites steeped in ancient tradition, could then have evolved, incorporating offerings of precious possessions to water, along with cremated ashes or bones. Bone and wood rarely survive in such an environment, and we are thus left with relics of only metal goods.

As temperatures dropped during this era, rainfall increased and coastal waters crept inland. Soils were depleted, fields became waterlogged and bog blanketed what was once fertile high country. Wet places, becoming more abundant, may have become the focus of a new water cult. The power of water came to the forefront, its healing potential growing with the rise in death and disease that accompanied over-population, just as the curative waters of the Middle Ages burgeoned after the plague.

Did our ancestors erect stones at healing springs as a permanent residence, a kind of storage battery for Earth energies that otherwise animated the water only for a short time each year? Did the monoliths of their stone monuments act like acupuncture needles to regulate Earth energy? Did megalithic architects, who had a fondness for seacoasts, rivers and islands, build funerary and other monuments to mark the meeting places of underground water lines or geomagnetic Earth currents? We will never know for certain, but the possibility remains intriguing and appealing nonetheless.

SPIRITUAL FITNESS

"And he cried with a loud voice:
Hurt not the earth,
neither the sea, nor the trees."

– *Revelations*

Why are we here? For many of us, our life's purpose is a great mystery. Manifesting on the Earth plane gives us an opportunity to experience individual, physical consciousness while still maintaining our essential divinity. When we bring to the Earth the qualities of a spiritual identity, we recognize and honor the Earth and all its elements and features.

There are countless ways to tap into the Earth's energy, and we have covered many of them in previous chapters.

"Healthy feet can hear the very heart of Holy Earth," the great Sioux leader Tatanka Yotanka (Sitting Bull) once said. Walk barefoot in the grass or in the rain. Plant a garden. Consider cultivating an herb garden. It can even be grown indoors, in the smallest of spaces.

Like water, life is constant movement. All water is going somewhere. We may not know where or how it is traveling, what obstacles it might meet or what places or situations might temporarily contain or restrain it. But the important thing about the flow of water *and* of life is that we move with it, making the best of circumstances. As Eleanor Roosevelt once wrote, "Do the best you can, with what you have, where you are."

A fountain — indoors or out — can sharpen our awareness of change and movement in life. We are also soothed by the sound of flowing water. In the earliest Arabian hospital in Alexandria, fountains lulled patients to sleep. Water can likewise help each of us enter a state of peaceful rest.

Incorporating the use of quartz crystals in our lives can help us keep awareness of the benefits of water close at hand. Like ice, quartz is hard, clear and bright. It is transparent, conductive and healing. We can wear quartz crystals as amulets or use them as part of our décor. They can enhance our mindfulness and sense of well-being.

Bring water into your spiritual/emotional life wherever possible. And remember too, that the physical body needs at least eight glasses of water a day.

CHAPTER 9

SACRED AND SECULAR

"SACRED IS REAL.
THEREFORE ALL IMPORTANT REALITIES
OF LIFE PARTICIPATE IN THE SACRED."

– *Encyclopedia Britannica*

I N SO-CALLED "PRIMITIVE" SOCIETIES, there is no division between the sacred and the secular. The ways in which Neolithic and Bronze Age megalithic architecture functioned secularly as *boundaries*, *landmarks* and *memorials* or as *meeting places* for trade or lawmaking all probably had a sacred dimension. For this reason, the emphasis in this section is almost exclusively on the sacred, covering *ritual* and moving on to *festivals*, *processions*, *dance* and *totems*.

SECULAR

"NOW ABSALOM . . . HAD REARED UP FOR HIMSELF
A PILLAR. FOR HE SAID, I HAVE NO
SON TO KEEP MY NAME IN REMEMBRANCE;
AND HE CALLED THE PILLAR AFTER HIS OWN NAME;
AND IT IS CALLED UNTO THIS DAY, ABSALOM'S PLACE."

– *II SAMUEL 18:18*

Our Neolithic and Bronze Age ancestors may have had any number of secular purposes for the standing stones they raised — markers for routes, boundaries, mineral formations, site lines, meeting places or memorial records of ancestors or special events.

One of the few instances in which we can more or less accurately deduce the purpose of a standing stone is Carreg Stone in North Wales. Carreg stands a mile east of Harlech Castle and is one of thirteen similar stones that move from Llanbedr village to Moel Goedog, where there is a collection of prehistoric cairns and hut circles. These stones almost certainly delineated a safe track across rough and mountainous terrain, just as moor stones – both crosses and pillars – still direct travelers across the Yorkshire Moors (PLATE 45). Today, a narrow lane runs approximately parallel to the Carreg Stones. We can find other standing stones in North Wales along major routes into the highlands, suggesting some seasonal movement in prehistory between summer camps and winter camps.

The ancient Greeks used an upright stone called a Herma as a boundary or landmark. In the Middle Ages, stone rows were sometimes used as field boundaries. The relatively small number of Neolithic tombs and stone circles we've found suggests some other function beyond the burial of the dead. They may also have been boundary markers for tribal territories, for example.

Stones like Clach Mhicleoid, or Macleod's Stone, (PLATE 46) on the Isle of Harris may have marked a primary landfall in a vast expanse of silver sea, black isles and rugged inlets. Standing on a blustery autumn day in the early 1990s in the shadow of Clach Mhicleoid, a wonderfully tall monolith, that is both wide and thin, I looked out to empty Toehead, a three-mile-long peninsula poking out into the wild Atlantic. Still emptier Taransay Island lay on my right. On the flank of Aird Nisabost hill, Macleod's Stone quite likely marked the strand line of Traigh Lar Beach below, just as the Penloic Menhir (PLATE 47) in Brittany probably marked a former estuary.

Chambered tombs required cooperative and communal labor, and had no uniformity of positioning. We see them on hilltops or in valleys, but rarely on what would have been the best agricultural land (PLATE 48). Even today, when our contemporary architecture soars skyward, we are still impressed with the size of Neolithic burial chambers. Part of their purpose may have been to display the power of a tribe or a clan and its leaders. As populations grew, ancestral bones deposited in grand monuments announced title to the land, discouraging newcomers from settling too close.

Tombs in the Orkney Islands may represent some thirteen tribal territories divided by arable land, each supporting twenty-five to thirty people. We will never know for certain, but these tombs may even have been raised with the help of other tribes, just as neighborhood collectives gathered for barn raisings in our more recent past. By their imposing size, burial chambers were a visible expression of a community's right to surrounding lands. When one group continually produced surpluses, it eventually gained control over tribal rites and rituals because of its status as apparent favorites of the gods. With acquired wealth, that power could then be displayed in elaborate communal tombs.

By the Bronze Age, the round barrows of chieftains, overlords or warriors were very often placed grandly on a hillside, as at Cuween Cairn in Scotland. Seen from below and silhouetted on the skyline, they could duly impress. With an emphasis on the ancestors they immortalized, these boundary markers clearly had a sacred dimension.

We can probably say the same thing about megalithic memorials or "stones of memory," such as Absalom's monument. Monoliths have commemorated important events, dates, or persons for thousands of years. More recently, we have Plymouth Rock, which marks a landfall in the New World, and Scotland's Cumberland Stone, which identifies the historic battlefield at Culloden.

Meeting places, too, have a sacred component. As sites of judgment, lawmaking, trade and festivals, prehistoric stone circles, henges and causewayed enclosures were probably the town halls, community centers and county fairs of their day. And they quite likely began as sacred spaces that recognized the sanctity of kingship or some hallowed feast day. The Viking *Orkneyinga Saga* speaks of a "Hauga-

Thing" —"a place of meeting by a haug or barrow." Courts in the Scottish Highlands were held at stone circles into the fourteenth century. One was convened at the standing stones of Rayne, in Gairlock, in CE 1349.

SACRED

"HOLD EVERY MOMENT SACRED."

– Thomas Mann

The sacred is imbued with divinity; with the vital life force we call spirit. Spirituality by definition – "of, relating to, consisting of or affecting the spirit" – is inclusive, allowing for recognition of the sacred in *many* forms and in *all* forms. There are many paths up the mountain. Religion by definition – "man's *relationship* to that which he regards as holy" – excludes, by virtue of "the chosen few." Or as U2's Bono says, "Religion reduces God."

Every religion has at least some of the following elements – sanctified places, rites and rituals, holy days, charismatic leaders, higher truths, rules, laws and "inspired" literature. Through the centuries, many of these have caused humanity a great deal of trouble, as they still do today.

Both ritual and dance have spiritual applications. Festivals, processions and totems are more firmly "religious." Our Neolithic and Bronze Age forbearers may have considered all of these in the design and function of their megalithic structures.

RITUAL

"WE TAP THE ENERGY OF THE UNIVERSE THROUGH RITUAL."

– Encyclopedia Britannica

> "Ritual is the technology we use to address the subtle energies that create healing."
>
> — Connie Kaplan

Ritual is the primary mechanism we use to control the uncontrollable and approach the unseen. Rituals help us shift from ordinary space and time to sacred space and time, by focusing our minds on a clear intent. The world's religions are loaded with rituals, many of them broad and profound — baptism, prayer, circumcision, mourning, purification, marriage, victory, fasting, confession, warfare and sacrifice. We often put purification, which brings us a sense of solidarity, at the top of the list. Purifying rites are perceived to protect our communities from "contamination" from violated taboos, childbirth, puberty, bloodshed, death, menstruation and so on.

Through prayer, magic, sacrifice, incantation and a recognition of the sacred in nature, "primitive" societies worship with rites of passage — birth, initiation, naming, warfare, death and burial. Plants and animals, the sky, the sun, the moon and the stars are all manifestations of the sacred in our natural world. Nature is not worshipped in and of itself, but rather as a transcendent revelation of the power of divine activity. Not an altogether bad idea.

Contrary to popular understanding, the nature rituals of "primitive" societies are not generally geared to control. We don't try to hold back winter, for example, with a ritual. Our goal is to ensure that we will survive the winter. Rituals may annually retell our community's story with myths that explain and perpetuate our existence in harmony with the Divine. Christians ritualize the thirty-three years of Christ's life into one year, delineating that year by his birth, childhood, teaching, crucifixion and resurrection.

In agricultural societies, the days and years have always been filled with the stuff of ritual. We've preserved revered last sheaves as "corn dollies;" opened a new plowing season by feeding sacred seed held back from a prior harvest to our farm horses or mixing it with seed corn to "teach it to grow." We recognize the sacred in the cycle of plant life — germination, growth, harvest, death and resurrection — a connection that led us to a suffering, but resurrected, god.

We can only truly understand any religious tradition — the melding of ritual with artistic expression and mythology — by viewing it from within the tradition itself. This is, of course, impossible with our Neolithic and Bronze Age ancestors, but we can venture a likely guess. Both lived in predominantly agricultural societies. From this, we can surmise that, like more contemporary agricultural societies, they sanctified the stages of their agricultural year with festivals and sacrifices and recognized the seasonal cycle of an Earth Goddess. For example, we know that the Celts used the seasonal rhythms of the sun and the rise and fall of vegetation in designating their yearly feasts of Imbolc, Beltaine, Lughnasadh and Samhain, a ritual repetition that annually recreated their world.

The tombs of our megalithic predecessors may have been religious centers that played a part similar to our parish churches, creating a social and religious focus for scattered but often related farm families. Relics from round barrows like the one near Avebury, where a punctured boar's tusk and other animal bones were found, suggest the ritualistic involvement of a shaman, as do deer antlers discovered in another burial chamber, the growth and shedding of stag horns representing the cycle of regeneration.

Similarly, the use of prehistoric stone circles as meeting places for ceremonies and rituals geared to observation of the night sky or the stages of the agricultural year seems quite plausible. Even today, we may define our sacred spaces with circles, and the largest stone circles of prehistory — the Ring of Brodgar, Long Meg and Her Daughters and Avebury, for example – seem too monumental for simple astronomical calculations. Key moments in the agricultural year may have been celebrated inside them with fairs, markets, feasts or other ritual gatherings.

We've found cremations in unmarked pits inside some stone circles. These may be indicators of the foundation sacrifices that initially sanctified these meeting places. Remains – particularly of women – have been found buried at the entrances to stone circles; the entrances identified by the width and/or height of flanking stones. Burnt grains have sometimes been discovered nearby as well. In some parts of Scotland today, a small, thin pastry cake called a "black bun" – rich and dark with molasses and filled with raisins, currants, cherries and citrus peels – is still passed around and eaten just after midnight on New Year's Day. Our traditional Christmas cake may have had its beginning in Neolithic rituals now lost to the mists of time.

FESTIVALS

"CELEBRATE WHENEVER YOU CAN."

– ANONYMOUS

Public rejoicing is one of the touchstones of our human history. All over the world, we acknowledge special occasions, notable events and annual cycles of the life force with entertainment and performance. The first celebratory observances probably came about as our ancestors gathered in sacred places to celebrate their relationship with the Divine, bringing some respite from the toil and apprehension of their daily lives.

"Feast" and "festival" have the same root word in the Latin "festus," meaning "solemn," related to the Latin "feriae." Meaning "days of rest" or "holidays," "feriae" gives us the word "fair." In the present, all fairs are "fun fairs," but in times past, "beast fairs" – like the Cattle Fair, Goose Fair, Sheep Fair and Horse Fair – coincided with specific religious festivals. These sacred festivals eventually developed into periodic markets for wares, livestock and workers – milkmaids, shepherds and other farm laborers looking for employment. The word "holiday" derives from the Old English "halig," meaning holy, and "daeg," meaning day. Holy days restore us to both wholeness *and* holiness, offering reprieve from the difficulties of daily living and sanctifying our very lives.

The ancient world, particularly Greece, is well known for its festivals, many of which probably developed from age-old Egyptian and Mesopotamian celebrations directed by priests. These included elaborate processions and the ritualistic bathing of sacred images and played a central role in worship of the gods. In a region of city-states, the celebrations of Greece were intensely local; the Olympic, Pythian and Delian games, for example. Plato advised the inhabitants of his "ideal republic" to seek out the shrines of local spirits, introducing celebratory festivals there at pertinent times.

Under Roman influence, mystery cults, whose participants were strict devotees, grew in importance. The mysteries at Eleusis, which included dance and other dramas, were preceded by a daylong procession during which pilgrims left offerings along the way at shrines dedicated to Demeter. For the most part, Roman festivals centered on mandated civic holidays, though on the "Day of Blood," priests gashed their bodies with knives in homage to the ancient fertility goddess, Cybele. During Saturnalia, the lengthy festival when belligerent and up-tight Rome let its hair down, excess and over-indulgence were the norm.

In early religious expression, the words *feast* and *festival* are interchangeable. When the religious, social and tribal aspects of a culture were one and the same, our ancestors annually recreated their sacred history through feast and festival. Events of our past recurred – and continue to recur – eternally. Repeatedly honoring the cosmic order of the Divine, year after year, we bind our living to our dead, our past to our present, ourselves and our families to the tribe.

New Year festivals, for example, represent the chaos before creation. In "primitive" societies, where the primary features of the past – day and night, winter and summer, sun and moon, rainfall and natural growth cycles – still rule the present, this tribal cosmology is transmitted through oral myth. Lives are considered meaningful to the extent that they imitate or reflect what the gods did in the beginning. The inauguration of a chief in the Fiji Islands, for example, is celebrated as a recreation of the world. Navajo sand paintings function in much the same way.

When ancient populations were nomadic, their festivals probably included sacred rites involving hunting or fishing. But seasonal celebrations geared toward the agricultural growth cycle of planting and harvest, along with the movement of domesticated animals, are more prolific in our history. In Northern Europe, our "pagan" Germanic, Celtic and Slavic ancestors all had such observances, marked with excessive feasting and drinking. These were also times when surplus goods and services could be exchanged.

Our earliest annual celebration may have been Midwinter (December 21), marking the rebirth of the sun. What better time to celebrate the life force of death and regeneration than on the shortest day of the year, when the night is still long and frightening? Long before Christianity, Northern Europeans like the Saxons and the Scandinavians celebrated Midwinter with dancing, feasting, gift-giving and religious rituals that involved ivy, holly and mistletoe, stand-ins for the Christmas tree. The Scandinavians called Midwinter the time of "Yule," a word that derives from the Old Norse "jol," the name given to the Midwinter feast that was adopted by Christianity as the birth date of Christ.

The longest day – the Summer Solstice (June 21) – was another major celebration. There is no mention of Midsummer festivities in early Celtic literature, but all across Northern Europe, our ancestors celebrated Midsummer by lighting bonfires as the sun set, a ritual probably imported from Anglo Saxon or Viking areas, where torch-lit processions circled sun-wise around bonfires to bless the crops. Any farm not contributing fuel for this fire might face harmful consequences. Among Slavic people, Midsummer festivities included ceremonial bathing, a form of baptism. Christianity disguised the Summer Solstice in the Feast of St. John the Baptist, on June 23 or 24. Our ancestors also gave the Equinoxes – Spring, March 20, and Autumn, September 23 – some attention, as indications of a waxing or waning sun.

The four seasons of the Celtic calendar were marked by the four cross-quarter days we've discussed earlier. Imbolc or Oimelc, on the first of February, was the spring lambing season, recognized especially in Ireland and in the Western Isles and Highlands of Scotland. We now know Imbolc as the Feast of St. Brigid in the Catholic Christian calendar, and most of us identify spring's beginning with Easter, from the Anglo-Saxon goddess of spring, Eostre. The hot-cross buns traditional to some Good Friday rituals may have originated in the cakes once offered sacrificially to pre-Christian spring deities.

Beltaine, or May Day – also known as Beltene, Beltane, Bealtine or Beal-Tene – on the first of May, was a festival originally common to all Celtic people. We still see May Day folk festivals being conducted annually from Ireland to Russia. In the British Isles, May Day has been celebrated for centuries, though records of the traditional festival at Padstow in Cornwall, including its drums and famous hobbyhorses, date only as far back as 1803. Once widespread English traditions, "Bringing Home the May," "Mummers' Plays," and the "Hobby Horse Dance," have been lost in other regions but still make up Padstow's annual celebration. When Padstow villagers were asked where these traditions had come from, they said they symbolized the death and rebirth of a god and/or sacred king. How did they know this? "Modern experts" had told them so.

Beltaine festivals were established to mark the coming of summer. With the return of the summer sun, our ancestors drove their flocks and herds to summer pastures. The most important part of Beltaine was the lighting of great hilltop fires believed to represent the power of the Sun God. These fires invoked divine protection for the season. Ashes from Beltaine fires were set aside for good luck. They were also scattered on fields to promote fertility, health and prosperity, and firebrands from Beltaine fires were distributed to rekindle family hearths that had been extinguished before the festival.

We've seen vestiges of May Day, like dancing sun-wise around a Beltaine fire and driving cattle between two fires for protection, in Ireland and Scotland in the very recent past. Sick animals were sometimes sacrificed on these fires, and, in the Highlands, broken Beltaine cakes were placed in a sack with one marked portion or a charcoal-blackened bit. Whoever drew that piece had to leap three times through the Beltaine flames, a likely remnant of human sacrifice. In some cases, the unlucky chooser was dubbed the "cailleach bealtine," the "Hag of Beltaine," a term of great dishonor.

Another symbol we associate with May Day is the Maypole or May Tree. Medieval villagers in Europe carried trees, garlands and branches in procession to honor the fertility and lushness of summer. "Bringing in the May" or "going a-Maying" meant that we collected flowers or other vegetation for decoration and dressed the Maypole with ribbons and wreaths.

Lughnasadh, a harvest festival, was the great two-week Celtic celebration that took place either side of the first of August. Lughnasadh is probably most comparable to our present day Thanksgiving, celebrating the gathering of crops and other blessings of the past year. Thanksgiving falls at various times, from late November in the US – a commemoration that dates to the autumn of 1621 – to early October in Canada. Of course, harvest celebrations are as old as civilization. Dependent on the whims of nature, actual harvest times are very much out of our hands; though as the culmination of growth cycles, they are naturally autumn events.

The word "harvest" comes from the Old English "haerfest," meaning "autumn feast." "Haer" is akin to Old Norse "haust," meaning "autumn." We also know harvest celebrations as First Fruits – the term derived from the earliest fruits of the season once offered to the Divine in thanks for the gift of fertility – and as Harvest Home, for the gathering and bringing home of the harvest. I came across one of the most moving contemporary expressions of this ancient ritual on the trip to Great Britain I took with my mother back in 1991. A gathering from the local harvest was laid out in the south porch of the Church of St. Mary in Ely, Lincolnshire. A long rosewood table had been pushed up against the east wall, a sheaf of wheat propped up in one corner. Red-berried sprigs had been placed on the broad stone sill of the window to either side of a vase of chrysanthemums, dahlias, zinnias and marigolds, all vibrant with the colors of autumn. The bench below was overflowing with ripe tomatoes, turnips, parsnips, red and green bell peppers, apples, oranges, pears, cucumbers and cabbages. And at the base of the shock of wheat, next to a second gathering of fall flowers, lay several sliced loaves of homemade bread. It was a beautiful sight.

For the Celts, the festival of Lughnasadh marked the beginning of the fall harvest, the "season of plenty," which began with the reaping of cereal crops and went on to the gathering of fruits, such as the sacred apple — whose cut center reveals a perfect mandala — and, finally, nuts. According to tradition, everything would be collected and stored by the first day of Samhain. Held October 31-November 1, Samhain marked the last of the great seasonal fire festivals. The first fruit celebrations of Lughnasadh — gatherings for feasting and races in honor of the Celtic god Lugh — are thought to have taken place in Ireland, generally on hilltops or near springs, for at least 1800 years.

The ancient Tan Hill Fair in Wiltshire, England, was celebrated until 1932. Some historians believe that this farming-oriented fair — a gathering of farm animals, crops and drovers — existed for more than 5000 years, until agricultural developments like the advent of the truck brought it to a close. In the Middle Ages, the fair, then known as St. Ann's Fair, was held on St. Ann's Day, and by 1541 it was held on St. Ann's Hill, a name corrupted by the seventeenth century to Tan Hill.

The Puck Fair in Killorglin, County Kerry, Ireland is still held in mid-August. For many years, the fair was associated with Lughnasadh celebrations. Part of the festivities still involves a goat or "puck" elevated on a platform, perhaps a traditional remnant of an ancient Celtic feast involving goat sacrifice. Another explanation of the festival's roots as a goat fair suggests that a local landowner renamed it because this was the only animal on which he could legally levy a toll. An act of the British Parliament in the early nineteenth century gave the British government's representative in Dublin the power to outlaw the collection of tolls at Killorglin's ancient August fair. At the time, tolls were monetary levies collected by local landlords for each animal brought to a sheep, cattle or horse fair. The landlord of Killorglin was on the outs with Irish authorities at the time and his right to collect such tolls had been rescinded. Goats, however, were not among the livestock restrictions.

Another facet of Lughnasadh involved "Handfast" marriages — trial unions of one year — which were sealed during Lughnasadh as "formal engagements." If a couple was still content a year and a day after their handfast ceremony, they would then agree to be married. As the Lughnasadh festival evolved over time, Christianity associated it with the mythic hero, St. Patrick.

A major Irish pilgrimage still takes place annually during Lughnasadh, with faithful participants scaling County Mayo's Croagh Patrick, some on hands and knees. This ritual involves not only climbing the mountain, but also chanting while circling standing stones on top. This commemoration is the most prominent remnant of age-old visits to holy wells and other sacred sites established in honor of the Celtic god Crom on Lughnasadh — then also known as Black Crom's Sunday.

Over time, the offering of our ancestors' first fruits to a harvest deity evolved into the fashioning of corn dollies, also known as harvest dolls, harvest mothers or harvest queens. Decorated with grain and flowers or constructed from the last sheaf of grain cut in the harvest, corn dollies are also called "kirn babies," from the Greek "keirein," "to cut." The plated-reed Cross of St. Bridget is probably a similar remnant of a first fruits offering.

Christianized Anglo-Saxons held their own harvest festival called Lammas on the first of August, a date we still know as Lammas Day. Lammas comes from the Old English "hlaf" — "loaf" and "maesse," meaning "mass." The Catholic mass, from the Latin "messa" — "the dismissal at the end of a religious service"— in turn comes from the Latin "mittere," "to send or dismiss." This mass is a commemorative sacrifice of the body and blood of Christ, as symbolized with bread and wine. Loaves of bread — Mass Loaves — baked from the first ripened grain of the harvest were consecrated on Lammas Day, when by old English law, private lands held during the crop-raising season were returned to common pasturage.

There is no consensus about the place the last of the great seasonal fire festivals, Samhain, held for the Celts, who divided their year into a time of light and a time of darkness. Imbolc and Beltaine were festivals of a waxing sun; Lughnasadh and Samhain celebrated the waning sun. We also know that the twenty-four-hour cycle of a Celtic day began at sundown. Thus, though they can't be certain, many scholars surmise that the Celtic New Year (November 1) may have opened with the eve of Samhain, October 31, which heralded the coming of winter.

As night descended, hilltop Samhain bonfires were lit to encourage the warmth of a fading sun, the fires' ashes scattered on barren fields to promote fertility. Herd animals were returned from summer pastures. Because not all of them could have been wintered over, many must have been slaughtered for the feast. Laws and land tenures were renewed, and genealogies were advanced. Hearths were rekindled for the coming year with the embers of Samhain fires, accompanied by widespread feasting and dancing in hopes that the fertile power of the sun might be taken up to sustain participants during the darker months ahead.

Samhain also involved divination, a supernatural process associated with seeking guidance from the dead, whose souls were said to revisit the earth during the festival. Hollowed turnips held candles — precursors of our modern-day Jack-o-Lanterns — and masqueraders attempted to confuse or frighten away malignant spirits. For many centuries, a general assembly of Celtic Ireland convened at Tara on Samhain probably once every three years. Legend says that its opening rituals included sacrificial victims being consumed by fire on the Hill of Tlachtga in County Meath, twelve miles northwest of Tara.

A celebration like Samhain, a time when the barriers between the human and spirit worlds were considered to have dissolved, is very likely pre-Celtic in origin, with the memory of the dead being kept alive in hopes that they would rest in peace and not disturb the living. Like so many other traditions, this "pagan" feast of the dead – impossible to eliminate – was taken over by Christianity as All Saints' Day, a commemoration of saints. October 31, the eve of All Saints' Day – All Hallows' Eve – became our contemporary Halloween. On All Souls' Day, November 2, prayers and Soul Cakes were offered to the departed faithful who had not yet been received into Heaven. But for pre-Christian Celts, the end of Samhain most likely meant that the old year had been laid to rest and the dead had once again returned to their graves.

We have reason to believe that these important Celtic festivals – Imbolc, Beltane, Lughnasadh, and Samhain – as well as observances of Midwinter and Midsummer, originated in our prehistoric past. Ongoing traditions often reflect forgotten memories, and the rites of one society or belief system often evolve into the rituals of another. Christianity is the prime example of one religion usurping and adapting the sense of the sacred, the feasts and the rites from other belief systems.

In the same way, the traditions of our Neolithic and Bronze Age ancestors could easily have been maintained, with cultural adaptations, in the Celtic Iron Age. Lughnasadh, for example, has long been associated with Neolithic cairns and stone circles. Until very recently, offerings of wine or blood, barley cakes and flowers were tendered at harvest time to prehistoric stone monuments like Finn MacCool's Fingers, which were seen as protectors of the fruitfulness of the land and purveyors of health and prosperity. St. Barnabas' Fair in Yorkshire used to be held at the Summer Solstice, in a field near standing stones called the Devil's Arrows, an arrangement now encircled by highways and bypasses. Sited to sunrise in early November, Swinside Circle in the Lake District of Great Britain may have anticipated Celtic Samhain celebrations by thousands of years.

As sacred temples, stone circles like Castlerigg in Cumbria created appropriate barriers for spiritual protection. Our ancestors may have used some as "rings of life" for spring and summer festivities, with others, in autumn and winter, being used as "rings of death." As we've seen from recent research, stone circles have resonant properties that might be analogous to the acoustics of cathedrals, though on a much smaller scale. The interiors of large circles like Long Meg and her Daughters could easily have accommodated up to 400 ritual participants, and five of the cromlechs in the Carnac area of Brittany could hold about 250 each, with plenty of elbow room. Incorporating music and voices within these ancient places of worship must have dramatically increased their aura of power and mystery.

We also see evidence of prehistoric ritual fires at stone circles, burial chambers and alignments — like charcoal and ashes found near monuments and remnants of charred grains discovered in post-holes or beside entrance stones. Could these have been precursors of Soul Cakes and Lammas Bread? Were they offerings deposited at holy sites on some particularly auspicious occasion? And were they carried to those sites along sacred processional routes?

The sanctity of ancestral shrines quite likely extended to the paths approaching or joining them. Avebury, Carnac, Callanish and Stonehenge all have alignments that may well have denoted a sacred seasonal processional pathway or the means by which a deity could enter a site. We can imagine night processions, illuminated by torches and bonfires, which must have been particularly stirring. "It's very probable this walke was made for processions," John Aubrey, in the seventeenth century, wrote of the alignment connected to Kennett, the burial chamber near Stonehenge. Impressive stone avenues on Dartmoor (PLATE 49) – lines of uprights four or five feet apart – are just wide enough for a single-file procession and generally lead to circles or burial cairns.

Some paths join a stone circle to a nearby funerary monument, symbolically connecting life with death. Double rows most often lead to cairns and often increase in height as they near. They also frequently have paired monoliths, one a tall pillar (male) and one a low, flat-topped or triangular rock (female), another figurative union of opposites. At Midsummer Sunrise at Callanish, local legend says that "The Shining One" – the sun or moon? – "walk(s) up the avenue, heralded by the call of a cuckoo."

Well into the modern era, megaliths are still an important part of celebration, worship and assembly. In Wales, for example, iconic circles and pillars of Gorsedd Stones are still being raised as an integral part of the National Eisteddfod, a festival of druidic origin featuring costumed bards and poets, folk dancers, musical fanfares and a symbolic horn of plenty. At Imbolc, people in Ireland still congregate at specified stone circles to honor the Earth goddess. Likewise, Stonehenge has probably been the site of outdoor festivals for more than 3000 years. Even the parish enclosures of Brittany – a stone wall that encircles the cemetery, the church, the charnel house and the calvary (a sculpted representation of the crucifixion, many of which have been attached to ancient standing stones) – reflect a contemporary spiritual affinity to ancient stone monuments.

During and after the Protestant Reformation, however, the fairs, feasts and holy days of Western and Northern

Europe were largely suppressed. To the Puritans, Maypoles were "stinckying idols" about which people would "leape and daunce as the heathen did." Yet for much of our prehistory, such celebrations must have been timeless, significant components of the necessary notions that kept our ancestors in harmony with the divine forces that were believed to control their world.

While the passage of time has obscured their true purpose, the megalithic structures of our Neolithic and Bronze Age ancestors were undoubtedly spiritual centers of some kind, whether to recognize the season of efficacy of a peculiar Earth spirit, to invoke the rebirth of the sun or to celebrate a harvest of plenty with exuberance and gratitude. Though most of the answers will always be hidden, asking questions of such a past can lead to a present-day awakening, the transcendence of secular boundaries to a more spiritual plain.

DANCE

"WE HAVE NO IDEOLOGY. WE HAVE NO THEOLOGY. WE DANCE."

– SHINTO PRIEST

In some languages, saying "to dance" is another way of saying "to pray." We see sacred movement as a way to meld with the Divine, to raise power or to induce a visionary state. In Hindu mythology, the creation of the world is known as "The Dance of God." Shiva – the original "Lord of the Dance" – brings matter into being and maintains order in the cosmos with dance and rhythmic sound. "Everywhere is Shiva's gracious dance made manifest . . . he dances with water, fire, wind and ether."

266

We think of dance — "motion that rises from emotion" — as the foundation of almost all of the arts. Throughout history, people around the world have demonstrated a natural and expressive reaction to rhythm. We've danced out of joy, sorrow or fear; for birth, death, fertility, illness, praise, hunting, sunrise, rainfall and crops. "Praise the Lord . . . praise him with timbre and the dance," we read in the Hebrew Old Testament. Serbs and Hopis, among others, dance for rain. Quechuan and Aztecs danced for the sun.

Sacred dance is a sacrificial act. We offer ourselves in tribute to or as a channel for the Divine. With communal dances, we weave individuals into one, a unifying concept that has appealed to many organized religions. A spontaneous release of energy can be transformed into the deliberate fixed pattern of a religious ritual. When we hold hands, we increase this communal feeling, explaining in great part why chain dances or choruses of dancing singers are among our most ancient forms of worship and celebration. As evidence, chain dancers are depicted on ancient Greek vases and in ritualistic Egyptian rock carvings of Anubis and Horus from 4000 BCE Luxor. Long ago, our ancestors recognized the power of harnessing movement to channel emotions and make concerted requests of their gods.

Secular dances were rare in ancient Egypt. Dances of adoration and entreaty, with the chanting of prayers and hymns, celebrated the relationship of participants with the Divine. A "Dance to the Morning Star," for example, took place at dawn, sometimes accompanied by the sacrifice of a white camel. Similarly, during the Festival of Isis, dancers representing the goddess as "dawn" or as "the spring wind" reenacted the search for her husband/brother, Osiris. Funeral rites included mourning dances, performed mostly by women; though those at the "Feast of Eternity" — a celebration that, like All Souls' Day, honored the dead

— featured participants of both genders.

Greek drama grew directly out of ancient spring festival celebrations, which included the ceremonial temple and torch dances often present during other major Greek occasions. Frenzied funeral dances featuring self-laceration were replaced in the sixth century BCE with less violent performances accompanied by instruments like the flute and the harp. Beginning as early as the eighth century BCE, the Pythia, the priestess of the Delphic Oracle, was said to receive divine messages during a hypnotic dance in which she was believed to imitate a snake.

At country wine-harvest festivals, Bacchic, or Dionysiac, dances — in which celebrants positioned on a circular dance-ground stomped ecstatically around a central symbol of the winemaking god — seem fairly obvious imitations of the pressing of grapes. The Spartans of the sixth and seventh centuries BCE held Pyrrhic war dances, and Virgil mentions a Trojan maze dance he associated with initiation rituals. Notably, outside of wedding feasts, most secular Greek dances, usually accompanied with singing, mimicked manual labor — reaping, milling and weaving for men and spinning and cooking for women.

The Romans, especially upper-class intellectuals, were not much for dancing, though their early history included some agricultural dances, orgiastic religious dances and rapid war dances by priests who drummed up the proper martial frenzy. During the Roman Compitalia Festival marking the beginning of summer — on the same day as Celtic Beltaine — blood sacrifices were offered with accompanied dancing at crossroads in the countryside, a remnant of which we see in the European country folk dances that were later held in similar spots.

Our basic forms of dance — the circle and the line — are nearly universal in initial formation, though with great variation in performance. Some of our dance lines interweave. Some dancers double up into parallel lines or move in a snaky fashion symbolic of fertility, as is the case with the Bavenda. A tribe in the South African Transvaal, the Bavenda's processional spring dance imitated an awakening python representing the Earth energies that stimulated spring growth. Spring "turning dances" through mazes were performed in Britain for many centuries. In the early twentieth century, the people of North Yorkshire remembered treading one in the ancient maze on Ripon Common. Native Americans still regularly hold circle dances, and ring dances likewise take place at some harvest festivals in lowland Scotland.

As we often see circles and spirals as pathways between worlds, it's not surprising that one of our oldest forms of dance is the sacred spiral, a circular in-turning followed by a complementary reversal. Spiral dances fold and unfold the world, recreating cosmic chaos and rebirth as they wind and unwind. In the United Kingdom, the Cornish Snail Creep, a spiral dance led by musicians, was performed into the last century. A related dance still takes place in Scotland at the New Year. Participants hold hands crossed at the wrists and stomp their feet while moving in to the center of the circle and back out again. Their pattern symbolizes the end of the old year and the beginning of the new.

With spiral dances, we mirror the movements of the cosmos, especially the clockwise movement of the sun. A sun-wise dance at Beltaine was performed in Scotland as late as the 1830s, while the Abbots Bromley Horn Dance — possibly the oldest surviving ceremony in Britain, predating the Norman Conquest — reenacts an ancient deer-hunting dance. Lines of dancers, some wearing sets of antlers, weave snakelike between each other before imitating the sun's circular course in a round dance. Separated lines then advance on each other and retreat. One set of the antlers used at Abbots Bromley has been carbon dated to about CE

1000.

Frenzied religious dances like those of the Mevlevi, or Whirling Dervishes, spiral the universe into being, the right hand raised and active to receive divine transmissions, the left hand returning them to the earth. These Sufi mystics, members of an order founded in thirteenth century Turkey by the poet Rumi — who would spin around a pillar in the mosque while scribes took down his words — whirl clockwise, seeking an ecstatic altered state of consciousness that brings insight from and union with the Divine.

Whirling movement symbolizes celestial spheres in orbit and by extension all the spheres of existence. At the center of the spiral, we defeat the monster of our own hidden nature — the Minotaur of the Minoan labyrinth — and are reborn into a state of renewed wholeness. Without language, dogma or separation, such dances are as close as we may come to God.

Ecstatic dances include the rituals of voodoo, which bring about "possession" through rhythmic motion. Trance dances like those of the Australian Aborigines, the Batak of Malaysia or Siberian shamans are likewise in this category and might also include drug-induced states of altered consciousness. These could be hunting dances, dances of appeasement or dances that accompany a soul to its final resting place. Shamanic trance dancers often seek to honor, identify with or even *become* a power animal or other totemic being.

All hypnotic religious dances have a built-up surge of emotion at their core. By ecstatic, rhythmic display, we try to create an environment in which the Divine — whatever we perceive that to be — responds by providing us with game animals, rain or some other kind of help. The Divine might even conjure up life itself as, for example, with ancient dance dramas meant to resurrect divinity as green corn or as rain clouds.

The very shape of prehistoric stone circles suggests that

our ancient ancestors performed rhythmic and possibly even hypnotic dances within or around them. We have countless tales involving petrified dancers in connection with standing stones – the Merry Maids (PLATE 50) and their two solitary outliers, for example. Pagan spirits in the guise of pipers are said to have persuaded nineteen women to dance on the Sabbath. From a clear blue sky, the story goes, a bolt of lightning transformed all of them into stone. The children of two Irish giants met the same fate, becoming the Seven Stones of Lissyviggeen.

All such tales may allude to the ancient pre-Christian rituals or pastoral festivals of our prehistoric forbearers in which wild, energetic dancing around or inside of stone rings produced alternate forms of consciousness. Such activity may also have been thought necessary to accumulate bio-energy that was then stored in the stones or conducted back into the earth. Then again, such tales may represent something more than the memory of ancient ancestral rituals. They may simply be another example of Christianity's interference with ancient venerated sites in an attempt to denigrate them or exploit their perceived power. This was probably especially true in late Tudor and Stuart times, when campaigns against "profaning the Sabbath" were particularly virulent.

And yet we have long used communal dancing, an important part of pre-Christian ritual, as a natural way of expressing gratitude or placating the Divine. In fact, all rituals in their many manifestations may have originated with dance, perhaps as part of first-fruit celebrations for the bounty of gifts received from nature/deity like maple syrup, corn, beans, wild rice, berries, squash or cactus fruit.

We have intriguing hints that prehistoric stone circles could support the idea of celebratory dance. When accumulated peat was removed from the recumbent circle of Reenascreena in the south of Ireland in the

271

1960s, the ground near the entrance showed evidence of erosion, thought to have resulted from countless generations of walking or dancing inside the circle. We have no definitive answers, of course, but there are other megalithic monuments — the Irish stone circles of Drombeg and Bohonagh among them — that have similar areas of compressed turf and trampled pebbles, suggesting ritualized dancing.

Off the fuchsia-lined road to Owenahincha, Drombeg Stone Circle rises pale-gray from a hillside of heather, bracken and gorse. Beside the circle stand the remains of two round huts with a stone causeway leading to a hearth, a well and a cooking trough. Visiting this wild and wind-blown spot back in 1992, I could easily imagine our ancient ancestors dancing away the seasons within the sacred precinct of their stone circle. Other circles likewise show evidence of deliberate paving or leveled gravel inside and outside of the rings.

In Celtic folk belief, fairies and witches dance inside round or ring formations to raise power or induce visionary states. As part of their legendary rituals, they also dance around prehistoric burial chambers. Could this be a folk memory of a shorter, darker people who inhabited Ireland before the Celts arrived, their dances the residue of Neolithic and Bronze Age activity? Very possibly.

Borrowing and innovation mark the cultural history of dance, which evolved into sacred groves or plazas or into the underground shrines of Pueblo kivas. Our dances through the ages have been masked, costumed or painted, like Morris Dancers or Hopi Kachinas. For luck or fertility, we've dressed our men as women. We've added flowers, rattles, flutes, drums, greenery or song, along with symbolic procreative leaps or power stomps. Before English carols became associated with Christmas, they were sung and danced in a circle to celebrate a variety of holy days — the coming of spring, for example. Along with later vernacular biblical "miracle" plays, the Mumming Play, a dance-related re-enactment of the Midwinter visit of unidentifiable beings, was the beginning of English theatre.

From Medieval Christianity forward, we've transformed early sacred dance into predominantly social forms, giving rise to the contemporary Maypole and gypsy dances of Europe, belly dancing in the Middle East, the Scottish sword dance – possibly a remnant sacrificial dance – and the hula, the ancient dance of Hawaii.

As Jill Purce writes in her book, *The Mystic Spiral*: "To each and to all it is given to dance."

TOTEMS

"(THE) SOULS OF ANIMALS INFUSE THEMSELVES
INTO THE TRUNKS OF MEN."

– WILLIAM SHAKESPEARE

The word "totem" is thought to be of Ojibwa origin and denotes a plant, animal or other object recognized as the symbol of a clan or family. Totemism is the mystical relationship or kinship between the totem and an individual or group. We may fear, imitate or hunt a totem animal, like the brown bear of North America, the wild boar of Europe or the Near East's auroch – the ancestor of domestic cattle. Our plant totems may be our principal foods, like blue corn, representing a deity of vegetation identified with the life force of procreation, birth and death.

Totemism appears to predate sedentary societies. The Swiss Drachenloch caves, for example, have revealed altars 70,000 years old dedicated to the bear. A totem's primal purpose may have been a means by which our forbearers distinguished one clan from another. But once this practical origin was forgotten, the totem name itself was used to suggest a relationship between a clan group and the totem object — frequently a dangerous being — on which the clan was dependent for survival.

Such a psychological link creates a magical, harmonious bond between a totem object, through which the sacred manifests, and those who carry its name. Through totemism, animals become our teachers and protectors, sources of ancestral power for a group that traces its descent from them through half-animal/half-human progenitors. This makes the animal a "cousin" or a "brother," applying a close family concept to a larger and more beneficial social setting.

In totemism, as in other religions, laws of control are subsequently developed, including taboos related to when and if a totem may be eaten and by whom. The regulated prohibitions and superstitions surrounding marriage between members of different clans further unite a tribe. And just as stories and legends explain the origins of Medieval crests and coats of arms, totem relationships and clan origins are expressed in myth.

Precise parallels for totems are not definitively known to have existed in the Iron Age Celtic cultures that followed the megalithic societies of our Neolithic and Bronze Age European ancestors. But the names of Celtic tribal groups such as the Scottish Clan Chattan ("Clan of the Cat"), the Caerini ("People of the Sheep"), the Epidii ("Horse People") and Brannovices ("Raven Folk") are suggestive of such a relationship. Just as native North American hunting cultures developed a connection between their material and spiritual wellbeing and the power of a specific animal, the large numbers of animal bones we've discovered in certain Neolithic tombs may imply a similar totemic veneration.

In the early twentieth century, twenty-four dog skulls and five human skulls were found at the prehistoric burial chamber of Cuween in the Orkneys. Similarly, a large collection of deer antlers was unearthed at Holm of Papa Westray North. At the Tomb of the Eagle (Isbister), also in the Orkneys, 16,000 disarticulated bones of 312 people were uncovered. Human skulls had been placed with an abundance of white sea-eagle carcasses, and there were also skeletal remains of cattle, deer and sheep. At Knowe of Yarso, a heap of excavated bones represented at least thirty people, along with the partial remains of thirty-six red deer. Twenty-six skulls had been separated and stacked neatly together. Might the red deer, the sea eagle and the dog have been symbols — totems — of the communities to which these tombs belonged?

On the other hand, in some Orkney tombs, like Unstan, where only piles of broken pottery were found scattered with the remains of five people, there were no animal remains at all. The broken pottery might simply indicate that spirit guides had been released from these objects.

The Orkney Tomb at Point of Cott held the bones of thirteen humans, along with those of cattle, rodents, fish, sheep, dogs, birds, deer and otter. The latter had likely used the tomb as a "holt," a burrowed lair. Intermingled with human remains, the Orkney chambered tomb of Blackhammer contained the bones of twenty-four sheep, along with gannet, cormorant, deer, oxen and goose. Some of these were undoubtedly nothing more than carrion dragged in by prey, or the remains of animals that had taken shelter there. Still, if totem animals *were* interred in burial mounds, we could say, with a smile, as Ronald Hutton has in his excellent book *The Pagan Religions of the Ancient British Isles*, that Blackhammer must have belonged to the "Clan of the Menagerie."

SPIRITUAL FITNESS

"To dance beneath the diamond sky with
one hand waving free."

– Bob Dylan

"One day, Ramakrishna, the nineteenth century
spiritual leader, was praying and doing his ritual,
and he suddenly had the perceptual cognition
that his ritual was meaningless because what he
was praying to **was** God, and so were the
utensils of the ritual, the idols, the floor, the
walls. Wherever he looked, he saw God in all
its infinite variety. And he was so overwhelmed
by this experience that he had no words; he just
danced for hours, he danced with exaltation."

– Gabrielle Roth

At the very least, we celebrate the human spirit when
we dance. At the highest level, where movement is
the spiritual essence of life, dance is vibrant, palpable and
unaffected. "It is where we find ourselves with God," says
Gabrielle Roth, who teaches dance as a spiritual practice.
"Turn on the radio, wherever you are. Let yourself move
with the rhythms, not with any great purpose or goal in
mind, except to feel yourself moving." This kind of dance
is empowering, passionate and liberating, emphasizing the
importance of keeping a "pagan," freethinking spirit.

Dance can also be a gift to our spirits when it is formally
structured — as with Tai Chi — or serves as exercise, as with
Jazzercise, for example. Even the concept of dance as a
metaphor can be supportive and sustaining. "I try to dance
with what life has to hand me," pop singer Stevie Nicks has
written. Dance is movement and movement is life.

What can we say about festivals and rituals but to celebrate whenever we can? Commemorate important events; observe anniversaries and feast days; acknowledge and connect with the seasons. With a few significant exceptions, such occasions almost always call for unqualified rejoicing and thanksgiving. Birthdays should be especially gratifying, as an opportunity to honor and appreciate our own unique manifestation of the Divine into the universe.

We can also celebrate spiritually with the use of fetishes in our daily lives, like a St. Christopher's Cross; talismans that represent and remind us of what we most revere. Familiar whimsical fetishes, like a horseshoe or a four-leafed clover, help us to focus, to organize our thoughts or to concentrate.

A fetish can also represent a totem animal. From a realm where there is no separation between the internal and the external world, "power animals" may come to us in dreams or through meditation. With their likenesses worn as a talisman or amulet, they not only bring us awareness of the beauty of animals in the material world and of the link between humans and our collective environment, but they can also serve as images of Divinity that bring us healing, energy, inspiration and advice.

In Native American and Celtic lore, specific animals offer specific gifts, creating a special personal bond. Working with a power animal as a totem is a personal endeavor, but here are a few more or less universal animal attributes you might consider if choosing one.

The Badger: *Tenacity*

The Bear: *Primal Power*

The Bee: *Community*

The Blackbird: *Enchantment*

The Bull: *Potency*

The Dog: *Loyalty*

The Eagle: *Courage*

The Fox: *Cunning*

The Hawk: *Nobility*

The Hind: *Gracefulness*

The Otter: *Joy, Play*

The Owl: *Wisdom*

The Rabbit: *Shyness*

The Stag: *Independence*

Chapter 10

BODY AND SOUL

"BODY AND SPIRIT ARE TWINS:
GOD ONLY KNOWS WHICH IS WHICH."

– ALGERNON CHARLES SWINBURNE

I N A SENSE, THIS LAST INTERPRETIVE section is the one most clearly connected to our own times. The use of prehistoric megalithic monuments as healing agents or as repositories of myth and legend is very much alive in our contemporary world. The magical curative properties of stones, and the stories of the mythological beings linked to them, are not limited to reflections on "big" subjects like life, death, heaven, earth and the sacred. Both are still actively with us.

Under Body, we're going to talk about aspects of stones in *healing*, both curative and prophylactic. Under Soul, we'll take a look at the *fairies*, *gods and goddesses*, *heroes* and other *"peopled" stones* that, through legend or myth, are said to inhabit or otherwise animate Neolithic and Bronze Age megalithic architecture.

BODY

"HEALING IS A MATTER OF TIME, BUT IT IS SOMETIMES
ALSO A MATTER OF OPPORTUNITY."

– HIPPOCRATES

I n many cultures, we look on sickness as a learning experience, a chance to acknowledge and then to correct an imbalance. The use of stone is not an uncommon result of such healing traditions. We've used oath stones, cursing stones, healing stones, weather stones — all of these, in one way or another — to achieve equilibrium by manipulating divine energy to more fully serve us. This reliance on stone

279

is sometimes evidenced in the very words we use to define wellness. The Irish word for physician, for example, is "lia," meaning "cures." But the word "lia" can also mean a pillar-stone, figuratively indicating the capacity of a stone to serve as a tool in healing. We have long looked on stones as guardians of our health and our well-being, as well as phallic symbols of fertility. Our veneration of stones, therefore, extends not only to healing, but also to the creation of life itself.

One of the most powerful healing stones of our past is the holed stone (PLATE 51), believed for many centuries to be particularly effective — not surprisingly — in matters of virility, fertility and childbirth as well as in the treatment and prevention of bone disorders like rickets. The Men-an-tol, a complex on Penwith Moor in Cornwall made up of several stones, one of which has now fallen, has a lengthy folklore history of such magical appeal. Until very recently, babies and young children were passed through this "female" holed stone three times for purification — a sort of rebirth to encourage good health — and for protection against rickets. Adults, seeking healing for back problems especially, were required to crawl around the stone nine times.

Over seven feet tall, the Tolvan Stone, also in Cornwall, stands behind a cottage at Tolvan Cross. In the recent past, newly married couples who successfully maneuvered their naked bodies through its seventeen-inch-wide opening — a challenging feat in our obesity-plagued times — were assured a fertile marriage. Similarly, in Brittany, the health of a newborn was believed to improve if passed through a hole in one of the megaliths of the Trie-Château dolmen. Most such stones have circular centers, though the one at Tobernaveen in County Sligo, Ireland, through which sick children were once passed in hopes of healing, has a rectangular core.

Healers through the ages have reached through a holed stone's opening to lay hands on the sick. Young people have been betrothed reciting "Wodden Prayers," while clasping hands through the opening of a holed stone, as was once done at the long-demolished Stone of Odin in the Orkneys. This ritual followed the bride making an oath to her groom at the nearby Stones of Stenness, and the groom's reciprocal pledge at the Ring of Brodgar. Occasionally, the sick still walk around the Stones of Stenness three times sun-wise, in search of healing.

Our fascinating juxtaposition of old beliefs with new was demonstrated at a holed-stone ceremony held on Ardmore Bay in Ireland in 1833. During the Festival of St. Declan, a hundred people passed through a holed stone while chanting aves and counting rosary beads. It's very possible that the bones of our prehistoric ancestors were similarly passed through the porthole entrances of some Neolithic or Bronze Age tombs, as if entering another world. As in the Celtic Cult of the Head, the skulls missing from some of these burial sites may have been those of powerful leaders whose remains were used in processions or other rituals. Considered the home of our human essence, other skulls, found shattered, may have been purposely broken to release the spirit of the deceased.

As we've already seen, water is also perceived to have magical curative properties. Well dressings and offerings are gifts to the Divine, another medium through which our ailments can be addressed. A rag tied on a nearby bush, for example, is believed to take up sickness. As it disintegrates, so does our ill health. When connected with stone, such power is augmented. We can still find cursing or curing stones placed at ancient holy wells or on altars, especially in Ireland. These stones were significant companions to other traditions of the day.

The Druids used weather stones to dry up rivers, to produce springs or to hold back rainfall, which they also *created* at times by tossing holy water in the direction from which storm clouds needed to come. The Breton legend we examined earlier, of water being tossed over the shoulder or poured over Merlin's Stone to call up a storm, clearly suggests the ageless power believed to be inherent in stone and water. The cup-and-ring markings near some megaliths may have served the same purpose, indicating a similar reverence in our prehistoric past.

In more recent times as well, standing stones were ritually washed, the water then being used for healing baths, mixed with herbs for poultices or brewed into teas. Water that had washed over the Giant's Ring, a stone circle near Belfast, was said to heal both illnesses and wounds.

In the eighteenth century, a rock basin in Grampian, Scotland, was filled with water and used for healing divination. If a worm — representing the primal healing energy of Divinity, manifested as a snake — were placed in the water and still lived when the patient arrived, he or she would also live. But if the worm were dead, that would be the supplicant's unfortunate fate as well.

Stones buried in the earth come into contact with this same divine power in its manifestation as Earth energy, just as stones left under a full moon are empowered by contact with divine energy manifested as moonlight. In all likelihood, the worship of the sun, fire, water, the moon, a tree, a spring, an animal — all of these in our ancient past — began as a focusing or a condensing of the omnipresent Divine into one simple representation of deity. Throughout history and prehistory, we may all have been acknowledging the same unknown and unknowable force; simply calling it by different names. What sets "believers" of one chosen aspect of the Divine apart from "believers" of any other is simply the contrived sense of superiority at the heart of organized religion; the sense of a "chosen people;" of a priesthood called upon to issue rules and regulations, to establish the hierarchies that impose control and keep the masses in line.

In this sense, too, the magical healing power which has been so often attributed to stone is a very ancient one. We can glimpse intriguing remnants of it in our age-old beliefs of the divine healing energy encompassed by and expressed in standing stones.

SOUL

"With us nothing has time to gather meaning, and too many things are occurring for even a big heart to hold."

— William Butler Yeats

We once *had* time for things to gather meaning. The stories our ancestors told about the beings that populated, connected with or otherwise animated prehistoric megalithic stone architecture – the gods and goddesses, heroes, giants, fairies and "peopled stones" of the following pages – all fall into the realm of myth, legend or folktale. By definition, they have gathered meaning through longevity, the retelling of their stories serving as a link between the past and the present; a way to impart cultural lessons or explain the unknown.

The Merriam-Webster Dictionary tells us that a myth is "a usually legendary narrative that presents part of the beliefs of a people or explains a practice or natural phenomenon." A legend is "a story coming down from the past, especially one popularly accepted as historical though not verifiable." A folktale is a tale "of, relating to or originating among the common people." Some of our legends and folktales may have begun as myths, and a single anecdote might fit into more than one category. For the most part, we have no way of knowing the specific mindset or intention of the people who created them. We simply know that each is a *story* that has survived the test of time, passed down through generations for a specific, though perhaps forgotten, purpose.

Myths serve a great many functions for us. They may be early attempts to explain our natural environment – celestial bodies, growth cycles, weather. They may be lyrical expressions from our earliest visionary shamanic cultures, the meaning of which we've long lost to time. They may be interpreted as the direct wisdom of Divinity, symbols of a universal collective unconscious, spiritual intuitions or instructional models governing individual behavior or group membership. Myths may be all of these. And we may often apply myth as readily to the present as to the past. Specific individuals pass, but the structure and inspiration of an extraordinary life remains.

In today's world, myths have often been turned into something negative. We too often see them as complete falsehoods, while, in reality, they speak the language of the spirit, metaphorically expressing profound universal truths. As sacred stories, they legitimize the rituals or customs that bring our communities together, while giving us allegorical explanations for otherwise incomprehensible ideas like gods, creation, death, the afterlife, kinship, fertility, kingship and evil. They also address the allegorical origin or discovery of elements and essences, such as fire, light or water that have had a profound effect on civilization's development.

In their spiritual context, we can only recite myths in sacred time and space, with specific storytellers as the designated voice. When myths *are* recounted, it is with no mere static observance. Myth is a kind of prayer, a recitation that recreates our world and takes it back to a state of primordial spiritual equilibrium. Certain myths of the Far East are prime illustrations of this. For example, the Dragon of Heaven and the Tiger of Earth – dual opposites of nature – are believed to have manifested from the same divine source. Every part of creation reflects some aspect of the fluctuating relationship between these equal energies, their relationships described through myth. Our goal in reciting them is the achievement of the balance and counterbalance of The Beginning.

Our deity and hero tales almost always contain the stuff of myth. Some scholars speculate that both of these may have originated in shamanic journeys. Hero tales, which usually tell of initiation or spiritual awakening through death and rebirth, might be traced to insight gathered on shamanic journeys, wisdom that was then fine-tuned for widespread education or enlightenment. Significantly, elements of hero training, like feats of magic, almost always mirror the action of a shaman. Over time, the shaman became the hero or the god of myth.

We can see a similar chain of transformation in the concept of witch flight. This ability – rooted in the "night flights" of Celtic shamans into other worlds – probably goes back, in turn, to Roman rituals in the north of Italy that involved, appropriately enough, the night flights of the moon goddess, Diana. The Iron Age Celtic goddess, Epona, took over the night flight tradition, presiding over the after-life with a herd of sacred foals.

The gods and heroes associated with standing stones, or said to be living in prehistoric chambered tombs, may have a similar connotation, a collective memory of our prehistoric ancestors – royal, shamanic or otherwise – who, their bones buried in mounds, became revered as god-like or heroic spirits.

The same can be said for legend, which probably has some fragment of truth at its heart – especially the fantastical adventures of heroic personages like Arthur, Ulysses, Gilgamesh and Beowulf. Legend is collective and carries within it, through the centuries, the wisdom, love, joy, fear and despair of all those people who lived in a specific land or region. In legend, we preserve the memory of people, places or events and embroider them with enchantment, vision and romantic glamour.

A legend surrounding the construction of the megalithic complex of Callanish is typical of this tendency. Callanish, according to this particular tale, is the work of the slaves of a priest/king who arrived on the Hebridean coast, robed in garments made of mallard duck feathers and accompanied by many ships. Perhaps such a story reflects a folk memory of one of the island's actual secular/spiritual leaders, a formidable personage who, backed by a significant retinue, directed the construction of the Callanish complex as a focus for some divine purpose now long forgotten. Water birds and feathered clothing are still associated with healing, healing centers and sun worship. Are such relationships hinted at in this Hebridean legend? We will never know for certain if rituals like those described in this tale took place among the stone builders of our prehistoric past, but the story does suggest some very real, very significant ancient experience.

Our folktales, full of simplicity, are most often seen as just plain good stories. They are "the very voice of the people, the very pulse of life," the poet W. B. Yeats wrote. Up until the very recent past, Irish storytellers—"Seanachie," pronounced "Shawn-ah-key"—would still gather to recite versions of the same story, voting on the acceptability of alternatives. In this way—as in all oral tradition—a long tale, like the tragic story of "Dierdre of the Sorrows," was recited almost word for word for centuries. A tale being told in the early nineteenth century was essentially the same one recorded in ancient manuscripts.

All around the world, folktales demonstrate great similarities in theme and story lines, suggesting dissemination by tribes, traders or other travelers who carried with them entertaining and universally adaptable stories of the brave and the virtuous, the wise and the crafty. Parallel stories, recited from untold antiquity generation after generation, might be a natural consequence of a common stage of our cultural development, a time when social behavior, moral conduct or taboos needed to be clearly defined.

By contrast, many of the legends and folktales involving the prehistoric stone monuments of Europe reflect Christianity's struggle to supplant and overpower our ancient beliefs (PLATE 52). Some story lines detail the threatening or challenging activities of a devil or a giant endangering the pious. Others represent, with "peopled stones," examples of the punishments incurred for a desecration of the Sabbath. Whatever their message, the intent of these dogmatic stories was the same – to replace traditional "pagan worship" with strict religious conformity. An exception to this subjugation is the survival of the "fairy story," which was often limited to a village or even a specific personality. This localization prevented any broader geographical influence, which may be why so many such fairy tales managed to survive intact.

As we know, myth, legend and folktale all overlap. The separation of stories into one form or another is the product of our contemporary thinking. Though we can't always put the subject of these stories neatly into one category or the other, we *can* look at gods and goddesses, heroes, fairies and "peopled stones," in a combined context, as we'll see in the following pages.

GODS AND GODDESSES

*"THE NEWGRANGE OF MYTHOLOGY . . .
is not a place of human habitation.
It is the domain of the gods."*

– MARTIN BRENNAN

The prehistoric megaliths of our European ancestors have been associated with gods and goddesses for many centuries. The Greek historian and geographer Strabo wrote in the first century BCE that ancient standing stones, grouped in threes or fours, were used by the indigenous inhabitants of the Iberian Peninsula for daytime rituals. These stones were "turned round by those who visit the place," who, "after pouring a libation, moved back again." Believed to be occupied by the gods by night, the stones were then considered out of bounds.

More recently, the myths and legends of the Iron Age Celts ascribe a similar divine habitation to megalithic monuments. Irish accounts tell us that the goddess of the River Boyne – Boand – lived in Newgrange, a burial mound within the ancient site of Brú na Bòinne. According to myth, the Celtic solar deity known as The Dagda stole inside and impregnated Boand, who then gave birth to Óengus, the Irish god of love. In the Irish Fenian Cycle, the warrior Finn describes Newgrange as the "house of Óengus of the Brú." Incidentally, the Irish king Cormac mac Airt, a convert to Christianity, refused to be buried there. Given the monument's position as a pre-Christian cemetery, perhaps he feared some divine retribution in the afterlife.

Newgrange is aligned to the Winter Solstice sunrise. It seems fitting then that Newgrange became the home of Óengus, whose father, at Óengus' conception, was said to have made the sun stand still for the nine months prior to

288

his birth. Eternally youthful, Óengus is thus known as a solar deity who personifies the day. The son/sun of the New Year is born of Mother Earth at the lengthening of days. Nearby Knowth is connected with Englec, Óengus' lover. While at Dowth, believed to be the oldest passage tomb of the Brú na Bòinne, the druid Bresial tried to build a Babel-styled tower to reach heaven. Notably, Dowth is sometimes referred to as Síd Bresial, "síd" denoting a dwelling place of gods.

In Celtic literature, the earliest inhabitants of Ireland were supernatural. Their gods were human. The Tuatha Dé Dannan, "the People of Light," for example, was an ancient Irish race overcome by Milesian invaders. Once defeated, they were driven into the hills to live underground as gods and/or fairies, in raths and mounds.

Crom Cruach or Crom Dubh, another ancient Irish deity, likewise has a direct connection to prehistoric stones. Also known as "Black Crom," Crom Cruach was a deity with strong eastern connections who had a stone idol erected to him in County Cavan by one of the early Irish high kings. A standing stone sheeted in gold, this image was surrounded by a circle of twelve stone "assistants" covered in silver. Many of the stone circles of our Bronze Age forbearers are likewise comprised of twelve evenly spaced stones. The annual Croagh Patrick pilgrimage, originally associated with Crom Dubh, involves a climb up the mountain of Croagh Patrick – a hill nicknamed "The Reek" – on Reek Sunday, the last Sunday in July. After reaching the summit, pilgrims – mostly men and often barefoot and even shirtless – celebrate the ascent with the ritualistic circling of a group of standing stones. Although a seam of gold was discovered in the mountainside during the 1980s, mining of the County Mayo site has been prohibited.

Numerous gods and goddesses of our prehistoric past may well have had stone-based observances similar to Black Crom's. However, the religion of the Iron Age Celts was intensely localized and not widely documented. Of the 375 noted Gallic deities, 305 appear only once in the era's historical record.

HEROES

All nations and tribal groups have heroes – legendary rulers, sages, saints or warriors; founders of faiths, lineages and settlements – to whom we ascribe exceptional attributes and abilities. Through the power of our collective imaginations, these heroes become larger-than-life giants. The evolution of this "hero cult," as an elemental idea, probably occurred spontaneously around the world. Specific heroes may have originated in one community and spread through trade or travel. Perhaps migrating tribes adopted the hero cults of the communities they encountered. However it developed, our tendency toward "hero worship" is universal.

The word "hero" comes from the Greek "heros" – plural "heroes" – a word whose etymology is unknown. Heros, as used in *The Iliad* and *The Odyssey*, refers to a man of great courage, strength, dignity, willpower and loyalty; often descended, in whole or in part, from some Divinity. Our notion of a hero changes with time and the cultural environment, though in its classic sense, a hero is differentiated from purely "heroic" action, such as the rescue of a child by a parent. The former is a distinct personality; the latter a specific action.

Heroic or epic literature generally derives from an early phase in civilization's history – a Heroic Age, during which humans were said to mingle with the gods. Considered by Greeks to be one of the five Ages of Man, this era depicts the adventures of a group of people whose heroic acts were said to mark the development of human societies. Through long winter nights, generation after generation, our ancestors told tales from a glorious past that quite possibly had some basis in fact. However, these stories were embellished over time to become allegorical legends.

When societies place trust in a specific leader, his or her followers find it difficult to discount the heroic aid rendered, even after the leader's death. Held by enchantment and so never completely gone, these undying heroes are willed to return to conquer new enemies or restore peace. After all, isn't it our overriding hope that goodness will overcome evil? We can find undying heroes like Robin Hood, King Arthur and Owen Glendower in most European cultures. *Gilgamesh, Beowulf, The Nibelungenlied, The Poetic Edda, The Icelandic Sagas, The Mabinogion, The Red Branch* — all of these are epic or heroic narratives in prose or poetry that recount the trials of our divinely descended champions.

Epic literature, much of which we've now lost, falls into one of three basic categories that generally overlap or grow from one another. The first group, prominent among so-called "primitive" cultures, concerns the purely mythical — the formation of an orderly world, usually by gods and their offspring, at the beginning of time. As culture heroes, the protagonists of these stories generally lose their influence as formulated religious beliefs take hold. Usually concerned with chaotic power struggles surrounding creation, these epics are ritualistic, beyond the scope of history. They feature cosmology, the birth of ancient divinities and warfare with later cycles of gods. They also encompass the ordering of the heavens, the Earth and the nether regions. The Greek Prometheus, who stole fire from the gods, can be seen as just such a hero. Prometheus, whose name translates as "forethought," was the son of Iapetus, one of the six Titan gods who ruled the cosmos before the ascent of the Olympians lead by Zeus. Prometheus was given the task of molding mankind out of clay. His devotion to his creation was such that he risked severe punishment for his theft of fire from the gods.

The second category of epic literature involves the hero of the quest or the voyage of discovery. These epics likely had their origin in the "dying god" or "dying goddess" of our Neolithic past, the never-ending birth, death and rebirth of the Earth's fertility. This divine cycle became associated with humanity's primordial memory of hunting rituals, in which our ancestors mirrored the wanderings of historic figures, totemic animals or ancestral deities. *Gilgamesh* of Mesopotamia, the earliest known hero of this type, probably grew out of the creation myths of the meandering Sumerian goddess Inanna, the Queen of Heaven (Ishtar), as she searched for her husband, Dumuzi.

Ishtar's quest included a descent into the underworld that recreated the annual death and rebirth of vegetation, just as the Greek goddess Demeter would later search annually for her daughter, Persephone. Such quest epics may also relate rites of passage — to manhood, for example — as they probably do in *The Odyssey*, which also features a descent into the underworld. Tales like these, which include *Beowulf* and *The Ramayana* from India, appear to reach back to the shamanic journeys of our Neolithic past. These heroes worked in company with nature, suffered loss, did battle with monsters and eventually achieved some emotional, spiritual or psychological transformation that brought them a new more harmonious life, a new world view or a new way of thinking. They were reborn.

The third hero category in epic literature involves the "heroic warfare" of historic migrations. In our European past, these developed from our Indo-European-speaking ancestors of the second millennium BCE, as they poured out of India and the Aegean world northward into Central Europe. This heroic tradition is one of transition and, like *The Iliad*, is generally independent of ritual, though it does have a legendary or mythological background. Within this genre, warriors, directed by the gods for good or for evil, struggled toward a destiny determined mostly by their own characters and personalities. Their battles were intensified by the warfare that surrounded them, and nature was subordinate to their personal triumphs and sorrows.

Produced in times of political instability, these heroic epics rely on individuality and independence. The King Arthur legends, with their loyalty conflicts and background of historical Saxon/Briton warfare, fit into this category. Such tales may also feature an embedded sword, a theme common to the Norse god Odin, as well as to both King Arthur and Galahad. This symbolism might stretch further back to a sword-god carving in a Hittite burial at Yasilikaya, Turkey, dating to about 1200 BCE. As epics of heroic warfare and adventure become more distanced from our everyday lives, we attribute to them the marvels and romance of far-off lands or, as in the case of Medieval Europe, of courts of chivalry.

Our greatest heroic epics are free of tribe or place. They rise above nationality and focus instead on the individual. Their heroes may be of noble birth, but the adventure itself is a journey of self-discovery. The hero's path mirrors and exaggerates our common rites of passage, such as birth, puberty, marriage, death and burial. The hero — as Everyman —ventures from our everyday world into a place of supernatural wonder, where otherworldly powers are dealt with, including a passage through darkness; descending into the "belly of the whale," so to speak. After enduring immense hardship, the hero returns with some gift for humankind, as did Aeneas, Jason and Prometheus.

A hero's return to society, however, may be difficult, misunderstood or even denied. Tribal or local heroes, such as Moses or the Aztec Tezcatlipoca, bring boons specific to their people or their tribes; universal heroes like Jesus or Buddha bring gifts the whole world can use. The hero/seeker and whatever treasure is found become one, inner and outer manifestations of the same divine mystery. "The great deed of the supreme hero," wrote American mythologist Joseph Campbell, "is to come to the knowledge of this unity in multiplicity and then to make it known; release the flow of life into the body of the world."

Most of our concepts of heroism dismiss women altogether or make them subordinate or peripheral. The *man*, Prometheus, stole fire from the gods and became a hero. By contrast, the *woman*, Eve, ate the apple and became an unholy evil. This attitude still influences what we think of as "appropriate" heroism for women, the criteria we use to raise our children and how we deal with women's wisdom or purity. Even in the present day — and certainly throughout much of history — a woman's place is too often considered secondary in a man's world; as a victim, reward, assistant, decoy or scapegoat. The role of "woman" is still too often seen as a means to further or flatter male heroism.

Similarly, we also still see heroism most often as the sensational, as physical strength, bravado and daring rather than quiet diplomacy, compromise and patience. Traditional male heroes separated themselves from home and family, while women generally worked to preserve them. This "women's work," such as American women pioneering in the Old West, is still too often seen as mundane, when it was actually essential to life itself. Though their sacrifices and courage have not been historically lauded, the truth is that women have been heroic in all ages. They've had to be.

Folklore condenses time to conform to our heroic legends. This accounts for the name "Queen Maeve's Tomb"

(PLATE 53) being given to a prehistoric burial chamber on Knocknarea Mountain in Ireland. The tomb's construction actually took place in the Neolithic Era, much earlier than Queen Maeve's Iron Age days, but its name was inherited after the legendary queen was said to have been buried there, dressed in full battle regalia.

Another example of folklore's penchant for condensing time is found in the Neolithic burial chamber called Arthur's Stone (PLATE 54) on the Gower Peninsula in Wales. According to legend, King Arthur found the stone – the twenty-five ton capstone of the tomb – in his boot as he traveled to the battle of Camlann in CE 539. He removed the irritation and tossed it over his shoulder. It landed on the high sandstone ridge of Cefn Bryn. King Arthur's Stone is the name given to another Neolithic burial chamber near Clehonger, also in Wales. (PLATE 55).

On the other hand, the Eightercua Alignment in County Kerry, Ireland, is known as the burial place of the wife of Amergin, poet-chief of the legendary Milesian invaders of Ireland. According to the Irish annals, the Milesians arrived on the island about 1700 BCE, a time well within bounds for the actual building of Eightercua.

FAIRIES

"CAROLAN SLEPT UPON A FAERY RATH.
EVER AFTER THEIR TUNES
RAN IN HIS HEAD, AND MADE HIM
THE GREAT MUSICIAN HE WAS."

– WILLIAM BUTLER YEATS

The word "fairy" did not appear in our language until the Middle Ages, and it was originally applied most often to a mortal woman with magical powers. The flowing robes and gossamer wings of today's Walt Disney creations come mainly from Shakespearean literature, where fairies were most often depicted poetically as the dainty, delicate, richly dressed and magical denizens of nature.

Derived from the Latin "fatum," meaning "fate," the Middle English concept of "faierie" or "fairyland" refers to a state of enchantment that was eventually assigned to supernatural beings or "fairies." We'd long known these as pixies or pisgies in Cornwall, brownies in lowland Scotland, peights in the Orkney Islands, korrigans in Brittany and elves, dwarfs and trolls in Scandinavia.

Our folklore cautions that most of these hidden people are ignored at great peril, even in modern times. In Iceland in the late 1970s, a medium was consulted to handle "elves" who, because of constant mishaps on a job site, were believed to have objections to blasting during road construction near the city of Akureyri. On the outskirts of Reykjavik, another road crew carefully relocated a "dwarf-owned" boulder known as Grasteinn that thwarted the expansion of a highway. Without such attention, workers believed, the costs of construction could double – employees might sicken, machines might malfunction.

In the Scottish Highlands, fairies are known as the Sith, (pronounced "shee"). In Ireland, they are called the Daoine Sidhe ("theena shee"), the Folk of the Mounds. These terms come from the East Indian word "siddhi," meaning "something which controls the elements." Fairies themselves apparently prefer to be called "The Good Neighbors," "The Good Folk," "The Sealie Court," "The Strangers," "The Gentry" and so forth. Though our "fairy" terminology may differ, there are common themes in our viewpoints.

Three basic theories account for the development of

our fairy beliefs. These involve the dead, ancient races and dwindled gods. Of course, all of these can overlap and mingle. As we've already seen, the burial cairns of our Neolithic and Bronze Age farming ancestors had a strong connection with death. Since the dead, it was believed, may either protect or punish survivors, their appeasement was essential. Soul-sized, the spirits of the Neolithic and Bronze Age dead may have evolved into the small-in-stature Celtic Sidhe. In the Highlands, "second sight," a fairy gift that enables some of us to communicate with the Sidhe, may have begun with the state of altered consciousness a shaman used to approach our ancestral dead. This talent may have been common among our very early forbearers, originating as a shamanic ability. Fairies might also reflect a belief in fallen angels or in elemental spirits whom the dead eventually joined in order to bring us their wisdom and power.

Some of our dead may also be, of course, an ancient race. The fairy-like creatures of the Scottish Orkney Islands, for example, are known as "peight," from "Pict," the ancient pre-Celtic, presumably indigenous, people of eastern Scotland.

In the third theory of the origin of fairies, we see them as waning gods or fading nature spirits who live in caves, springs or ancient burial chambers called fairy hills. As abandoned beings, we've reduced them in our popular imagination to mere physical smallness. In Ireland, fairies are considered the survivors of an ancient prehistoric immortal race called the Tuatha Dé Dannan, the children of the goddess Danu, They are slight, dark-complexioned people who, when conquered by Milesian invaders, took refuge in hills, glens and forests and under "the hollow hills," the fairy mounds of prehistoric cairns, barrows and huts.

Our Bronze Age ancestors built circular wattle and daub huts sunk two to three feet into the ground, and roofed them with turf on which grass, bracken or even small bushes grew. These had the appearance of small hills or mounds, in which fairies, as members of that ancient race of gods, were said to live. There they became the earth spirits, nature spirits and elementals who directed the growth cycles of the land. One of these monuments, Newgrange, was one of the primary fairy palaces of the Tuatha Dé Dannan, a place where visitors might encounter the fairy folk and gain the wisdom of venerated ancestors, vanished races or elemental spirits.

To be abducted by fairies – known as "taken by fairies" or "stepping on a stray sod" to the Celts – is like taking a shamanic journey into the spirit world. The "victim" is lured by fairies and falls into a deep sleep, often brought on by the singing of magical birds. A resulting illness or depression – said to last about seven years – is blamed on the work of fairies. The Celtic hero Cúchulain, for example, was fairy struck as he slept near a standing stone. Two fairy women – the birds he was hunting – caused him to fall into a great sickness for a year. The day before Samhain, a visitor arrived with a pledge to cure the hero if he would accept an invitation to visit the stranger's daughters in the Otherworld. Cúchulain returned to the menhir at which he'd been sleeping when the fairy women had first appeared. One of them came again and carried him off in a "boat of bronze" to the Otherworld of the Sidhe, from which he returned cured. In traditional cultures, such attention from the fairies would be a call to become a shaman. If such a shamanic call is rejected, the target of a fairy's summons could become severely lethargic or even die.

Fairies have had a lengthy and imaginative connection with all manner of prehistoric megalithic architecture. Fairies were said to have delivered the red shale boulders that make up the Roche aux Fées, or Fairies' Rock, at Esse, France, from an outcrop three miles away. One of the stones, the nearby Menhir of Rumfort, was dropped and left behind in the process. Also in Brittany, Merlin the Magician's tomb is a megalithic ruin in the Brocéliande woods. Nearby, another such ruin is said to house the fairy, Vivian, whom the poet Robert Wilbur called "a creature to bewitch a sorcerer."

Similarly, dolmens in Brittany are thought to shelter others of the korrigans, the fairies or dwarf-like spirits of Breton folklore. Stones like the one where the Irish hero Cúchulain dozed, mark spots of powerful Earth currents connected to the fairy underworld. It is said that fairies regularly dance inside stone circles, around single standing stones and beside ancient burial chambers.

One typical fairy tale is taken from Janet and Colin Bord's *Ancient Mysteries of Britain.* "Willy Howe in Humberside is a prominent round barrow which housed a fairy dwelling, seen by a drunken villager late one night. He heard people singing and went to see who it was. Through an open door in the side of the mound, he could see people banqueting at large tables. One of the people saw him and offered him a cup. He took it but threw away the contents, not wishing to come under the spell of the fairies, and ran off with the goblet, which was made of an unknown material."

Such stories suggest that fairies and their many colorful counterparts may be one more way by which our ancestors creatively expressed the manifestation of the Divine into the universe. Such explanations of supernatural involvement in the human experience remain in our cultural psyche today.

PEOPLED STONES

"THE DEVIL GOT ON THE VERY TOP OF THIS PEAKED HILL
AND SANG OUT 'AULBORO TOWN
I WILL DING DOWN,' WHICH HE ACCORDINGLY DID,
WITH HUGE BOLTS OF STONE OF WHICH
THE INCREDULOUS MAY SEE NO LESS THAN THREE STICK-
ING BOLT UPRIGHT IN THE
GROUND NEAR THE DOOMED AND MISERABLE TOWN."

– JOSEPH PENNELL

"IT IS LEFT BY TRADITIONE THAT THESE [CALLANISH]
WERE A SORT OF MEN
CONVERTED INTO STONES BY ANE INCHANTER."

– JOHN MORISON (1680)

C ountry dwellers of even our most recent past
traveled very little. As a result, they developed
strong attachments to and familiarity with the forests,
springs, pools, hills and standing stones of their immediate
surroundings. Thus, they produced tales to explain the
origin of unusual features in the landscape, including ancient
burial chambers and stone circles.

We find tales of "peopled stones" in many forms. The
veneration of stones as power sources essential to a
community's well-being may have played a significant role in
our prehistory. But as time passed, we lost our understanding
of this role. Tradition, however, held the stones to be sacred,
and our forbearers peopled them with spirits and other
entities. Some tales were probably inspired by a stone's
shape or a specific grouping. To give just one example,
during a recent visit to the two squat stone circles on

Dartmoor known as Grey Wethers, it became immediately apparent to me why legend has long identified these circles as petrified sheep. But for the distant grouping of these stones, the moorland is flat and grassy and as I looked over the heath, the Grey Wethers undoubtedly resembled a gathered flock. In fact, one Grey Wethers legend claims they were once sold as such to a passing stranger, who having overindulged in drink at the nearby Warren House Inn, misidentified them through the moorland mist and bought the lot of them.

We've attributed other stones to famous people such as King Arthur, Robin Hood and even Oliver Cromwell. Wayland's Smithy's Chambered Tomb, for example, housed a well-known tenth century blacksmith. A horse and a coin left outside this ancient Ridgeway Path grave were supposedly taken in by the legendary Wayland the Smith; the horse to be shod and the coin in payment.

Most "peopled stones" belong to one of four basic story lines, two of them contrived by Christianity to usurp the power of "pagan" sites, to denigrate them or to discourage people from gathering at them. The first story line involves the devil. In tales surrounding the Devil's Arrows of North Yorkshire, the devil is said to have thrown stones at the town of Aldborough, shouting "Borobrigg keep out o' way, for Aldborough town I will ding down!" In the Orkneys, the Dwarfie Stane on the Isle of Hoy (PLATE 56) is said to be the result of the devil having hurled boulders at believers and their church. Some time later, a local dwarf named Trollid supposedly moved into the Dwarfie Stane, giving it its present name.

According to Yorkshire legend, Britain's tallest monolith, Rudston — weighing forty tons and standing twenty-five feet, nine-inches tall — was similarly flung by the devil in an attempt to demolish the parish church of All Saints in the tiny village of Rudston. Setting legendary interpretation aside, the lofty stone, a slab of moor-grit conglomerate has two possible origins. It was either hauled up from nearby Cayton Bay, or it was dragged down from the adjacent Cleveland Hills. Erected between 1600 BCE and 2000 BCE, the massive monolith probably extends as far down into the earth as it rises above it.

I reached Rudston, just out of Bridlington in Yorkshire, on a warm and windy day in mid-August 2009, just as the church clock chimed four o'clock. Smoothly tapered and capped with metal to protect it from erosion, the stone soars above a sea of grave slabs, one smaller prehistoric grit stone marker and a slab cyst grave. At its base, I found a small collection of coins and a glass-enclosed candle. The literal and figurative high point of Rudston's peaceful churchyard, the monolith clearly seems to mark prehistoric holy ground.

The second category of tales of peopled stones concerns animated stones that dance, talk, wash, drink, walk or otherwise have life. Such stories might reflect a time when our ancestors made use of stones or mounds to manipulate natural Earth currents. The standing stone of St. Martin-d-Arce, for example, is said to turn at midnight. Culey-le-Patry moves at the sound of a crowing rooster. According to ancient lore, the alignments at Carnac — said to be 3000 Roman legionnaires turned to stone for pursuing St. Cornelius — go down to the sea for a swim on occasion, and the standing stones at Plouhinec take a drink from the river at midnight on Christmas Eve. In contemporary society, we can no longer fathom such personification of the inanimate. However, these beliefs were not discounted for many generations.

The third story line ascribed to peopled stones involves the work of giants or wizards. As country folk in the Middle Ages, our forbearers could not possibly accept that such thoughtful arrangements of huge and unwieldy boulders could be the work of mere humans. There had to be other forces at work. Stonehenge, they presumed, was built by the magician Merlin. Tre'r Ceiri in Gwynedd, an arrangement in Wales, means literally, "the Town of Giants" and is named after its supposed creators. In Ireland, the seven stones of Lissyviggeen are considered the stony offspring of giants. Similarly, the central stones of Callanish (PLATE 57) were viewed as thirteen local giants – the "Fir Bhreige" or "False Men"– who'd been turned to stone for rejecting the Christian faith. On that same windy day when I first encountered Callanish, the sun, slipping in and out of clouds in a watery sky, made deep shadows of the stones, turning them, in my mind's eye, into hunched giants draped in long black robes. Although I knew in a literal sense that the image was no more than my imagination, I was momentarily transported in time to an era long ago when such conjecture seemed much more real.

As we see in two Irish burial chambers – the Great and Small Griddles of the Fianna – heroes may *become* giants. The passage of time often gives a boost to both legend and physical stature. Of the now forgotten throngs who once walked the hills worldwide, often only the "giants" are remembered in myth, legend and folklore. "There were giants in the earth in those days," the Bible says. If by "giant," our ancestors meant superior intellect, knowledge or supernatural wisdom, could the standing stones of our ancestors and the tales they spun hint at some prehistoric local power spot, Earth current or magical spring that impacted the development of civilization? Perhaps we could answer such questions if only more evidence remained.

In contrast to the lore of giants, animated stones and acts of the devil, the fourth of the themes concerning peopled stones involves abuse of the Christian Sabbath. Some of the most prominent yarns we tell are connected to Sabbath Day violations and their exacting consequences. The Hurlers of Bodmin Moor (PLATE 58), for example, are personified as gamesters turned into stone for playing on that holy day. Long Meg and her Daughters are said to be a coven of witches turned to stone for gathering in defiance of Christian authority. (PLATE 59); Stanton Drew, a wedding party for which the devil himself played fiddler, was likewise in violation of proper Holy Day observation. Although it began innocently enough, the Stanton Drew celebration continued into the early hours of the Sabbath. By dawn, the legend says, 'the revelers had all turned to stone.

Similarly, at Neant-sur-Yvel in Brittany, St. Meen is charged with changing drunken monks into rock. The Merry Maids — along with their nearby Pipers — were all petrified for dancing on the Sabbath, as were the young women who danced at vespers at Langon and St. Just in Brittany. A Bristol priest who'd neglected mass was likewise turned to stone, his fate an everlasting reminder of Heaven's punitive wrath. To our Medieval ancestors, such stories were prime fodder for sermonizing about "the wages of sin." The fear of petrified damnation undoubtedly inspired a greater level of compliance to the doctrine of the day.

SPIRITUAL FITNESS

"It does me no injury for my neighbor
to say there are twenty gods or no god.
It neither picks my pocket nor breaks my leg."

– Thomas Jefferson

"We must restore the ability we had as children
to see the heroic in the everyday.

– Miriam Polster

304

"THE HERO IS SYMBOLICAL OF THAT DIVINE CREATIVE
AND REDEMPTIVE IMAGE WHICH IS HIDDEN
WITHIN US ALL, ONLY WAITING TO BE KNOWN
AND RENDERED INTO LIFE."

– JOSEPH CAMPBELL

"For the One who has become many, remains the One undivided," St. Symeon the Younger wrote many centuries ago. The individual – all individuals – with the world itself, seem eternally interconnected through the manifestation of divinity. Yet in our modern world, religion is too often dogmatic and divisive, lacking in any spiritual significance.

A good place for us to begin to recognize the Divine in our world is to appreciate the heroic in our everyday lives. "God will bring people and events into our lives," said Father Thomas Keating, "and whatever we may think about them, they are designed for the evolution of his life in us."

Can you identify and acknowledge one person or one event in which a divine plan has manifested in your life? If not, consider that spiritual inspiration and heroes are everywhere, more numerous and diverse than popular stereotypes would have us believe. People of integrity, spirit and courage, our heroes may be our mentors, guides, teachers and parents, whose influence is individual and sometimes instantaneous. They empower us daily through their encouragement and unwavering examples.

Our heroes may be our role models, close to home or far away. Not every hero needs to undertake a great quest to be worthy of our admiration. Sometimes it's better just to work with what's at hand. "You've got to live with your dreams. Don't make them so hard," Bono of the Irish rock band U2 has written. All we need is for heroism to oppose whatever depletes life, to inspire us to accept both our responsibilities and the consequences of our own actions.

The concept of healing discussed earlier provides us with an opportunity for positive thinking. Create your own affirmations and always express them in the present tense. Let go of a bad habit. Be more open with yourself, more "wholistic." Practice meditation, tai chi, yoga or some other exercise that brings balance and harmony. On a simpler level, storytelling, if only for fun, helps families bond.

Keep a personal journal. Get to know your body and your own thought processes better. When we become aware of what brings us happiness, personal fulfillment and the realization of our goals and dreams, we improve our relationships by becoming more cognizant of the needs and wants of others. We can all be heroes, in harmony, body and soul.

Epilogue

Stones of Memory

"Greetings to you, sun of the seasons,
as you travel the skies on high, with your
strong steps on the wing of the heights; you are
the happy mother of the stars.
You sink down in the perilous ocean without
harm and without hurt;
you rise up on the quiet wave
like a young queen in flower."

– Traditional Scottish Folk Prayer

"Truth is one; the sages call it by many names."

– The Rigveda

In a rare, black-velvet sky, I watch a broad and bluish shimmer of stars, thick and brilliant, dip down to wash the ancient monoliths of Callanish. The full moon rises, and in that moment, when a silver luster crosses the highland grass and settles on stone faces, old stories become real again and very near.

For untold generations, through the long centuries, this same curtain of moonlight and darkness has dropped down out of the hills, bringing civilizations through the ages the same indistinct shadows in place of the colors of day. The scene has the same familiar singularity to us today that it had for the long-dead fishermen, farmers, warriors and others who lingered to watch so long ago. In it, we feel the remarkable permanence of beliefs that profoundly stirred

307

our human imagination. We sense a unity across time and space.

The standing stones and burial chambers of our Neolithic and Bronze Age past have this to tell us and more. They encourage our boundless appreciation of the natural world — of wood and wave, rhythm and rainbow, of sunsets and seasons and sacred space. They help us understand that we've had, from the earliest of times, an innate sense of the unity and divinity of all things. The sun, the moon, the stars, our ancient Earth Mothers, Earth energy, fire, water, light — all of these are manifestations of the same divinity expressed over time and place. The idea of essential Oneness; God in the trees.

Rabbi Lawrence Kushner expressed this basic truth when he wrote, "There's a very compelling metaphor I heard first from [the philosopher] Jacob Needleman. He says that there is a mountain, and the mountain is very high, and the top of the mountain is being with God. But because the mountain is so high, its base is so big that it is in several different climate zones. And people have different traditions for how to climb the mountain. People in the tropical climate have a tradition that says wear short pants and pith helmet and mosquito netting. And people in arctic climates have a tradition that says you wear a snow parka and goggles and boots.

"When the people in the tropical climates get about halfway up the mountain, it gets a little chilly and they have to go back for a sweater. And when the people from the arctic climates get about halfway up, it's getting a little bit warmer, and they shed their outer layer of clothing. When they get to the top, of course, everybody's dressed the same way. The problem is when people walk around the base of the mountain and argue about how to dress."

In our present world, we argue an awful lot about how to dress. Our prehistoric ancestors had their own view of the mountain and how to climb it, a view as valid at its simple, truthful core as any other. All societies have the same basic impulse to see the Divine in our natural world, to be touched with awe and wonder. Our call to return to this ancient precept is part of the legacy of standing stones.

We give value to these structures of our Neolithic and Bronze Age forbearers not only for their intrinsic beauty, but for that sense of spiritual continuity. We, too, can be alive in the present, revel in our journey rather than in our destination. "This is the day the Lord hath made," the Psalmist wrote. "We will rejoice and be glad in it."

In our recent past, seventeenth century material astronomy focused a reason-based attention on the heavens. Views of the nineteenth century emphasized the Earth's practical biology; the twentieth century, anthropology and the psychology of our human condition. Effectively, we buried the old mysteries. We stowed away their force and their function.

In examining the standing stones and prehistoric burial chambers of our past, however, we have uncovered mystery and message on many levels. Through them, we can rediscover the inexhaustible, multifaceted and wonderfully divine existence that is the life in all of us.

Glossary

Alignment: a series of standing stones in a straight line, in avenues, fans or single lines.

Anti-chamber: the front portion of a tomb separate from the chamber.

Antiquary: a student of ancient relics.

Barrow: an artificial tumulus or mound of earth, chalk or turf construction used to cover one or more burials; probably from an Old English word meaning "small hill." Many barrows contain cairns.

Cairn: an artificial mound of a megalithic tomb covered or once covered by pebbles or small stones; "a heap of stones." Most extant cairns are in Wales and Scotland.

Causewayed Enclosure: a circular ditch interrupted by causeways to form a broken ring.

Chambered Tomb: a tomb built of massive undressed stones sometimes combined with dry stone walling, covered with an earthen mound or stones and divided inside into separate chambers. They are of two main types, passage graves and gallery graves. The last Neolithic tombs were chambered tombs.

Cist: a short, rectangular stone ossuary; a box-like structure covered with a capstone and built for a single inhumation or cremation; usually covered with a cairn of stones; Probably from the Latin "cista," meaning "small basket with cover."

Corbelled Roof: a roof formed by small, flattish stones in successive overlapping layers.

Court Cairn: a burial chamber with a stone-built forecourt at the broad end leading to a stone chamber.

Cromlech: a Welsh term for a dolmen; the early name for megalithic tombs; once used in Brittany to designate a stone circle.

Cupmark: a small rounded hollow made in a slab or rock.

Dolmen: a Breton word, "dol-maen," meaning "table-stone," now associated with the large freestanding megalithic chambers of portal tombs. Most are single chambers composed of three uprights and one or more capstones. An original covering of earth or stones may have been eroded or dispersed.

Drystone: a building style using stone slabs piled on top of one another to form walls or kerbs without using any bonding material such as clay or mortar.

Erratic: a rock moved some distance by glaciers.

Four-poster: a stone circle made up of four stones; most commonly found in central Scotland.

Henge: a circular or oval enclosure with a ditch and outer bank, usually with one or moreentrances; may include or have included a stone or wood circle inside.

Kerbstones: large stones surrounding the base of a passage mound.

Ley: an alignment of ancient sites with ancient trackways.

Long Barrow: a tomb with an earthen mound over a capstone monument with a timber or dry-stone wall to retain the soil; length greater than width. The earliest Neolithic tombs were long barrows.

Megalith: a term coined in the mid-nineteenth century. From the Greek "megas," meaning "great" and "lithos," meaning "stone."

Megalithic Avenue: parallel settings of three or more pairs of upright stones.

Megalithic Tomb: a tomb built of large stones usually covered by a mound.

Megalithic Monument: any structure built of large stones usually set upright in the earth.

Menhir: a single standing stone; from the Welsh meaning "long stone."

Monolith: a single standing stone; from Greek "monos," meaning "sole" and lithos meaning stone.

Outlier: a standing stone outside a stone circle or henge.

Passage Tomb: a usually circular tomb covered with an earthen mound with a long passage lined with upright slabs leading to the central chamber; generally 4000-2000 BCE.

Portal Dolmen: a stone chamber with tall uprights and a sloping capstone; some with mounds, but many exposed.

Recumbant Stone Circle: a stone circle with uprights arranged in ascending order toward a large stone – the recumbent – laid between two flanking uprights.

Recumbent Stone: a stone in a circle lying down on the circumference of a circle.

Ring Cairn: a roughly circular ring of small stones that encloses a level area used for cremation burials.

Round Cairn: a round burial chamber usually covered with stones, though time may have covered them with vegetation making them discernible only because their covering differs from their surroundings.

Stone Row: a prehistoric linear setting of regularly spaced standing stones, uninterrupted by any other structure. There are about seventy stone rows on Dartmoor in England.

Thermo-luminescence: a constituent of all pottery that has been fired which decays at a known rate and enables pottery material to be dated as to time of firing.

Tomb: from the Latin "tomba," meaning a burial stone, simple or monumental.

Trilithon: two megaliths set upright with a third placed across the tops of both.

Tumulus: a barrow.

Wedge Tomb: a generally oval gallery tomb tapered in height to the back, narrower and lower toward the rear, in a wedge-shaped ground plan, probably once covered by a cairn; generally post 2000 BCE.

İNDEX

ABOUT THE AUTHOR

Diane Beeaff

A native of Kitchener, Ontario, Canada, Dianne Ebertt Beeaff has traveled extensively and combines a lifelong love of history with a quest for present-day understanding.

An acclaimed artist and writer, Dianne has authored two works of nonfiction—*Homecoming* and *A Grand Madness, Ten Years on the Road with U2*. Her award-winning first novel, *Power's Garden*, was published in 2009; her poetry, watercolors, graphite sketches and magazine articles have been featured for decades throughout the United States and Canada.

Bringing Western Europe's monolithic architecture to the contemporary forefront, *Spirit Stones* reflects both the richness of Dianne's professional writing and her personal thirst for knowledge and spiritual growth. She and her husband, Dan, reside in Tucson, AZ and are the parents of two children.

ABOUT FIVE STAR

Linda F. Radke

Linda F. Radke, veteran publisher and owner of Five Star Publications, has been ahead of her game since 1985—self-publishing before it was commonplace, partnership publishing before the rest of the world even knew what it was, and producing award-winning traditionally and nontraditionally published fiction and nonfiction for adults and children.

Five Star Publications produces premium quality books for clients and authors. Many have been recognized for excellence on local, national and international levels.

Linda is also is the author of *The Economical Guide to Self-Publishing* (a 2010 Paris Book Festival first-place winner in the "How-To" category and a Writer's Digest Book Club selection, now into its second edition) and *Promote Like a Pro: Small Budget, Big Show* (a Doubleday Executive Program Book Club selection). She is a founding member of the Arizona Book Publishing Association, was named "Book Marketer of the Year" by Book Publicists of Southern California, and received numerous public relations and marketing awards from Arizona Press Women.

Five Star Publications dedicates a percentage of profits to The Mark Foster Youth Fund and other charities chosen by the authors.

For more information about Five Star Publications, the Mark Foster Youth Fund, or charities supported by Five Star authors, visit www.FiveStarPublications.com.

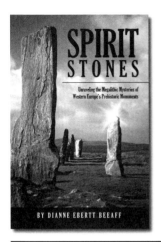

SPIRIT STONES
·ORDER FORM·

ITEM		QTY	Unit Price	TOTAL
Spirit Stones			$19.95 US $20.95 CAN	
			Subtotal	
* 8.8% sales tax – on all orders originating in Arizona.			*Tax	
$8.50 for the first book and $1.00 for each additional book going to the same address. (US rates) Ground shipping only. Allow 1 to 2 weeks for delivery.			*SHIPPING	
Mail form to: Five Star Publications, PO Box 6698, Chandler, AZ 85246-6698			**TOTAL**	

NAME:

ADDRESS:

CITY, STATE, ZIP:

DAYTIME PHONE: FAX:

EMAIL:

Method of Payment:
❏VISA ❏Master Card ❏Discover Card ❏American Express

account number   expiration date

signature   3-4 digit security
number

❏ Yes, please send me a Five Star Publications catalog.
❏ Send me info about the author speaking at my event.
How were you referred to Five Star Publications?
❏ Friend ❏ Internet ❏ Book Show ❏ Other

Five Star Publications Inc
A Resource for Every Author & Publisher Since 1985

P.O. Box 6698 • Chandler, AZ 85246-669
(480) 940-8182   866-471-0777   Fax: (480) 940-878
info@FiveStarPublications.com   www.FiveStarPublications.com